I0120804

Financial and Fiscal Instruments for Catastrophe Risk Management

Addressing Losses from Flood Hazards in Central Europe

John Pollner

THE WORLD BANK
Washington, D.C.

Contents

Boxes

Figures

Tables

Acknowledgments

This report was prepared by a team led by John D. Pollner, Lead Financial Officer, of the Private and Financial Sector Development Department (ECSPF) and Country Sector Coordinator for the Central Europe and the Baltics Country Department (ECCU5) of the Bank's Europe and Central Asia Region (ECA). The team included Intermap Technologies (Consulting Firm), Aon Benfield (Consulting Firm), Martin Melecky, Financial Economist (ECSPF), Eugene Gurenko, Lead Financial Sector Specialist (GCMNB), and Claudio Raddatz, Senior Economist (DECMG).

Chapter 1 of the report was written by John Pollner. This chapter is the main section of the report and summarizes the main findings and develops design options for a flood disaster catastrophe insurance pool for Central Europe.

Chapter 2 was written by Intermap Technologies based in the Prague Office and edited by John Pollner. The firm Intermap specializes in hazard risk mapping based on digital terrain mapping technologies and has a practice in flood risk modeling. This is the main data analysis section of the report, which details the methodology and individual country risks. It also builds the loss distribution functions used for the probabilistic estimation of events as well as pricing of insurance or alternative financial instruments for coverage.

Chapter 3 was prepared by Aon Benfield, a catastrophe reinsurance analysis firm and reinsurance broker, and reviewed and edited by John Pollner. This section analyzes the statistical correlations between different flood magnitudes in each country and historical and projected insured losses in flood affected areas. The objective was to determine predictable correlations between threshold floods and monetary losses so that parametric-based contracts could be built with associated financial compensation based on surpassing of any such physical thresholds.

Chapter 4 was written by Eugene Gurenko. This section reviews and analyzes the private sector insurance markets in the V-4 and their degree of coverage of catastrophic events. It also analyzes the public sector mechanisms in place by central governments, such as budget reserve funds, their characteristics, and mode of application for funding disaster events.

Chapter 5 was written by Martin Melecky and Claudio Raddatz and edited by John Pollner. This section covers a large sample of countries globally, that are subject to natural disasters, and analyzes the GDP recovery path and post-disaster fiscal sustainability (when using deficit or debt financing) based on a countries' economic, financial sector, debt raising, and insurance characteristics.

The peer reviewers for the final report were Olivier Mahul, Program Coordinator (GCMNB), and Francis Ghesquiere, Lead Disaster Risk Management Specialist (LCSUW).

The Sector Managers for this report were Lalit Raina (ECSF1) and Sophie Sirtaine (ECSF2). The Sector Director was Gerardo Corrochano (ECSPF). The Country Director was Peter Harrold (ECCU5). The Regional Vice President was Philippe Le Houerou, (ECAVP).

Abbreviations and Acronyms

API	Antecedent Precipitation Index
CAT	Catastrophe
CDF	Cumulative Distribution Function
CEE	Central and Eastern Europe
CRED	Center for Research on the Epidemiology of Disasters
CRESTA	Catastrophe Risk Evaluating and Standardizing Target Accumulations
CORINE	Coordination of Information on the Environment (for soil erosion)
CZ	Czech Republic
df	Degrees of Freedom
DTM	digital terrain models
ECB	European Central Bank
ESA	European System of Accounts
EUR	Euro
EURIBOR	Euro Interbank Offered Rate (interbank lending rate)
EUSF	European Union Solidarity Fund
FLEXA	Fire, Lightning, Explosion, Aviation
HU	Hungary
GDP	Gross Domestic Product
GIS	Geographic Information System
GMR	Geomorphologic Regression
IRF	Impulse Response Function
LAU	Local Administrative Unit
LEC	Loss Exceedance Curve
MARS	Multiple Non-linear Regression Analysis
NACE	Classification of Economic Activities in the European Community
NUTS	Nomenclature of Units for Territorial Statistics
OEP	Occurrence Exceedance Probability
p	Probability
PL	Poland
PML	Probable Maximum Loss
PPP	Purchasing Power Parity
PVAR	Panel Vector Autoregression
RTP	Return Period
SK	Slovak Republic
SPV	Special Purpose Vehicle
TIV	Total Insured Value
UN	United Nations
VAR	Vector Autoregression
V-4	Visegrad-4 Countries (Poland, the Czech Republic, Hungary, the Slovak Republic)
WDI	World Development Indicators
XL	Excess-of-Loss (a catastrophe insurance coverage)

Executive Summary

This report addresses the large flood exposures of Central Europe and proposes efficient financial and risk transfer mechanisms to mitigate fiscal losses from natural catastrophes. In particular, the Visegrad countries (V-4) of Central Europe—namely, Poland, the Czech Republic, Hungary, and the Slovak Republic—have such tremendous potential flood damages that reliance on budgetary appropriations or even European Union (EU) funds in such circumstances becomes ineffective and does not provide needed cash funds for the quick response and recovery needed to minimize economic disruptions.

The report is primarily addressed to the governments of the region, which should build into their fiscal planning the necessary contingent funding mechanisms, based on their exposures. The report is addressed to finance ministries and also to the insurance and securities regulators and the private insurance and capital markets, which may all play a role in the proposed mechanisms. An arrangement using a multicountry pool with a hazard-triggered insurance payout mechanism complemented by contingent financing is proposed, to better manage these risks and avoid major fiscal volatility and disruption.

The historical and more current flood losses in the region have been substantial, given the countries' river basin topographies and exposures to weather events. In 2010 the V-4 demonstrated their historical and topographic vulnerability to floods and associated loss exposures. Poland suffered US$3.2 billion in flood related losses, comparable to its US$3.5 billion of losses back in 1997.

The economic vulnerability generated by flood events can be immensely catastrophic. Flood modeling analysis of the V-4 shows that a disaster event with a 5 percent probability in any given year can lead to economic losses in these countries of between 0.6 percent to 1.9 percent of GDP, as well as between 2.2 percent to 10.7 percent of government revenues. Larger events (albeit with lower probabilities) could quadruple the size of such losses. Although Poland has the highest overall exposure to loss, the Slovak Republic is quite vulnerable given its lower share of the government budget in the overall economy. The Czech Republic and Hungary fall in between and have substantial exposures.

The European Union Solidarity Fund (EUSF) is available as a mechanism to channel EU member budgetary contributions to disaster-stricken states. But it comes into effect at very high levels of losses in relation to government revenues, and does not provide sufficient funding. It is also not nimble as a mechanism to provide immediate funds for recovery and emergency—thus it is utilized mainly for medium-term post-disaster reconstruction. The governments of the V-4 maintain modest budgetary reserves for catastrophic events, but a more optimal system should include financial mechanisms to supplement the funding gap between budget reserves, EUSF resources, and actual losses that occur requiring immediate financing for fast recovery.

In the insurance sector in Central Europe, protection against loss damages for private households and business counts on a well-developed industry. The insurance industry provides coverage to between 50–75 percent of households in the V-4 countries, showing a relatively high level of development of the sector. Government assets and infrastructure, however, as well as potentially less advantaged households, are not broadly insured, implying contingent loss liabilities to the state.

An insurance-like mechanism for national governments can be tailored for 'macro-portfolio' country needs. Fiscal support in the event of country-level disaster losses, by virtue of their broad territorial scope, should use mechanisms that provide payments triggered by physical flood intensities (rather than exact site-by-site losses as in the traditional insurance industry). This is accomplished via innovative yet ultra-safe financial instruments. For example, if infrastructure losses near a flood zone can be historically shown to have high correlations to flood levels, then financial counterparties can accept contracts that pay solely when the flood level is exceeded, in exchange for a fee or premium. This is called a parametric-based contract since the physical parameter, not the monetary level of loss, triggers the payout.

A multicountry mechanism for pooling of risks to protect government assets and infrastructure can also provide major cost efficiencies to all governments, using parametric-based contracts. Since a coverage-provider can rely on a larger more diversified and predictable portfolio with a greater number of participants, savings on a V-4 country pooling mechanisms can range from 25 to 33 percent of the financing costs that each country would otherwise have paid if it obtained such financial coverage on its own.

There is also evidence that countries' use of insurance-like instruments improve their long-term fiscal sustainability prospects. The economic and statistical analysis of disaster events occurring globally in several countries with hazard exposures shows that those countries with deeper financial and insurance markets, recover more quickly in terms of the post-disaster GDP growth path. As well, they experience reduced public sector deficits compared to those countries with little or scant use of financial and/or insurance mechanisms.

There are several instruments and options for both risk transfer/insurance and risk financing/debt mechanisms for funding catastrophes. Governments should consider both classes of instruments to optimize the coverage-versus-cost benefit. Both instruments can be analyzed based on equivalencies in terms of market spreads, taking into account the probabilities of invoking them. A hybrid-like instrument, the catastrophe bond, is really a risk transfer instrument but structured as a debt security. Under this instrument, financial investors take the risk of a loss of principal if the disaster occurs (benefiting the bond issuer with free funds to pay for recovery). This report conducts an analysis of a possible four-country catastrophe bond that the V-4 countries could partake of, to finance large flood disasters if they occurred in their territories.

Contingent loans or debt can be also used as stand-by facilities that cost less than insurance when unused. However, their application should be for higher levels of losses so that they are invoked less frequently. This would avoid an excessive buildup of debt if such instruments were used for frequently recurring hazard events.

Individual countries need not be concerned about subsidizing others' losses if the pricing approach under a multicountry initiative is risk adjusted. A pooled mechanism using risk transfer instruments such as the ones discussed above, can use pure risk-based pricing considering each country's individual exposure profile. The opposite would be pricing of coverage equally among all participants. A balanced approach might be to consider a combined risk-pricing approach with a portion of the pricing based on solidarity (that is, some equal pricing as well as some based on individual country risk). This would bring benefits to all participants through the "large portfolio effect," as well as build in a partial solidarity element to share the highest exposures.

Legal provisions and institutional governance requirements are also required to ensure that any such scheme operates with clear rules of loss assessment and payment. To implement the above, an institutional set up would be needed under a legal entity, meeting minimum capital reserves (in the case of a pooled parametric insurance mechanism) or underwriting costs (in the case of a catastrophe bond) and needing the establishment of an issuing trust vehicle. A simpler approach could also involve directly contracting with international insurers or reinsurers, though such pricing may be higher in the long run than setting up a funded vehicle.

A feasibility analysis needs to be completed to provide an additional level of reliability of the potential losses involved, and their likelihoods of occurrence. To design the approaches contemplated, further validation of asset and property values and vulnerabilities need closer analysis. Governments have several choices and can also select specific assets or amounts they wish to protect, to receive compensation under a custom-designed loss financing scheme.

Setting up flood-level based contracts would require additional physical and hydrological risk modeling. This ensures that flood magnitude correlations with qualifying losses are closely linked. If catastrophe bonds are used, a market pricing test for the final spread asked will be needed. For all the above, governments should count on a small team of independent experts to monitor such contracts, ensure financial management of funds, oversee the trust vehicles, and assure the requisite governance procedures and trigger verification mechanisms needed to invoke payments under the proposed disaster funding schemes.

The V-4 countries should therefore begin to set up the financial mechanisms to prevent major fiscal losses from future catastrophic floods. The instruments proposed can be market tested under a final feasibility analysis and implemented with a relatively streamlined institutional infrastructure. Political agreements will be needed among the participants to launch these mechanisms which, with collective participation, are shown to be highly cost effective.

CHAPTER 1

Risk Analysis and Financial Instruments for Managing Catastrophe Exposures

Planning for the Fiscal Exposure Impacts of Major Flood Losses in Central Europe

This catastrophe risk management report examines financial mechanisms to apply for fiscal contingencies including the design of innovative funding approaches. These are proposed for large catastrophic events and climate change risks in the four Visegrad countries (V-4)—Poland, Hungary, the Czech Republic, and the Slovak Republic—and demonstrate how risk transfer instruments can improve fiscal smoothing to manage major expenditure outlays. The report is addressed to country governments, particularly the Ministries of Finance as well as the insurance and securities regulators and the private insurance and capital markets. The report examines the disaster-funding arrangements in the context of the European Union Solidarity Fund (EUSF) that is used to help finance European Union (EU) members following natural disasters. The report proposes optimizing the financial and fiscal mechanisms to tackle large future losses that disproportionately impact country budgets and economies.

The report focuses on assessing the flood risk exposures of the public sector in the V-4 countries and proposes financial mechanisms that can be used to mitigate governments' resultant fiscal losses. The report examines how catastrophic events for the V-4 and their loss exposures, compare with shares of national gross domestic product (GDP) and fiscal budgets. It then demonstrates that risk pooling arrangements for these countries are feasible to cover major losses before and after EUSF financing kicks in, and also reviews other available instruments (budgetary, reserves, risk insurance, catastrophe bonds, parametric contracts, contingent loans and other) that may be appropriate to complement funding and avoid fiscal disruptions from major disasters, which are mainly floods, but also could potentially be used for hazards such as earthquakes, droughts, wind storms or extreme temperatures.

The years 2009 and 2010 demonstrated once again the return of peak floods in Central Europe. This showed how significant the exposure and vulnerability to floods continues to be for the V-4. As can be seen from experience in the last two decades, flood losses do not occur annually at catastrophic magnitudes; however, when they do occur, the impacts are significant in terms of overall economic losses and public expenditure commitments (see table 1.1).

Table 1.1. Central Europe Floods: Economic Losses in Selected Years (in Nominal US$ Million Equivalent)

Country	1997	1999	2001	2002	2004	2009	2010
Poland	3,500	—	700	—	—	100	3,200
Czech Republic	1,850	—	—	2,420	—	150	60
Hungary	—	293	—	—	—	—	358
Slovak Republic	60	113	—	—	383	—	—

Source: Center for Research on the Epidemiology of Disasters (CRED).
Note: — = not applicable.

The Fiscal and Macroeconomic Framework and Its Relation to Disaster Impacts

The fiscal and debt adjustment process following natural disasters is dependent on initial conditions in the financial sector's structure and the fiscal and/debt accounts. In this context, the report also considers the impact of natural disasters on public finance sustainability by characterizing how government spending and debt typically responds to catastrophes. The strategies followed by different governments regarding the combination of expenditures, revenues and borrowing depends in part on their access to loans or market financing, their cost, and the demand for government services, all of which are related to the degree of insurance in the economy. While this part of the study uses a much larger sample of countries worldwide to arrive at more reliable estimations of fiscal response effects, this larger sample provide insights regarding government strategies, financial instruments, and market instruments to better handle disaster costs in the V-4 countries.

The analysis found that countries with more developed financial or insurance markets suffer less from disasters in terms of output declines. The way this is achieved differs in each case. In financially developed markets, governments are able to raise funds and increase deficits. This response helps alleviate the impact of the disasters. In countries with high insurance penetration, the smaller impact of disasters on GDP occurs without a large fiscal expansion. Financial markets and development institutions can thus help in the design and use of fiscal insurance policies or hedging debt instruments to further diminish disaster consequences. Surprisingly, those countries that were more indebted seemed to be those with better access to debt. Thus, debt levels on average also appear to proxy for better access to capital markets rather than constrained fiscal space. However, those with deeper insurance markets suffered less from rising fiscal deficits when financing post-disaster growth (see box 1.1).

Box 1.1. Fiscal and GDP Response Based on Insurance Depth in the Economy

An analysis of insurance depth in the economy shows its effect on the recovery process following a disaster. Figure B1.1 shows the cumulative impulse response functions (IRF) for GDP, government expenditures, and government revenues. These are for climate-related disasters for a set of countries with high and low levels of insurance penetration. Time 0

(Box continues on next page)

Box 1.1 *(continued)*

(x axis) is when the disaster strikes. The solid lines show the impact of a type of disaster for countries with high levels of insurance penetration (thick black line) and for those with low levels of insurance penetration (solid thin line). The dotted lines show one standard deviation confidence bands. The availability of insurance results in a much better GDP recovery which in turn helps government revenues and allows for a less constrained expenditure path. Details and scenarios are further discussed in chapter 5.

Figure B1.1. Cumulative Impulse Response Functions versus Insurance Penetration in Economy

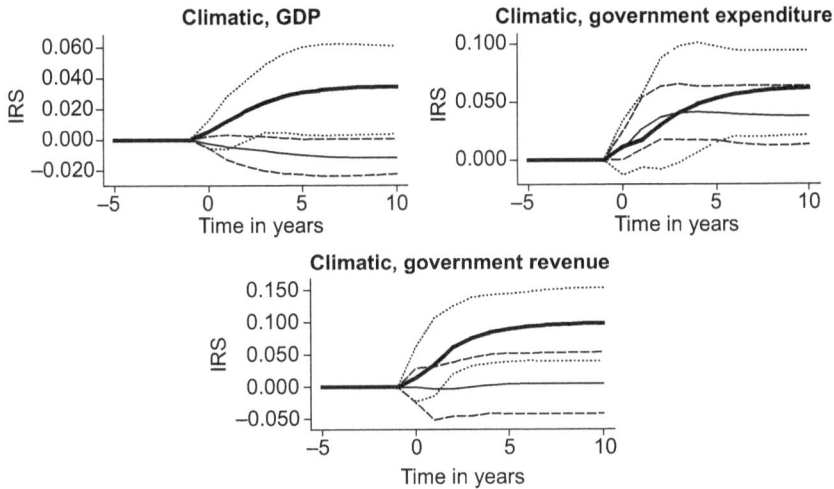

Source: Melecky and Raddatz 2011.

The Role of the EUSF in Disaster and Fiscal Management

The EUSF was established in late 2002 in the aftermath of major European floods. The EUSF is used to partially compensate public budgets for damage suffered as a result of natural disasters. The eligibility to use EUSF funds becomes available once disaster losses equal EUR 3.0 billion or 0.6 percent of GDP, whichever figure is lower.

The amount of aid provided under the EUSF is 2.5 percent of losses below EUR 3 billion equivalent, plus 6 percent of any losses above that threshold. If the loss, for example, is exactly EUR 4 billion, aid would amount to 2.5 percent of 3 billion (75 million) plus 6 percent of 1 billion (60 million) or a total of 135 million.

For a large disaster, while EUSF outlays provide extra funding, they can at times be very small in relation to total losses (see table 1.2). Given its 'trigger points' the funding is also small in relation to the average size of the economies of EU members. Hence there is a need to examine additional targeted risk management and disaster financing mechanisms that further reduce the gaps generated by emergency disaster funding out of government resources.

Table 1.2. Outlays Incurred by the EUSF (EUR Million)

Outlay	2002	2003	2004	2005	2006	2007	2008
EUSF total aid provided	728	107	20	205	24	445	281
Average amount of aid per event/country	182	18	20	205	12	74	56

Source: European Commission.
Note: 2002: Austria, Czech Republic, France, and Germany; 2003: Spain (2), Italy (2), Portugal, and Malta; 2004: France; 2005: the Slovak Republic, Estonia, Latvia, Sweden, Lithuania, Romania (2), Bulgaria (2) and Austria; 2006: Greece and Hungary; 2007: Germany, France (2), United Kingdom, Greece, and Slovenia; 2008: United Kingdom, Greece, Slovenia, France, and Cyprus.

Measuring the Level of Risk and Potential Financial and/Fiscal Impacts

In the Czech Republic in 2002, the flood disasters amounted to 3.5 percent of GDP, putting strains on the government budget. Even though EUSF payments became available these arrived with substantial delays and were essentially used to refinance costs already incurred. Such levels of losses generate economic and social vulnerabilities with associated disruptions that require immediate government responses and a quick resolution of the event impacts.

This report therefore quantifies the exposures and risks, and provides policy and instrumental solutions. Such solutions, including financial or insurance-like mechanisms which are meant to stabilize the fiscal risks that may materialize, are used to supplement and render more effective the public actions needed to prepare for, and address future catastrophic losses whether they are caused by periodic natural perils or climate change induced events. The methodology for quantifying exposures and risks is shown in box 1.2.

Box 1.2. Risk Modeling Methodology

The methodological elements for estimating financial impacts used in this report comprise expert risk modeling techniques that link physical hazards with loss outcomes. The model elements used are shown in figure 1.1 and essentially cover the stochastic, hazard, damage, and financial modules. Digital terrain mapping and risk modeling methods are used to create uniform high-resolution three-dimensional digital models of the earth-surface including elevation data and geometric images based on geographic information systems, engineering and hydrology variables, and insurance risk factors, in order to determine the potential frequency and severity of major flood risks and associated losses (affecting the State's resources as well as private sector assets).

The sources of data on inventory and values of assets including infrastructure in the economy were obtained from statistical institute information classified according to EU standards. Where assets, buildings or infrastructure were not valued, monetary information was obtained from economic and market sources. Missing data was based on interpolating information from similar assets based on standard construction costs, population centers, income information, and other economic and social variables. The technical chapter 2 that follows, explains the methodology in detail and the currency and other conversion factors used for data on the four countries.

Source: Prepared by the authors using World Bank data and other financial market information.

Figure 1.1. Technical Modules of the Catastrophe Risk Model

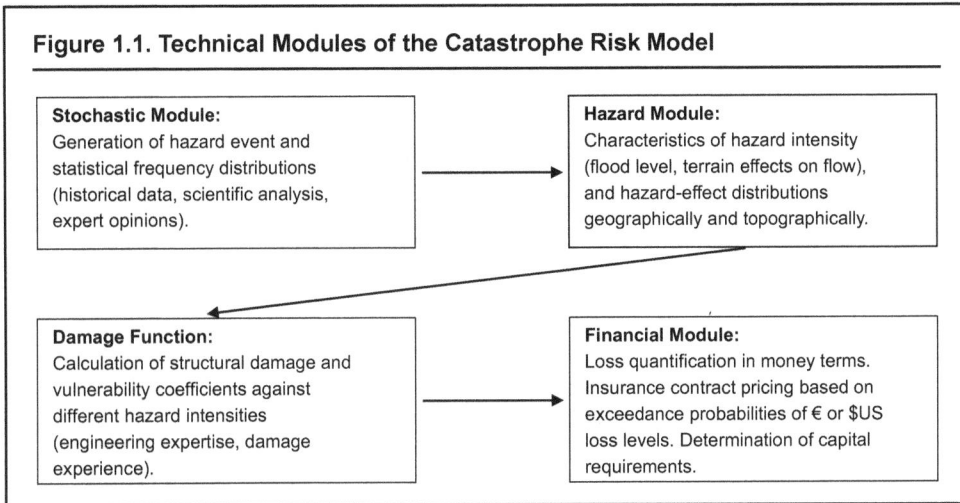

Stochastic Module:
Generation of hazard event and
statistical frequency distributions
(historical data, scientific analysis,
expert opinions).

Hazard Module:
Characteristics of hazard intensity
(flood level, terrain effects on flow),
and hazard-effect distributions
geographically and topographically.

Damage Function:
Calculation of structural damage and
vulnerability coefficients against
different hazard intensities
(engineering expertise, damage
experience).

Financial Module:
Loss quantification in money terms.
Insurance contract pricing based on
exceedance probabilities of € or $US
loss levels. Determination of capital
requirements.

Source: Prepared by the authors using World Bank data and other financial market information.

Structuring Financial and Fiscal Instruments for Funding Losses Ex Ante

For unfunded exposures, special forms of budgetary and 'insurance-like' financing should be considered. These can be used to fund both: (i) mezzanine (mid-level) catastrophe losses before EU Solidarity Funding becomes eligible, and (ii) high levels of losses where EUSF funding is limited. In the first case, reasonable allocations of emergency funding as well as reallocations of public budgetary funds need to be identified before determining the gap between such funds and EUSF funding. In the second case, after EUSF funding is provided at the highest level of losses (predefined in monetary terms) the unfunded part of these highest losses can be subject to special financing and macro insurance-type arrangements discussed below.

Loss prediction tools, however, are first needed so that mezzanine mid-level and highest-level loss funding can be invoked based on accurately modeled losses. Modeled losses are estimated from physical phenomena (such as levels and intensity of water flow in key flood areas, earthquake intensities, or wind storms) that are correlated with historical damages and have a predictable relation to asset and infrastructure value losses (see box 1.3). Given the complexity of modeling floods and water flow, this report focuses on this particular peril which is the primary hazard in the V-4 countries and can be used as a "macro" predictor of loss.

Box 1.3. Parametric Trigger Events as an Alternative to Direct Loss Measurement

Physical event threshold triggers can be used instead of financial loss levels. In the insurance/capital market industry parlance, the physical (versus financially reported) loss triggers are referred to as "parametric" triggers. If a physical phenomenon such as a measured flood level can be associated reliably with potential losses to housing, buildings or infrastructure, then an insurance contract can pay for losses once that certain physical trigger is reached (for

(Box continues on next page)

Box 1.3 *(continued)*

example, water/flood level) instead of paying out based on an ex post site-by-site examination of actual losses (the latter being the "loss adjustment" method in the industry parlance).

Flood magnitudes are thus directly associated with losses. To obtain estimates of such parametric triggers in a reliable way, hazard distributions, exposure values, vulnerabilities, and loss estimations are first calculated. Following that, correlation simulations of flood levels (measured as volume of water discharged over a time period) are calculated against financial losses associated with such flood levels/discharges as per historical experience and projected forecasts. This exercise can be done across a number of river basins within a country so that the measurement of flood events at each specific location can be correlated reliably with predictable losses under robustly tested risk models.

Source: Prepared by the authors using World Bank data and other financial market information.

Table 1.3 summarizes the link between the level of water flow and potential losses. The correlation results show country losses of EUR 500 million associated with the volume of water (cubic meters/second) discharged during historical and projected disaster events for river catchments in each of the countries examined.

Table 1.3. Water Flow Level/Discharge per River Catchment Correlated to a EUR 500 Million per Country Loss

Czech Republic		Slovak Republic		Hungary		Poland	
Odra-CZ	m³/sec	Dunaj-SK	m³/sec	Ipel-HU	—	Odra-PL	m³/sec
	2,410		14,014		—		4,344
Morava-CZ	m³/sec	Vah-SK	m³/sec	Dunaj-HU	—	Wisla-PL	m³/sec
	785		2,037		—		8,486
Dyje-CZ	m³/sec	Hornad-SK	m³/sec	Salo-HU	m³/sec	Narew-PL	m³/sec
	918		1,278		758		1,805
Vltava-CZ	m³/sec	Bodrog-SK	m³/sec	Hornad-HU	—		
	2,997		2,032		—		
Labe-CZ	m³/sec	—	—	Tisza-HU	m³/sec		
	3,751	—	—		4,810		
				Leitha-HU	m³/sec		
					276		

Source: Aon Benfield, Czech Republic.
Note: — = not applicable.

While a financial contract based on flood levels is innovative and simpler to execute, it can result in errors known as "basis risk." By using river-catchment flood measuring devices with automatic transmission of data to a centralized information station to prevent manipulation, financial/insurance contracts can be designed to pay countries predefined sums if the water level exceeds the threshold levels. This can involve some "basis risk" meaning that the flood level might occur (though with lower losses than projected) but the contract would still have to pay out. Alternatively, the flood level may not reach the threshold level specified in the "contract trigger" (even though substantial damages occurred) but the contract would not pay out. These are risks in such an approach, although its simplicity is beneficial and this "basis risk" can be borne by national governments more easily than by a single private party. This is because governments operate on a large country-wide "asset portfolio" of risks where such discrepancies would be smoothed out across the entire territory and over time.

Country Loss Distributions on Account of Flood Hazards

Historically, the four countries analyzed have experienced major flood events, aggravated by both heavy rain storms as well as higher average temperatures. Temperature increases at times generate a more voluminous water flow from melting ice and snow. While these countries can partake of EUSF which are essentially budget contributions from other member states in the event of major catastrophes, the funds 'kick in' at only very high level of losses as described, and only cover a small portion of such losses. Thus fiscal disruptions occur well before EUSF assistance is activated for mega sized events.

Figure 1.2 estimates the probabilities of occurrence and potential losses to state and/public property and infrastructure from major flood events. The return period expressed in years can also be seen as an annual probability of occurrence or loss at the levels shown (in euro millions). This does not necessarily reflect a loss from a single event (such as one major flood) in a given year, but can also reflect the accumulation of several flood losses during the year which add up to the annual loss level. For example a 100-year return period means a 1 percent chance of the loss occurring annually.

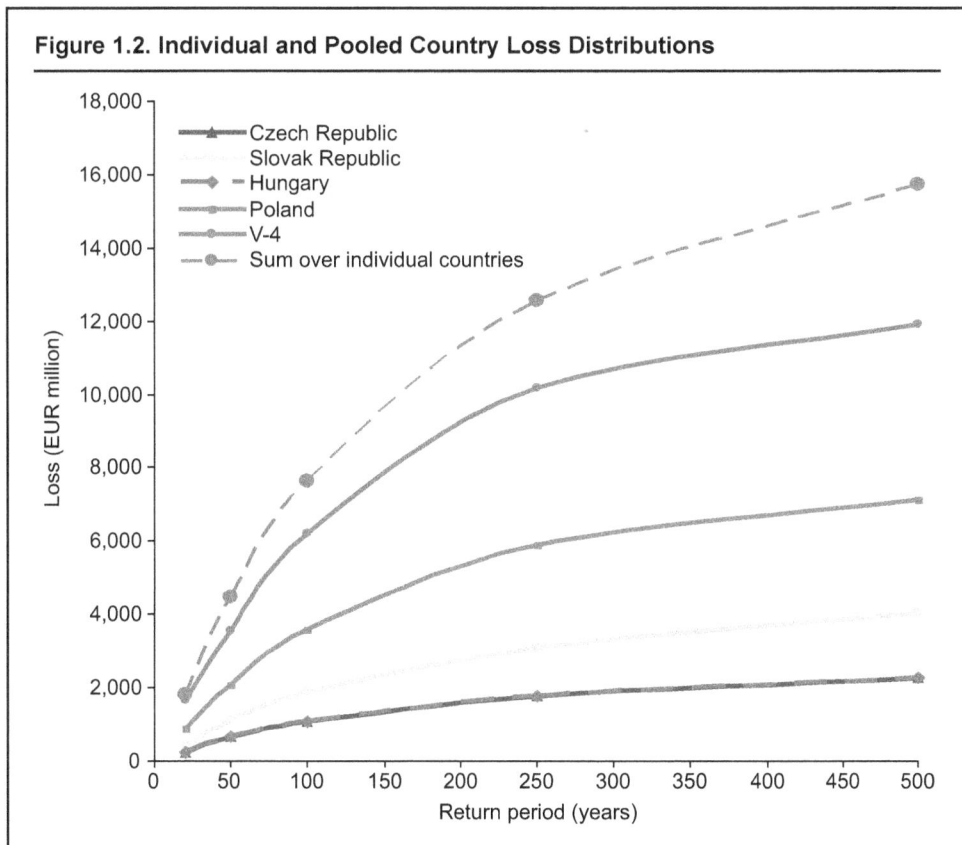

Figure 1.2. Individual and Pooled Country Loss Distributions

Source: Intermap Technologies.

Given the rare catastrophic nature of these events, the 1 percent probability, however, has a wide variation of uncertainty. Such an event can therefore at times occur more frequently within such a variation/range. As can be observed, for a 2 percent annual probability (assuming a 50-year return period) the four-country combined loss exceeds 4 billion euros (Sum curve). As this report demonstrates later, given the ratio of annual potential losses versus government revenues, and each country's level of GDP, the existing budgets of governments would be severely strained before EUSF payments (which take several months to process) come into play. This would thus call for an intermediate mechanism of risk financing, to supplement the liquidity needed to augment budget resources, even before the EUSF funds are invoked.

The benefits of pooling risks across countries and reducing costs, becomes evident. In the figure 1.2, the "Sum" curve shows the simple aggregate of the losses of each country added together under the individual scenarios. Poland has the largest potential loss given that it is the largest economy with the most assets at risk. The "V-4" curve represents the statistical pooling of the four countries under a combined loss portfolio. What is notable is that this loss curve has lower aggregate losses (and would thus have lower premiums if governments insured these assets) than the simple "Sum" curve. This is because the "V-4" curve relies on lower overall standard deviations of losses given a larger number of event observations for the four countries combined, that is, a portfolio diversification effect that reduces volatility.[1]

In practical terms this means that if countries were to insure themselves individually the cost of catastrophic coverage would be significantly higher than as a group. An insurer of any kind would cost the premiums based on individual country exposures which would have higher individual variances (requiring higher pricing). This is because on a single-country basis, catastrophe events would occur less often than when observed as a group. If the countries combined their portfolios, the larger number of catastrophe observations would reduce the statistical variances within the larger event set, and allow an insurer to price them with fewer uncertainties about predicted loss events, and thus charge lower "group" rates.

The cost savings from pooling are directly quantified based on the V-4 combined loss distribution curve. Observing the graph above one can see that for a 500-year (0.2 percent probability) event, the summed losses for each country individually, amount to a potential loss of approximately EUR 16,000 million. Let us assume that a premium for insuring that entire amount (under a parametric trigger based contract) would be 2 percent of the loss covered, or EUR 320 million, which would be payable proportionately according to the risk level of each country. However, as a combined insured risk portfolio (the V-4 curve) the countries show a potential loss of EUR 12,000 million for the same event probability (due to the pooling effect and lower standard deviation of the combined country risks). Thus the premium, if kept at 2 percent in this case, would be EUR 240 million representing a collective savings of EUR 80 million, or a 25 percent reduction in the actuarial premium.

Rationale for Government/Public Sector Insurance Needs

The above analysis makes a strong case for consideration of a collective country fiscal insurance mechanism to cover losses. Similar schemes have already been implemented in other parts of the world (see box 1.4). Several instruments can be utilized for this

Box 1.4. An Operating Multicountry Catastrophe Risk Fiscal Insurance Pool: The CCRIF

The Caribbean Catastrophe Risk Insurance Facility (CCRIF) is the first multicountry risk pool using parametric insurance policies. The policies are funded by initial capital as well as by insurance and capital market instruments. CCRIF is a regional catastrophe risk fund for Caribbean governments developed with support from the World Bank to help mitigate the short-term cash flow problems that small economies suffer after major natural disasters. A critical challenge addressed by the CCRIF is the need for short-term liquidity to maintain essential government services until additional resources become available. Although post-disaster funding from budget sources, or bilateral and multilateral sources can be important financing sources, external assistance often takes months to materialize, and usually supports specific infrastructure projects.

CCRIF has in its first three years of operation, offered separate hurricane (wind) and earthquake policies. Caribbean governments may purchase coverage which triggers a "one-in-15-year" hurricane and a "one-in-20-year" earthquake, with maximum coverage of US$100 million available for each peril. The cost of coverage is a direct function of the amount of risk being transferred, ensuring no cross-subsidization of premiums and a level playing-field for all participants.

There are four main reasons CCRIF was designed as a parametric facility: (a) payouts can be calculated and made very quickly because loss adjusters do not have to be relied on to estimate damage after a catastrophe event, which can take months or years; (b) governments do not have to provide detailed asset values and other information prior to the insurance program commencing, and have just one form to sign during the entire claims process; (c) calculation of payouts is totally objective based on a few simple input parameters published in the public domain by the body responsible for estimating those particular parameters, and a set of formulae which form part of the policy; and (d) the risk which drives policy pricing is uniformly defined (there is no subjectivity in its definition).

The parametric insurance program was developed using physically measurable indicators of known hazards to trigger payments. This allows the CCRIF to estimate the loss on the ground by using data from the National Hurricane Centre (NHC) in the case of hurricanes and the United States Geological Survey (USGS) in the case of earthquakes, and a proxy relationship developed under a pre-agreed catastrophe risk model. The information provided by the NHC and the USGS are in the public domain and so are available for scrutiny, as are the variables in the risk model.

Under the CCRIF's impact measurement process, the loss is calculated through an index. The index represents the hazard levels (wind, storm surge, and waves for hurricane, ground shaking for earthquake) which are used as the driving variables to establish proxies for losses. It is important to note that the object of the Facility is not to cover the entire losses faced by affected states, but to provide in case of a major adverse event, short-term liquidity to cover both disaster response and basic government functions.

Payouts following disasters have been triggered under the CCRIF. In 2007, the CCRIF paid out almost US$1 million to the Dominican and St Lucian governments after the November 29 earthquake in the eastern Caribbean, and in 2008, CCRIF paid out US$6.3 million to the Turks & Caicos Islands after Hurricane Ike made a direct hit on Grand Turk Island. More recently, Haiti received a payment of US$7.75 million (approximately 20 times their premium for earthquake coverage) fourteen days after being struck by a devastating earthquake of magnitude 7.0 in January 2010. In September 2010, Anguilla received a payment of US$4.3 million following Tropical Cyclone Earl in August. In November 2010, after October's Tropical Cyclone Tomas, the CCRIF made payments to the governments of Barbados (US$8.6 million), Saint Lucia (US$3.2 million) and St. Vincent and the Grenadines (US$1.1 million).

Source: World Bank, CCRIF.

purpose. However, this does not mean that standard insurance contracts are a solution for covering potential fiscal liabilities from natural and climate induced disasters such as floods, given that such standard contracts would require extensive on-site damage assessments and costly loss-adjustment procedures. Rather, certain macro/fiscal insurance mechanisms may be more apt for this purpose and for uses by governments.

Catastrophic losses can be very significant in relation to macroeconomic accounts. In terms of macroeconomic planning, flood disasters in Central Europe generate substantial resource impacts when compared to national GDP and government budget revenues. Table 1.4 shows the impact of relatively modest catastrophes on macro/fiscal variables, for the V-4 countries, and where both total country assets (the sum of private and public property and infrastructure) are shown, as well as public property and infrastructure by itself. More severe events (such as those with an annual 0.5 percent likelihood) would escalate these losses significantly.

Table 1.4. Effect on Budget Revenues and GDP, from Reference Catastrophe Floods

Event	Poland	Czech Republic	Hungary	Slovak Republic
20-year event (5% probability)				
Euro amount				
Total property (€ million)	2,508	768	966	1,191
Public property (€ million)	904	245	248	412
% of Revenue				
Total property	2.2	1.4	2.3	10.7
Public property	0.8	0.4	0.6	3.7
% of GDP				
Total property	0.8	0.6	1.0	1.9
Public property	0.3	0.2	0.3	0.6
100-year event (1% probability)				
Euro amount				
Total property (€ million)	9,954	3,405	4,235	5,452
Public property (€ million)	3,586	1,086	1,087	1,887
% of revenue				
Total property	8.6	6.2	10.0	48.8
Public property	3.1	2.0	2.6	16.9
% of GDP				
Total property	3.2	2.5	4.6	8.5
Public property	1.2	0.8	1.2	2.9

Source: Intermap Technologies and IMF International Financial Statistics, 2008 and 2009.

In terms of loss ratios, for a 100-year 1 percent probability event, the impact from flood losses is very disruptive in relation to government revenues, and has significant loss impacts versus GDP. A 20-year event is less so, but not insignificant. For total public and private property, the losses from both events represent a significant as a percentage of budget revenues, with the Slovak Republic being highly affected (due to a smaller government sector) and with significant effects for Hungary and Poland. For public property exposure alone, under the 1 percent annual probability, the Slovak Republic and Poland appear most vulnerable. Interestingly though, in recent years, except for 2004, the Slovak Republic has not suffered from flood damages as much as its other three neighbors, though this is not a reason for complacency given its assessed risk exposure.

Large losses below and above EUSF eligibility thresholds present major fiscal challenges. Total losses as a percentage of GDP range from 2.5 percent to 8.5 percent for the V-4 countries for a 1 percent probability event. For public property, only the Czech Republic's losses are under 1 percent of GDP (and 2 percent of budget revenues). What is worth noting, is that for the 5 percent (20-year) probability event, with the possible exception of the Slovak Republic, none of the countries would be able to access solidarity EUSF funds if public sector losses fall below the threshold for access. In any case, even when private sector losses are included and eligibility for tapping EUSF resources exists, there are clearly significant public expenditures that would need to be deployed immediately for losses below the EUSF threshold, as well as to bridge expenditures pending the receipt of EUSF funds plus significant losses above and beyond amounts provided by the EUSF.

Budget reserves and insurance are thus complementary measures to be used as fiscal tools for disaster management. As mentioned, given the large variance and uncertainty of catastrophes, a 100-year event represents an average forecast and does not necessarily mean that the event will occur at that magnitude only every 100 years. Prudent government risk managers would actually budget reserves representing 1 percent of the loss each year to ensure funding for such a "big" event.[2]

As described further below, budget reserves are not necessarily the most optimal or efficient form to fund and protect against these disasters. While governments should count on budgets for relatively low-level losses, and on the EUSF for a portion of extremely high losses, the middle or mezzanine level of losses, and losses above EUSF funding eligibility should count on much more optimal risk management tools to stabilize fiscal outlays.

Market Insurance and Private Property Coverage

Flood catastrophes inevitably affect private property, particularly homes and dwellings, although the catastrophe insurance market is quite well developed in the V-4 countries. Insurance penetration (expressed as percentage of homeowners with catastrophe insurance) averages between 50 and 75 percent. This is positive and given that not all regions of any particular country are subject to catastrophic risks, it represents a rather high insurance penetration level.

The unique feature of the V-4 markets is that catastrophe insurance perils are traditionally included in the overall scope of coverage under homeowners' policies. In most other markets this represents an optional policy 'endorsement.' As a result, almost all households with a fire policy in the V-4 countries are automatically covered against floods, windstorm, landslides, hail and avalanches. In the Czech Republic, most insurers charge an adequate risk premium for the catastrophe portion of the risk while in Poland the risk premium is driven more by market competition.

Reinsurance for individual country subsidiaries is typically arranged in a centralized fashion through reinsurance departments of parent companies. The parent companies in turn place the cover for the whole group. This approach allows realizing considerable savings which translates into lower premiums for homeowners. In the case of the Polish state-owned insurer, the sheer size of the company allows it to pool the risk on a country-wide basis, which results in a well-diversified risk exposure and highly affordable pricing.

However, despite a relatively high level of insurance penetration, governments still carry a considerable budgetary exposure to catastrophic floods. Governments of the V-4 countries may consider changing the existing post-disaster compensation policies for housing reconstruction by introducing a strong element of private responsibility for losses inflicted by natural disasters. Such a policy change would likely increase insurance penetration among homeowners and would also help significantly to reduce government fiscal exposures to the private sector against natural disasters.

Based on the above factors there does not appear to be a case for government support for enhancing the capacity of the private catastrophe market in the V-4 countries. The market counts on a robust insurance industry and reinsurance support from the major European reinsurers, Munich Re and Swiss Re. Based on total country exposure and potential losses, further studies regarding the capacity of the insurance industry to absorb major losses (and its requisite capital) would be prudent, coupled with strengthened regulatory monitoring and risk assessment techniques, in order to ensure that actuarially such risks are well quantified, and covered by adequate appropriate insurance reserves. (See chapter 4 for more detail).

The Range of Catastrophe Insurance Instruments

Before laying out a proposed financial structure for pooling the V-4 countries' flood risks, recent developments in financial mechanisms for disaster contingencies should be disclosed. As shown in table 1.5, there are a range of financial instruments used in the past and more currently, to handle catastrophic risks. Table 1.5 shows in the first column, instruments which fully transfer the risk of loss to another party in exchange for a premium. The premium payment is a method of smoothing losses over time without the fiscal shocks that an outlay for single major loss creates for a country.

Table 1.5. Insurance and Financing Options

Insurance (risk transfer) instruments	Loss financing instruments
Indemnity insurance	Budget reserves
Parametric insurance/reinsurance	Contingent loans
Catastrophe ("cat") bonds	Bond guarantees
Catastrophe swaps	Catastrophe equity puts
Exchange-traded catastrophe options (index-based)	Contingent notes
Weather derivatives	Contractual/contributory solidarity payments

Source: Prepared by the authors using World Bank data and other financial market information.

However, these instruments (risk transfer, insurance) should be only used once other funding instruments have been exhausted or when they are no longer cost-effective. This would occur in situations where budget or debt financing are insufficient or uneconomical from a medium-term fiscal perspective. In the second column, the instruments shown are purely financing instruments. They do not transfer the risk of loss as in insurance but typically do not require any prior payment if no loss occurs. The different instruments are briefly described in box 1.5.

The deployment of debt for disaster financing is a useful instrument for smoothing losses but should be limited to certain thresholds of losses. Debt financing for disasters in the low to mid-level range of losses can result in being used frequently, thus building

Box 1.5. The Range of Catastrophe Insurance Instruments

Risk Transfer Instruments. The traditional form of insurance is *Indemnity Insurance*. A premium is paid annually in exchange for payment covering a loss if it occurs. However, the loss has to be on the specific property that is insured. For that reason it "indemnifies" the policy holder for the particular loss on the asset contractually insured. An insurance loss adjuster needs to verify this before the payment is effected. As discussed, *Parametric Insurance or Reinsurance* works more as a financial option contract where once surpassing a threshold of a measurable physical event or physical index (such as temperature) it results in a promise to pay a predefined sum of money, regardless of what the actual level of damage is. The difference between actual and 'modeled' damage is called 'basis risk' but for large portfolios such as a country's infrastructure, this risk is minimized, versus when applied to individual properties.

Catastrophe ("cat") Bonds can take the form of either indemnity or parametric insurance though more recently they have been mostly parametric. As further described below, they work just like parametric insurance contracts except that the insurer is an investor who receives a bond yield in lieu of a premium payment. While maturities of cat bonds vary, most congregate around the three–four year maturity range. The investor/purchaser is at risk of 'default' or losing his/her capital if the catastrophic event occurs, in which case the 'insured' party can use the bond principal proceeds to pay for losses. *Catastrophe Swaps*, another instrument, are simply a portfolio or instrument swap. One party who may hold catastrophe insurance risk (either as a cat bond or an insurance portfolio) can swap such instruments with another party in exchange for another type of portfolio (this can be either a regular bond/fixed income portfolio or a catastrophe portfolio but covering another type of risk or hazard than the one swapped). The objective is to diversify portfolios and thus minimize risk concentrations.

Exchange Traded Catastrophe Options are financial options which are triggered when industry-wide losses (or subregional industry-wide losses) in a given country, exceed a certain threshold which then allows the option to pay out. Typically the losses are expressed as an index (for example, the Dow or S&P being a constructed index) rather than as monetary amounts, to make measurement easier. Insurers that have potential losses associated with the index would find such contracts advantageous. *Weather Derivatives* are also option-like contracts which get triggered when temperatures (sometimes called the temperature 'index') exceeds or falls below a certain level. Such contracts are useful for both energy companies (who want to get compensated during extreme temperatures) as well as agricultural producers who could suffer crop losses with extreme degrees.

Risk Financing Instruments. These instruments are primarily funding mechanisms adapted to the needs of catastrophe losses. *Budget Reserves* as practiced by the V-4 countries, reflect allocations made annually for sole use in funding public losses (and some low-income private household losses) from disasters. Typically such reserves do not cover mega events in which case additional budget reallocations are made. *Contingent Loans* are pre-negotiated undisbursed loans which can be invoked quickly in the event of a major disaster to supply fast liquidity. Multilateral institutions as well as private commercial banks offer such facilities. *Bond Guarantees* can be considered supranational guarantees for bonds issued by a country in the aftermath of a disaster to raise funds. While countries can issue bonds without such guarantees, the latter can lower the financing cost during a period where economic and fiscal stress may have been generated by the disaster.

Catastrophe Equity Puts have been used by private companies and reflect pre-arranged contracts for a company to issue shares to raise funds if a disaster has affected its operations. This requires prior agreement with investors who are willing to purchase shares after such an event. *Contingent Notes* are similar to catastrophe equity puts but entail the issuance of notes or bonds to pre-agreed creditors who would invest in them to provide a company with liquidity in the event of a disaster. They would usually be priced above the going bond rate for such a company thus providing a yield benefit, but are not catastrophe (risk transfer) bonds. *Contractual/contributory solidarity payments* are multiparty contributory arrangements such as the EUSF discussed above where an economic community of sovereign or sub-sovereign entities contributes to a common "pot" to assist members.

Source: Prepared by the authors using World Bank data and other financial market information.

up unsustainable debt. Larger disasters require more financing but they occur less frequently. However, insurance premiums are also more expensive for frequent low-level losses as a payout claim would be more likely.

This would therefore call for using debt financing at less frequent, higher level losses (where repeat uses of debt would also be less likely). Insurance should be used at midlevel to high levels of losses (where premiums will not be so high versus at lower levels with more frequent losses). The optimality of the financing instrument can essentially be determined by conducting simulation modeling covering periods of several years, to demonstrate the cost effectiveness of each.

Structuring Catastrophe Mechanisms to Optimize Coverage at the Lowest Cost

Based on the several indicators and approaches discussed, complementary catastrophe financing mechanisms for the V-4 countries need to take into account three key considerations:

- Does the loss level of financing falls below the eligibility level of EUSF funding and substantially above budget funding available to make such a scheme worthwhile.
- If risk transfer mechanisms are used, are the benefits of risk-pooling significant enough, or should financial mechanisms be used on a single country basis.
- If risk transfer mechanisms are used, what type would be best suited, and should these mechanisms be supplemented by financing instruments such as contingent debt to optimize the long-term coverage/cost ratio and benefits.

In terms of economic loss and fiscal risk considerations, it is clear that a "mezzanine" layer of funding as well as a supplementary top layer are crucial to affront expected disaster costs. As table 1.4 earlier showed, a 5 percent probability event (a 20-year event) would cause significant losses to public property ranging from 2.2 percent to 10.7 percent of the respective governments' revenue bases. This would also generate losses ranging from 0.3 percent to 0.6 percent of GDP for public property alone and from 0.8 percent to 1.9 percent for all properties. A 1 percent probability event would cause losses that are multiples higher.

Several of these losses fall above the budget capacity of the countries and below the level where the EUSF funds may be invoked. Even when the EUSF funds are triggered, alternative funding mechanisms will provide quick needed liquidity and bridge financing for immediate recovery of destroyed assets and infrastructure life lines, as well as to supplement the loss financing at the topmost levels that cannot be covered by EUSF funding even when invoked.

The financial efficiencies obtained from multicountry pooling can be a deciding factor as to whether governments should use insurance-style mechanisms. In the country loss distributions shown earlier, and as discussed below, the benefits of pooling are substantial in terms of cost savings given the diversification advantage accruing to the insurance risk-takers or investors, in pricing this type of risk. Pooling can also be set up with an element of pure risk-based pricing across countries which benefits both the V-4 as a group as well as individual countries with risk-specific profiles without subsidies between countries.

A versatile mix of financial instruments will optimize the fiscal stability and debt minimization strategies of governments. Financing (versus risk transfer) mechanisms should be considered if the probabilities are so clear as to make a least cost case for using debt financing versus insurance instruments. As mentioned, financing should not be placed at overly low (more frequently recurring) loss levels since debt can buildup, unless the terms of such debt are sufficiently favorable so as to make such financing cost effective. Another option is to use favorable financing terms to fund insurance premiums or cat bond spreads——if the low cost debt is of a sufficiently long maturity, in which case the amortization of the premiums is spread out and, coupled with low financing rates, minimizes the impact on the budget.

Costs of Catastrophe Risk and Associated Market Pricing

The pricing nature of catastrophe instruments should be assessed across different instruments to make informed decisions regarding their long-term net costs. It is easiest to understand the instruments of insurance (including cat bonds) and risk financing instruments (loans, or standard bonds) and their pricing, when expressed in equivalent terms such as an interest rate spread over a risk-free rate. An excess-of-loss (XL) insurance contract typically used to cover only high catastrophe level losses, could, for example, command a premium equivalent to 3.7 percent of the amount insured, or expected to be paid out, if the qualifying event occurred.

As described in box 1.6 a cat bond is really an insurance contract with investors. It pays an interest rate which should reflect the insurance risk plus a basic risk free rate. Thus, if we use Euribor as a proxy for the risk-free rate (though admittedly it is marginally higher than an entirely risk-free rate), an insurance-like premium paid as interest to a cat bond investor could be equal to a 2.5 percent insurance-risk spread, plus a Euribor or similar "risk-free" base rate of 1.2 percent, for a total 3.7 percent interest rate paid on the catastrophe ("cat") bond.

The cat bond rate of return thus has several components. As can be seen in figure 1.3, the final bond return comprises the basic risk free rate obtained from investing the bond

---

Box 1.6. The Equivalency among Catastrophe Risk and Capital Market Instruments

Disaster Occurrence as a Market Default. The excess of loss (XL) insurance rate for a catastrophe level risk can also be seen in the context of a typical financial market instrument. In this regard the catastrophe probability risk spread is akin to a regular bond's default spread. If a corporation, for example, had to pay a bond spread of 2 percent over the risk free rate, the market would assume that its probability of default was 2 percent. Similarly in the case of a cat bond insurance contract, the spread above the risk free rate represents both the possibility of the disaster occurring (and triggering the contract), or the possibility of the bond defaulting. The default would effectively take place if the disaster occurred, as the bondholder would lose his principal which would be used to pay the 'insured' party for the disaster loss.

Operation of a Cat Bond. The pricing of a cat bond was briefly described above. However, it must be noted that the cat bond spread only represents the insurance risk but not the credit risk of the issuer. This is because the issuer is not the "insured" party as one would expect. In a cat bond transaction, as illustrated below, the 'insured' party (for example, the government) only pays the premium or risk spread for financial protection from catastrophes. The bond issuer is a legally separate and de facto protected special purpose vehicle (SPV) which is immune from any claims or from credit quality of the final recipient. This allows the SPV to be rated AAA. Being that it is a single purpose legal entity it does not carry any of the risks associated with SPVs or SIVs publicized during the 2008–09 financial crisis.[3]

(Box continues on next page)

Box 1.6 *(continued)*

An Alternative Nontraditional Design. An SPV is not essentially needed, however. If the government wished to be the direct issuer this could be done as well. However, in such a case the investor might require an additional spread for any existing sovereign credit risk.

Any such spread could be reduced though, via the use of supranational credit guarantees to investors, which, while costing a modest fee to the issuing government, might raise the bond rating to AAA thus reducing the credit risk spread by a larger proportion than the guarantee fee cost itself.

Features of the Special Purpose Vehicle. In the typical design, the SPV has three main functions: (a) to provide absolute credit risk protection to bondholders as per above, (b) to serve as the de facto insurance conduit providing the government catastrophe coverage, and (c) to issue the bonds to the investors and collect the risk premium from the government or other beneficiary of the insurance. A trust account is set up wherein the bond proceeds are deposited earning a risk free or similar rate. By earning a risk free rate, the government no longer needs to pay that portion of the bond spread as it is already paid out of investment returns from the trust. Thus the government only needs to pay the "insurance risk spread."

Investing in cat bonds has a significant "upside" for several investors. The approach described (also summarized in the diagram below) reflects a typical arrangement for investors in cat bonds. While it may appear like a loser's gamble, the benefit for investors are twofold: (a) they receive a relatively high yield compared to other market instruments (in the event of no default), and (b) the cat bond instrument helps diversify their portfolios with a risk (that is, natural or climate disaster related) which is not correlated to other financial market bonds or securities. Since cat bonds finance losses beyond a certain probability (for example, in the 1 percent range of probability) investors also consider that the "default risk" is worth taking to obtain the benefits described.

Source: Prepared by the authors using World Bank data and other financial market information.

Figure 1.3. Catastrophe Bond Financing Structure

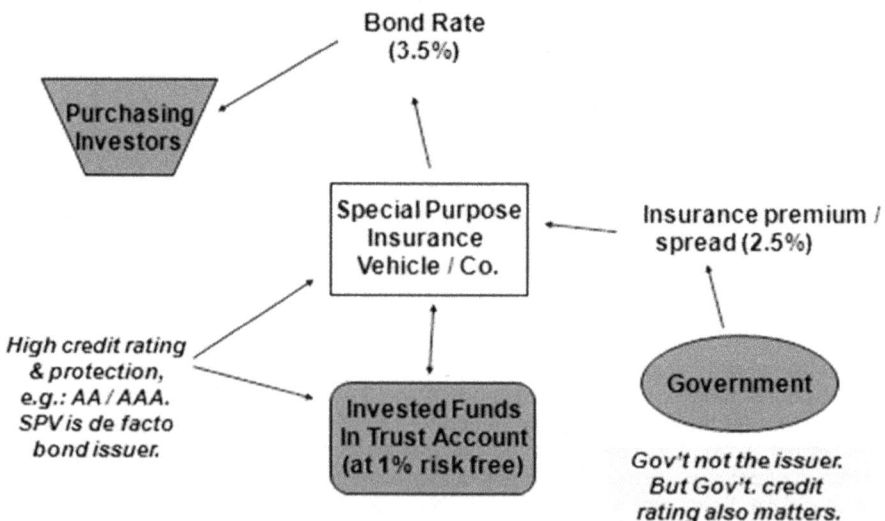

Source: Prepared by the authors using World Bank data and other financial market information.

proceeds in a protected account (with a 1 percent return assumed) plus the insurance spread reflected in a variance-adjusted probability of the occurrence of the catastrophic event (assumed at 2.5 percent). The total bond coupon interest rate (annualized) paid to investors is thus 3.5 percent in the example below.

It should be noted that there is no risk of principal default due to credit risk. This is because the government (or any other client) does not hold the funds nor is responsible for directly repaying principal. This is paid out of the trust account via the special purpose vehicle (SPV) if no catastrophe occurs to trigger any loss payment. As mentioned, if the catastrophe event triggers, then the bondholders lose their principal and the funds in the trust are transferred as an insurance payment to the government.

Comparing Insurance Premiums with Contingent Loan Pricing

In comparing debt financing versus insurance-type instruments, the long-term effect of expenditures and fiscal outlays for each financial instrument, needs to be quantified. Price comparability requires multi-period simulation since the instruments' funding characteristics and contractual conditions are unique. An approximation of equivalent pricing can be visualized under specific catastrophe scenarios (for example, probability-based events) where each instrument can be tested for its cost effectiveness. This is described in box 1.7.

Box 1.7. Equivalence of Debt versus Risk Transfer (Insurance) Instruments

Occurrence versus non-occurrence scenarios need to be first considered. If a probability of occurrence of a major flood event in a given river catchment in the Czech Republic is say, 5 percent in a given year (that is, p = 5 percent), and a EUR 300 million loan, is considered to fund such a loss, if it is priced at 3 percent over Euribor then the average annual payments, including principal and interest, over an assumed 10-year maturity period, would provide a "premium-equivalent" annual rate of approximately 22 percent for the total cost of such credit during that time period. On the face of it, this seems highly expensive. However, since there is a high probability (95 percent, the converse of 5 percent) that the credit will not be utilized at all, then the expected cost of such an instrument must weigh the two possibilities. Thus, the projected cost of the loan would be:

$$p \times (22 \text{ percent}) + (1-p) \times (0 \text{ percent}),$$

where p is the 5 percent occurrence probability and 22 percent is the all-in cost of the credit expressed as a fixed level payment (of principal and interest) over the average loan balance. No grace period is assumed. This therefore equals:

$$5 \text{ percent} \times (22 \text{ percent}) + 95 \text{ percent} \times 0 \text{ percent} = 1.1 \text{ percent},$$

which is lower than the insurance premium of 2.5 percent discussed above.

However, if the loan (or an additional loan) needed to be utilized again during the same time period, then the cost would of course rise and begin multiplying. Of course, once the loan is utilized, its effective overall cost of 22 percent (if treated as an insurance contract) is substantially higher than paying an insurance premium (which has no principal repayment) or a cat bond spread; as the loan is fully repayable debt and there is no risk transfer.

(Box continues on next page)

Box 1.7 (continued)

Advantages of Loan and Insurance Instruments. The loan becomes more cost effective at less frequent probabilities since in such cases, it is likely to be utilized less, in which case the cost of non-use is zero or close to zero.[4] However, since estimates of catastrophe probabilities require a large variance/range around the mean probability (which is one reason why insurers price premiums at a multiple of the expected loss probability) provisions must be made for such a variance. An incorrectly specified probability or a higher adjusted probability (for example, due to climate change effects), may indeed make insurance pricing more attractive if debt financing is triggered too often. While typically more expensive, insurance does not face the risk of unexpected large repayments and can be more easily built into public budgets as uniform level annual payments.

Source: World Bank.

Optimal Structuring of Funding Mechanisms for Loss Coverage

Combining the available financial and budgetary instruments would optimize governments' fiscal risk management against disasters. As discussed, for Poland, the Czech Republic, Hungary, and the Slovak Republic individual country disaster financing structures can be designed, as well as combined/pooled structures to gain diversification and pricing benefits accruing to the four countries. Any pooling structure would apply primarily to the middle mezzanine funding layer and above, as shown in figure 1.4, since the lower layer represents national government budget reserves for disasters, and the topmost layer is partially covered by EU solidarity fund payments. The mezzanine layer can also overlap with the top layer in order to provide quick liquidity and bridge financing while EUSF payments are processed and to fund any losses above those not covered by the EUSF. In the case of Poland, for example, the mezzanine layer could cover public property/infrastructure losses amounting to around 0.3 percent of GDP (as per table 1.4) under a loss scenario with a 5 percent annual probability.

Figure 1.4. Proposed Disaster Risk Funding

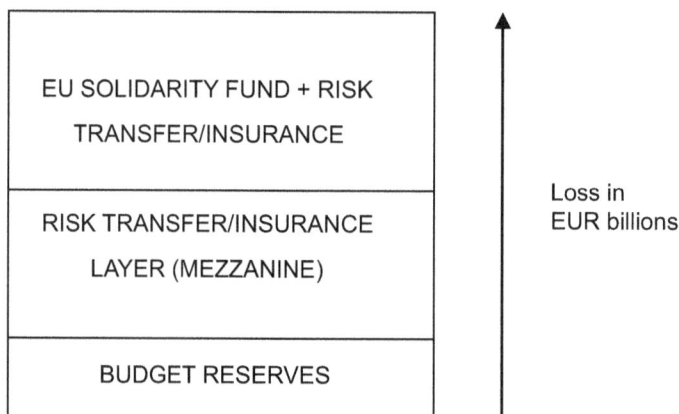

Source: World Bank.

If the mezzanine funding layer is specifically examined (see figure 1.5 for an expansion of "mezzanine" box from figure 1.4), it can comprise a hybrid of instruments to optimize the financial cost of catastrophic coverage. In the example of the structure given, a contingent loan is used to cover a pro-rata portion of the potential loss, while risk transfer instruments in the form of a catastrophe bond and/or a parametric insurance policy provide the remainder of the coverage. In the case of a catastrophe bond under a multicountry pooled structure, each country would pay the calculated portion of the insurance risk spread to the SPV which would issue the final bond to investors. Further below is the discussion of risk-adjusted spreads for each country, based on their respective loss exposures and probabilities.

Figure 1.5. Risk Coverage Mezzanine Layer

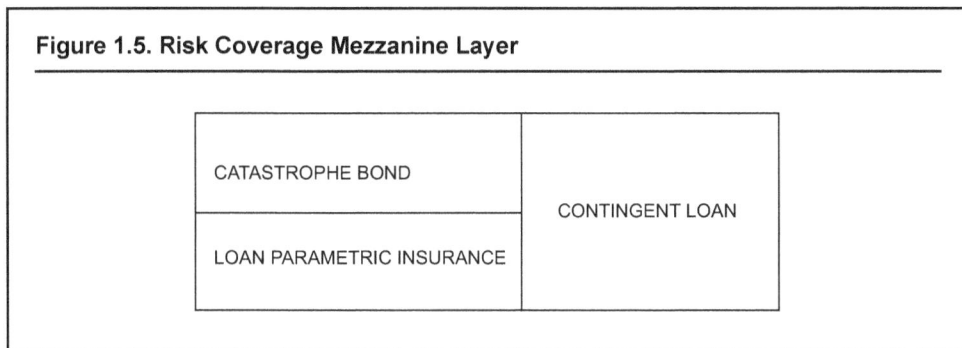

Source: World Bank.

Applying a Parametric Insurance Structure

Under the parametric-based contract, the flood level itself is the payout trigger. The parametric instrument can be used both with the cat bond instrument shown in box 1.6 as well as under an insurance policy within box 1.8, the "parametric insurance" box (the latter can be offered by an insurance arm of a major international reinsurer such as Swiss Re or Munich Re). The parametric contract works like a financial option: if the technical measured flood event is recorded above a certain threshold (such as flood height or water flow volume) the financial/insurance contract will pay out a pre-specified amount. Thus the flood level needs to be associated (with a degree of modeling accuracy) to actual historical or forecasted losses. The contract does not pay on a property-by-property basis since this mechanism is geared toward national governments with country-wide asset portfolios and ensuring a streamlined approach.

The trigger attributes can also be custom designed. In the example that can apply to both a parametric insurance contract or a catastrophe bond as explained earlier, the insurance payment trigger can be further calibrated depending on the flood height level and on the location of the flood in relation to population centers. The parametric contract triggers thus need to be specified according to the flood magnitude and location attributes, with payment amounts related to asset value characteristics of each country (and city). In the illustration in box 1.8, the principle is that, as the flood height becomes larger, the insurance payout becomes greater as well. In this regard, parametric contracts need not be only binary and can be calibrated along a graduated scale.

Box 1.8. Parametrically Triggered Payments Calibrated with a Two-Factor Index Scale

Measurement and Application of the Trigger. The payment is higher if the threshold flood trigger is breached within the city center (or within the perimeter established; see figure 1.6) and lower if the threshold flood is breached outside the central city limits (this is designed as such since typically asset values outside the perimeter are less concentrated and would thus suffer lower losses). The percentage (%) figure refers to the total available fixed limit insurance coverage under the contract for a worst case scenario (in this instance a full 100 percent payment occurs either when the flood height is 70 meters in the inner city grid, or 100 meters in the outer grid). In all other scenarios, the payment would only be a proportion of the total as shown in the threshold payment trigger table.

Technology and Data Validation. As such mechanisms require flood measurement equipment in each river catchment in each country, such equipment and its technical standards would need to fully certified across all countries. To enhance credibility and confidence in a multicountry scheme, a radio satellite device that picks up the flood readings from the equipment, should be attached to each site and transmit the flood data to a central office (for example, regional emergency or monitoring station) immediately so that the flood reading is not reliant solely on local based staff. This 'central data collection' location is also important for communication to investors (under a cat bond contract) so they can rely on one centralized location for reporting on whether triggers were breached or not.

Annual Event Occurrence versus Annual Cumulative Threshold. An alternative method to structure and interpret the contract triggers would be to make them cumulative or equivalent to several events, within an annual period. Thus, instead of the contract paying out only when the flood exceeds a certain level in a given location, it might be specified so that given flood levels receive certain "weights." If those flood levels and weights occur frequently within a year, the sum of the "weights" can be used to build a composite variable which if exceeding a pre-specified 'composite weight' threshold, would allow a contractual payment to be made even if this was not caused by one single event. This is somewhat akin to the case of Marcelo Rios (a Chilean tennis player) who achieved top seed status in world tennis in 1998 by winning the several smaller competitions, but without having won any of the Grand Slam Cups (that is, US Open, French Open, Wimbledon, Australian Open).

Source: World Bank.

Figure 1.6. Threshold Payment Triggers

Flood height (in meters)	40	70	100	Outer grid of city
% insurance payment Inner grid	40	100		Inner grid of city
% insurance payment Outer grid	20	60	100	

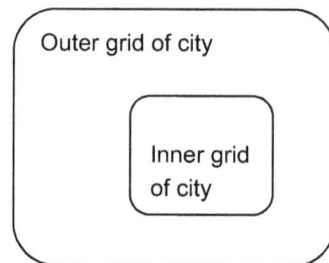

Source: Prepared by the authors using World Bank data and other financial market information.

Global capital market capacity allows an efficient diversification of insurance sources. The global insurance/reinsurance market capacity and its available capital may not be sufficient to cover large new risks such as those for central European floods. This would be determined by a market test and contract bids, and would also depend on the levels of coverage sought. This is why in the earlier diagrams, the 'parametric insurance' layers were split by cat bonds and parametric insurance to diversify and take advantage of additional funding sources to transfer such risks. For parametric contracts, a much broader funding source is the cat bond market since the capital markets have over 100 times the exposure capital than that of global insurers and reinsurers.

Risk-Based Pricing (Based on Loss Exposure and Probability)

Individual country pricing under pooled funding arrangements should be risk based to avoid cross-subsidies. One key concern of governments when participating in pooled insurance structures is the fear that they will be subsidizing their riskier neighbor(s) who will suffer more of the losses. A parallel debate is occurring in the banking realm within the auspices of the Financial Stability Board (FSB) with regard to burden sharing for potential cross border deposit insurance rules. Under flood insurance pools as described in this report, it is very straightforward to add risk-based elements to the pricing to minimize cross-subsidization across countries. The pooling effect in itself reduces the pricing margin for all participants anyway due to the larger diversified portfolio. A solidarity element is also an option that can be considered.

In table 1.6, alternate design options are shown regarding the financial risk-spread pricing cost for certain levels of coverage. In table 1.6, based on the country loss distribution analysis, an aggregate loss of EUR 7.6 billion is used for the countries combined.

Table 1.6. Price Advantages of Pooling for Country Flood Insurance (Based on a Combined Aggregate Loss of EUR 7.6 billion)

Country	Individual pricing non-pooled	Countries pooled with risk pricing	Pooled with solidarity risk pricing[a]
Poland	4.50%	3.02%	2.35%
Slovak Republic	2.40%	1.61%	1.64%
Czech Republic	1.50%	1.01%	1.34%
Hungary	1.60%	1.07%	1.37%
Average expected loss probability	1.00%	0.67%	0.67%
Average spread/premium[b]	2.50%	1.68%	1.68%
In euros			
Sum of individual premiums	190,000,000		
Sum of pooled country premiums		127,300,000	
Savings from pooling		62,700,000	

Source: World Bank.
a. Solidarity pricing means that half the pooling benefits are shared equally—the other half are allocated by risk to each country (i.e., those with lower risk getting the most remaining half benefits).
b. Over Euribor, which is currently around 1.2 percent. The spread reflects the pure risk probability premium (expected loss probability) plus the variance uncertainty premium (risk load) around the mean of the risk probability.

In the table's *first* column, is the financial spread that each country would pay if they would individually contract such insurance or use a cat bond on their own.[5] The *second* column shows the reduction in each country's financial spread or 'premium' if the public property/infrastructure was insured as a pooled portfolio. The savings in premiums (or financial spread) amount to EUR 62 million or 33 percent of the non-pooled amount when summed.

Contract sizes can also be scaled to individual country funding preferences. It should be recalled that since these are parametric contracts, they are structured as financial options triggered by threshold flood levels, therefore the total coverage amount can be adjusted accordingly (for example, one country may wish to have a coverage of EUR 100 million and another EUR 1 billion) according to each country's preference. This is because the loss payments that are made, are based on the technical model and triggers and not on actual damages sustained by individual assets on the ground. Of course the intent of the model is to capture a similar level of losses, given a specific flood magnitude. The scaling down of any contract coverage therefore, would result in a proportional reduction in the risk premium, to an amount equivalent to the individual country risk spread multiplied by the coverage amount desired. The probability levels (and thus the end-pricing) can also be adjusted depending on whether a government wishes to fund more frequent flood losses or rarer events.

While the pooling and/aggregation benefits are obtained up-front by all countries, solidarity pricing elements can also be built in. In such a case, and as shown in the *third* column of table 1.6, this would entail pricing for half of each country's risk based on its proportionate loss probability (that is, risk-based) and the other half split evenly among all participants (that is, a non-risk based, solidarity element). No more than this is recommended as a solidarity element, as any higher amount would result in over-subsidization by lower risk countries. Alternatively, the pricing can be left as purely risk-based price in which case even the highest risk country will still benefit from the pooling effect. The amounts shown above are entirely illustrative and could just as well constitute $1/10$th or $1/100$th of coverage levels individually selected by each country, with commensurate premium levels for such lower coverage amounts.

Pooled pricing as a portfolio, results in lower financing spreads than is achieved at individual average country risk spreads. As can be seen, the sum of loss probabilities for the four countries in the above example, in order to reach the aggregate loss level shown, represents a 1 percent probability when countries insure alone, but a 0.67 percent probability when they pool their risks. Due to the variance uncertainty of mega events the insurance pricing raises the spread to 2.5 percent, on average, when countries insure individually, since each country is assessed as an independent portfolio with a corresponding variance volatility.

Pricing is reduced to a 1.68 percent average cost spread when pooling the risks, versus the 2.50 percent average spread when insuring separately. Table 1.6 shows the average individual and portfolio costs and spreads for the cases of (a) individual based pricing, (b) pooled pricing fully adjusted for country risks, and (c) pooled pricing with half of the pricing based on country risks and half of the pooling benefits distributed equally among participants as a solidarity element.

Summary of Risk Management Efficiencies Applied to Specific Instruments

The choice or combination of funding instruments for the mezzanine and top levels of fiscal disaster coverage will require final market pricing tests. These include bids, available terms, more detailed physical risk modeling, and loss probability estimations before obtaining final figures for loss probabilities and risk pricing. However, based on the preliminary results of this study as reflected in the above analysis for parametric contracts, the pricing should have a range close to these figures.

In some instances additional financial service fees will exist beyond the risk spreads alone. Due to underwriting and other fees, a catastrophe bond contract for example may have a higher "all-in" cost. It will also have a coupon rate would include the risk free rate plus the risk spread whose pricing may need additional market testing. Alternatively, a contingent loan contract can also be used where its disbursement would be parametrically triggered.[6] To simplify the final analysis, the next illustrations focus on the parametric insurance component of the broader mezzanine layer within a risk funding structure.

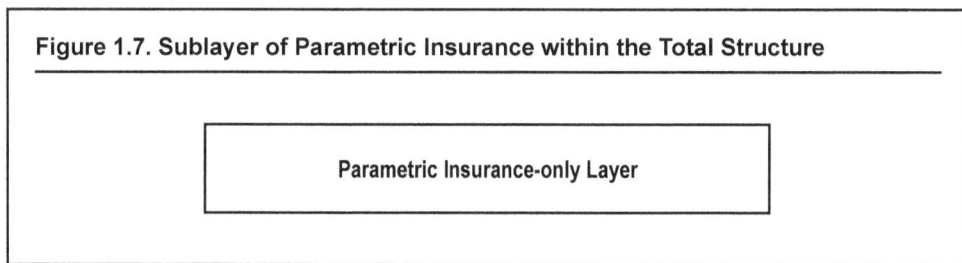

Figure 1.7. Sublayer of Parametric Insurance within the Total Structure

Parametric Insurance-only Layer

Source: World Bank.

If the parametric insurance portion of the mezzanine layer illustrated in figure 1.7 is split into individual country risk spreads and costs, these would be as shown in figure 1.8, assuming each country separately and individually contracted such insurance.

Figure 1.8. Individual Pricing: Non-pooled

Poland	Czech Republic	Hungary	Slovak Republic
4.5%	1.5%	1.6%	2.4%

Source: World Bank.

If the V-4 countries pooled their risks within a single mechanism, the spread/cost pricing would be reduced as per figure 1.9. In this example, the partial solidarity scenario is used where half of the reduction in spreads would comprise the proportional

Figure 1.9. Pooled: Collective Pricing (Solidarity and Risk-based)

Poland	Czech Republic	Hungary	Slovak Republic
2.35%	1.34%	1.37%	1.64%

Source: World Bank.

allocation of the pooled savings assigned to each country based on its exact risk profile, while the other half of the pooled savings are allocated in equal shares to each country. This would result in the following risk-cost spread(s) for each country:

Under this arrangement all parties benefit from the multicountry diversification of the fiscal disaster insurance coverage, with risk-sharing based half on country risk and half on the solidarity element. The option of only risk-based pricing would be represented by table 1.6, column 2, where there is no solidarity element.

An alternative or supplement to the risk transfer insurance portions of a fiscal insurance structure would comprise a multicountry cat bond (figure 1.10). Since such bond pays a risk free rate (approximated by Euribor in this report) plus the additional spread for insurance risk probabilities, its total cost appears initially higher than under the purely parametric insurance approach which does not have a base rate to contend with. But this is not the case, as the Euribor base rate component is invested and yields a return accruing to each country.

Figure 1.10. Pooled Catastrophe Bond Structure

Poland	Czech Republic	Hungary	Slovak Republic
Euribor	Euribor	Euribor	Euribor
+	+	+	+
2.35%	1.34%	1.37%	1.64%

Source: World Bank.

As discussed previously, since cat bond proceeds are invested in risk-free or similar securities, pending an event, this cancels out most of the Euribor cost. To illustrate, the current average euro government bond spreads approximate 1 percent. The "close to risk-free" three-month euro deposit rates approximate 1.04 percent. Thus, the cost (in interest payments) on a cat bond would not be Euribor plus the insurance risk spread, but rather Euribor minus the risk free rate returns earned, plus the insurance spread. The Euribor rate less the risk free rate base would thus only amount to about 0.2 percent and potentially less depending on the funds and securities that are invested in, with the cat bond proceeds.

Governments will likely be concerned about the issuance of a single bond covering all four country risks. However, there should be no concern at all since the de facto legal issuer of a cat bond is not a particular sovereign government but rather a special purpose legal entity vehicle that sells the bond to the investors (and on the other hand, acts as a captive single purpose insurance company to the governments).

Therefore the issuance of a single bond for the V-4 countries falls outside and does not affect national public debt limits. Essentially each country would pay its risk-based spread to the cat bond legal entity vehicle (that would be set up by the sponsoring insurer), and the sum of the country spread or premiums would be allocated for paying the required interest to the bond investors (in addition to the Euribor base factor, discussed above, which accrues for the most part from the bond funds invested). In this regard, the cat bond is not accounted for as public debt. Rather, the premium/spread payments into the scheme represent government budgetary obligations and an expenditure item.

If a catastrophe occurred in a given country under the cat bond mechanism, the affected country would be paid from a portion of the invested cat bond principal that had been set aside in the trust. The size of the payment assumes a graduated compensation structure based on the severity of the hazard as per the discussion above. The remaining funds would still accrue interest for the investors (albeit on a lower principal base) but still be available for disaster payments if a qualifying catastrophe occurred in any of the other countries. Figure 1.11 illustrates the structure and flows under such a mechanism.

Given the principal-protected design of the SPV under a cat bond, there is no 'issuer' credit risk for the repayment of principal. This of course excludes the event of a qualifying disaster which constitutes an insurance risk versus a credit risk. As mentioned, in addition to the insurance spreads paid per country, the differential of approximately 0.2

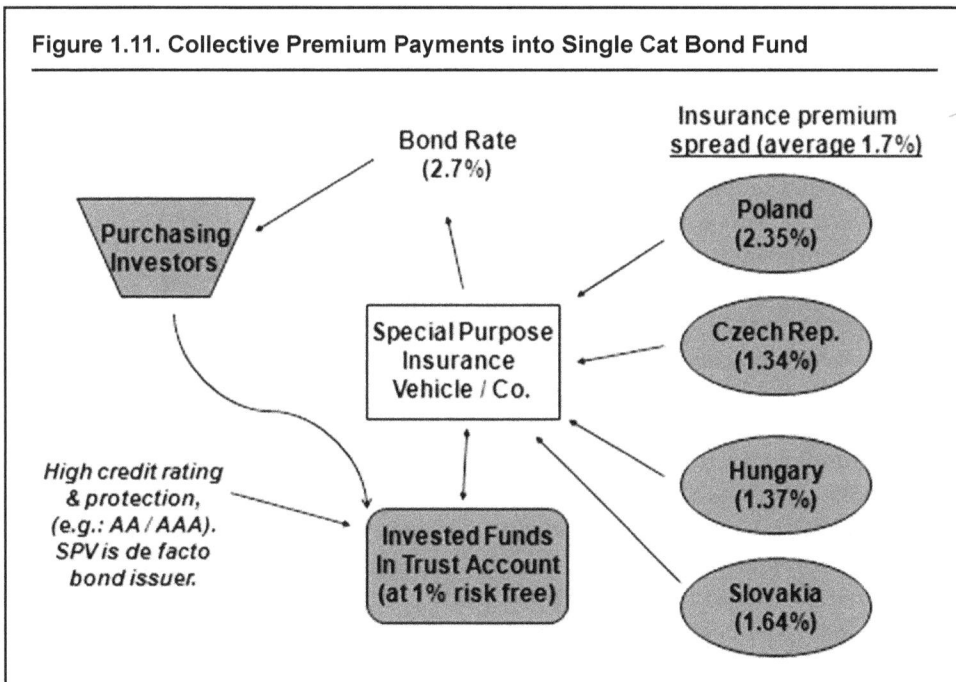

Figure 1.11. Collective Premium Payments into Single Cat Bond Fund

Source: Prepared by the authors using World Bank data and other financial market information.

percent between the Euribor rate to be paid as part of the bond coupon, and the risk free rate earned on the invested funds, would add another element to the cost. Bond preparation and underwriting fees would also need to be factored in.

To provide investors additional assurances, a credit guarantee can also be applied to the coupon interest which comes from public sector budgets. For example, the premium/coupon payments could potentially carry a minor credit risk depending on the market rating of each country and its reliability in making budgetary payments. If this was of any concern, a supranational guarantee could be provided to investors to assure the timely payment of the coupon interest. Since coupons are a small fraction of total principal, any guarantee fee would be very minimal (for example, 0.5 percent of a coupon representing 1.68 percent of total principal, that is, extremely small).

A coupon payment guarantee can be "rolling," which means that it would cover only the next payment incrementally, when it arises. If a guarantee of this sort is invoked by investors (in an overdue payment situation), the guarantee would first pay the investors and then deactivate (that is, it is not reinstated so any subsequent coupons would not be covered by the guarantee). While this would seem less than desirable from the investors' point of view they would have already been locked into the cat bond contract.

Investors would thus have also already accepted a lower coupon interest spread given the up-front existence of a guarantee. This spread would continue to benefit the government(s) until the end of the contract. The rolling feature of the guarantee, while not activated, would also make its fee cheaper as it would only cover coupon payments as they come due. Of course, a guarantee could not cover principal since by definition under a cat bond, the principal is at risk due to natural 'insurance' causes, until it comes due as a final bullet payment, assuming the absence of a qualifying disaster event.

Institutional Set-Up to Manage Pooled Structures

A four-country catastrophe insurance fiscal scheme with the options discussed above could be set up by creating a new legal entity owned by the V-4 governments. For example, this new legal entity could be based in a different country with a well established trust industry such as Switzerland. The legal entity would collect premiums from the participants and promise coverage based on up-the-line contracts engaged in with global insurers or reinsurers, as approved by the entity's Board which would include all the country governments.

In the case of a parametric contract for participating members, the entity would ideally require initial capitalization to meet minimum technical reserve requirements. This would help to lower the up-the-line cost of insurance since the initial capital would provide the first cushion of coverage. That means that additional purchased reinsurance coverage would only be contracted at higher loss levels, at a lower proportional cost. This design feature is important since premium payments made by members in the initial years would be insufficient to make up a sufficient cushion in case of an early disaster occurrence. Under such a parametric mechanism (excluding the use of a cat bond), a small initial capital contribution would thus be required from participating members. Such a contribution would also help lower the premium spreads beyond the benefits obtained from pooling alone.

An alternative arrangement would be to use an existing global insurer or reinsurer to provide direct coverage. This would result in a higher spread/rate because such an insurer would also need to recover a return on capital plus the pricing for the disaster coverage risk. Such an arrangement would be simpler to set up and would nevertheless provide the pooling benefits of a four country portfolio.

A multicountry catastrophe bond mechanism may not be the lowest cost mechanism but it would be a pioneering approach and the most innovative option. Using a multicountry catastrophe bond (whose final pricing would need validation from market offers) would not need any initial capital and would be priced based on the market's demand for an adequate risk-based spread, given the flood risk characteristics. A calculation of all costs and fees should be first quantified as well as establishing the trigger probabilities. Triggers for a lower likelihood (larger upper level loss) event would demand lower proportional premiums, and also compensate mainly at high loss levels which is the main purpose of these instruments.

Conclusion

The V-4 governments should consider it a priority to design and implement a joint catastrophe risk management scheme to ameliorate the fiscal impact of major disasters.

Flood based catastrophes require not only fast response and emergency relief services from governments, but also adequate financial and fiscal planning to ensure that such events do not unduly disrupt economic and fiscal planning or generate setbacks in the development path. Historical and projected flood scenarios can result in losses amounting to significant shares of budget revenue and GDP, not only for total country-wide losses but also for damages to public/state property and infrastructure.

While existing mechanisms such as government budget funds and the EU Solidarity Fund certainly provide needed funds in the event of major floods or other disasters, their quantum as well as their speed of deployment does not match the urgent short term needs of disaster situations. In this context, governments should analyze their potential nationwide risk exposures and determine the precise levels of losses and probabilities that would require pre-established funding for expected damages to provide immediate liquidity and smooth out fiscal costs.

For the V-4 countries which all share major flood risks, a pooling approach to fiscal funding insurance would also provide significant financial savings (estimated between 25 percent and 33 percent of otherwise individual country approaches) when setting up such mechanisms.

At a macroeconomic level, insurance payments to governments need not be based on site-by-site assessments of asset damages. Instead, using scientific risk modeling methods, reliable correlations between flood magnitudes (measured at river catchments) and large area estimated losses can be custom-designed so as to put in place physical event-triggered (parametric) contracts. These can be verified and paid out with speed, and meet the needs of immediate post-disaster financing.

Next Steps and Due Diligence Requirements for Setting up a Risk Pooling Mechanism

To proceed with any of the above options, additional due diligence analysis is needed to validate and obtain a sufficient degree of precision in the underlying data parameters, in line with the requirements of risk analysts, market players and hydrological experts. This would include the following steps:

▓ Validation of values of property and infrastructure exposures, loss exposures for such assets, and projected loss frequencies. This would involve refining the analysis of the likelihood of losses by country and by regions within each country, based on a higher resolution of the data and mapping illustrated in this paper.

▓ Refinement of correlation analyses is needed with respect to flood magnitudes associated with likely losses in each country's areas surrounding river catchments, and obtaining correlation coefficients of sufficient dependability to use and rely on, for parametric contracts.

▓ Obtaining further precision in the probability functions (severity and frequency probabilities) will be required to determine loss distribution functions with a very high confidence level (for example, 99 percent confidence interval) to allow precise and reliable expert and market pricing.

▓ Obtaining market final validation of cat bond pricing or parametric insurance pricing spreads is required. For cat bonds, an inventory should be done of the "all-in" funding costs including credit rating costs, modeling costs, other financial services in the SPV structure, and bond underwriting costs.

▓ Governments should select the public asset inventories and potential infrastructure losses wishing to be protected (for example, as a subset of total assets at risk) and determining the loss exposure probability functions for these, so as to arrive at the consequent quantification of insurance levels desired for loss compensation and affordable cost for such.

▓ An institutional structure and multicountry legal conduit should be set up as an insurance entity to pool the risks and channel resources for the respective options and mechanisms for risk transfer. The rules of operation, method of verification of payment triggers and management of funds would need to be defined depending on which option or instrument is selected.

▓ A small team with expert skills should be selected manage and oversee any institutional structure for the above purposes, and determine the overall final cost of the mechanism selected including carrying out oversight, maintenance and monitoring functions.

Next Chapters

Following Chapter 1, the report provides additional supporting analysis and data in the next chapters as background information. The next parts of the report cover the following:

▓ **Chapter 2**: Covers the physical risk and loss modeling methodology used to determine flood probabilities and effects in different regions of each country and to arrive at modeled losses, based on a range of public and private sector assets and infrastructure, mapped to topographic/terrain characteristics and flood behavior and impacts.

▓ **Chapter 3**: Examines, for the purpose of parametric contract design, the correlation analysis of flood frequencies and severities versus monetary losses, in order to establish reliable loss quanta associated with measurable physical flood magnitudes per country and per river catchment.

▓ **Chapter 4**: Reports on the institutional analysis of private insurance sector penetration and coverage for catastrophic and flood risks in each country, as well as the availability and scope of public sector budget mechanisms for funding natural disasters.

- **Chapter 5**: Develops a multicountry global econometric analysis based on worldwide data, showing fiscal sustainability effects from natural disasters and how different country pre-conditions (such as depth of financial, bond, insurance markets) affect the GDP path and the effectiveness and nature of the fiscal response in the recovery process.

Notes

1. If we make the analogy of investment returns instead of insurance losses, this is akin to having a pension portfolio of 3 bonds versus one of 30 bonds. A 30-bond portfolio would have more even and stable returns while a 3-bond portfolio may have a potential upside but also a large potential downside (loss). If a pension fund manager firm had to guarantee at least a zero rate of return on the investments, it would need a larger capital cushion for the 3-bond portfolio, as the chances of it yielding below-zero returns would be much higher.

2. Currently government budget allocations for disasters are rather modest, with the Czech Republic allocating EUR 4 million annually (but relying on ex post bond issuances for disasters), Poland EUR 170 million, and Hungary EUR 15 million.

3. Very few cat bonds experienced credit pricing problems during the crisis as the use of the Libor base rate implied underlying supporting securities with a degree of liquidity and credit risk. For cat bonds, floating rates are frequently swapped into fixed rates via 'total return swaps' and some swap counterparties (for example, Lehman) had credit risks because of this. These were for a very small minority of issuances, however, and now these latent problems are being corrected via the use of cat bonds with a spread over risk free Treasuries instead of Libor, and lesser use of swaps into fixed rates.

4. Commercial banks typically charge a commitment fee for undisbursed balances so there is an additional cost to consider. Multilaterals such as the World Bank used to charge commitment fees but the current rate on commitment fees for IBRD loans is zero.

5. The figures shown are only estimates based on available market and risk exposure information but would need to be validated in more detail if an actual transaction were to be engaged.

6. One possibility would be the use of a multilateral or IBRD loan where currently, a maturity up to 12 years would offer a rate of Euribor or dollar Libor plus a 0.6 percent spread. For dollar Libor, the effective all-in interest rate would be approximately 1.05 percent, and for Euribor higher at around 1.85 percent (using data as of Q1 2011). A loan could be a contingent facility (currently with no commitment charge while pending disbursement) to complement insurance mechanisms. It could also be alternatively used up-front to finance premium payments for a parametric insurance policy, or pay for bond coupon interest.

Catastrophic Loss Exposure Analysis: Flood Exposures and Probabilistic Loss Estimations in Poland, the Czech Republic, Hungary, and the Slovak Republic

Introduction

This chapter analyzes the possible property losses caused by extreme flood events in the four countries of Eastern Central Europe that include Poland, the Czech Republic, Hungary, and the Slovak Republic, often commonly referred to as the V-4 or Visegrad Group countries.

In the nineties and at the beginning of this century, the sub-region was hit with two unusually intensive floods that changed understanding of the risk of flood in the countries of the sub-region. Both floods started with extreme precipitation in areas of very high API_{30}[1]. The change occurred together with major changes in political and social arrangements in the countries. Even after the serious floods in the early summer 1997 in Poland and the Czech Republic, the risk of floods in the region had not been generally considered particularly serious. Decision makers as well as the population at large continued to believe that the region would not suffer from serious floods and that the safe period of the twentieth century would continue. Some risk managers in the insurance industry introduced tools based on geographic information systems (GIS) and sought support of GIS providers.

The situation for research in this field improved after the August 2002 flood. The forecasted flooded areas according to the developed models nearly coincided with the experience of the 2002 flood. As a result, the perception of flood risk increased. This allowed major support from the insurance industry for the research teams of Intermap Technologies and thus the study represented in this chapter is based on a yearlong experience of the research team[2] of Intermap Technologies (located in Prague), providing support for the insurance industry in natural hazard modeling, GIS and software development for reinsurance, underwriting, risk management, loss adjustment, product development, and other departments of the insurance companies, in close cooperation with partner companies and development teams, such as insurers and reinsurers, Nat Cat modelers and universities.

The main emphasis of this work was thus on the estimation of possible losses to publicly owned property caused by river floods. River floods are generally understood as mainly regional floods, or partially local river floods caused by heavy rainfall events. In contrast, pluvial floods are understood as surface water flow or "ponding" outside the floodplains caused by heavy rainfall, as well as coastal surges, and are not considered in the study. Public property in these countries usually includes not only public administration, social infrastructure (such as education, culture, and health care) and technical infrastructure (such as transportation and communication networks) but also enterprises that did not fully undergo the process of privatization during the period of economic transformation of these countries.

Based on the experience with the major regional floods in the last 15 years, the public sphere was also required to fund a part of the flood losses in private property, especially housing and infrastructure. While the situation has improved now with better insurance penetration, the root causes included relatively low prior penetration of household insurance as well as low limits of claims amount for insured properties due to heavy competition in the insurance market and a poor level of financial awareness among the clients of insurance companies. Therefore, loss estimations on private assets were also a part of the analysis.

The study comprising this chapter is divided into four parts and an appendix (available online) with detailed data.[3] The first three parts contain descriptions of the methods used in the analysis while the fourth includes the results. Basic terms, content and limitations of the study are defined in Part 1 while Part 2 lists the sources for the input data. The methodology itself is described in Part 3. Part 4 is divided into two parts, one describing the results of regional and sector distribution of assets, and the other containing the results of flood loss estimations. The online appendix includes all the detailed information that was not included in the body of the other parts. The appendix is subdivided into three constituent units, the first one includes detailed data mostly on the inputs, the second one on the outputs, and the third one is mapping loss estimations in a very deep detail.

For possible loss estimations, a scenario method of flood exposure modeling was used. This method was originally developed for the insurance market in close cooperation with some leading Czech insurers in order to estimate the overall risk of their portfolios and check the conditions given to them by the reinsurance companies. Several territorial scenarios were selected for each country including the territorial extent of the recent major flood events, various catchment areas of the major rivers as well as complex geographic areas like such as geomorphologic or historical-cultural units.

The results for different scenarios may well represent the eventual range of losses, however, a single typical or mean value of losses had to be found for each country, and given the fact that the possible loss of a compound territory was not an additive function of partial possible losses of its component territories, a typical value for the whole V-4 Group had to be found. Therefore, an extrapolation of a stochastic method of flood exposure was done using the information on the regional structure of property, its location in the flood zones and possible losses under different scenarios. The stochastic method that is one of the main inputs in that extrapolation was built up in close cooperation with the Nat Cat Team of the Swiss Re reinsurance company. At the theoretical level, the flood loss modeling is explained in section 3.1 in general, in paragraph 3.9 for scenario-based modeling, and in section 3.10 for the stochastic modeling and its extrapolation. The territorial scenarios themselves are described in section 3.6 and listed in appendix section 5.1.9. (The Appendix referred to in this chapter is available online at: http://documents.worldbank.org/curated/en/2012/01/16242871.)

As the main output of the study, loss functions have been constructed for the V-4 Group, the individual countries as well as the distinct scenarios, namely the Loss Exceedance Curves and the Survival Functions. The Loss Exceedance Curve is a functional dependence of the possible loss on the return period of the loss while the Survival Function represents the per cent probability of exceeding a certain loss within a period of one year. In addition to that, possible regional distributions of the losses were estimated and projected to maps of administrative divisions in the countries. The possible loss estimations can be found in section 4.2.1 and, in more detail, in the appendix section 5.2.1. Their possible territorial distributions of losses are mentioned in appendix 5.2.4 while the possible distributions into institutional sectors as well as industry branches and asset categories are included in appendix section 5.2.5. appendix section 5.2.3 reports on loss purpose classification of losses for each scenario and appendix section 5.3 contains deep details of the loss estimation for each scenario.

To better understand both territorial and sector structure of the property in the countries that are subject of the study, the outputs also include a split of the assets according to the sector of economic activity (that is, Industry Branches), physical constitution (that is, Asset Category), and ownership structure (that is, Institutional Sector) as well as their territorial split into first (that is, provincial) or second (that is, district) levels of the state administration. On the methodological level, this topic is covered by sections 3.2 by sector, and 3.4 for the regional distribution, respectively, with listing ancillary data for regional distribution in section 4.1.2 and appendix section 5.1.13. The results are presented in the appendix sections 5.1.5 by sector and 5.1.12 for the regional split.

During the course of the work, the team was looking for the best available data on the structure of the assets in the respective countries as well as their regional distribution. Initially, governmental institutions such as ministries of finance, education, health, interior, and so forth. were contacted. However, it turned out that only incomplete lists of governmental property were available at those governmental bodies with even less complete information on the values of those properties. Furthermore, all of the V-4 countries went through a significant deconcentration and decentralization process whereby substantial parts of public administration, social infrastructure and public enterprise became a property of regional or local governments. Those properties are not listed by central governments anymore and to obtain a full list of public assets would have meant collecting the lists from up to 80 provincial and approximately 15,000 local administrations in addition to the central governments in the V-4 countries. Recognizing this, an alternative way of collecting information was chosen. The four national statistical offices provided lists of assets aggregated nationwide and for the largest statistical territorial units such as the NUTS-2 or NUTS-3 of the pan-EU classification. Even if using the same methodology of a three-dimensional split of the assets, there were slight differences in the availability of those data between individual countries. Therefore, additional interpolation was required for the countries with data gaps in both nationwide as well as territorial classification of the assets.

Even less complete were the records of the losses caused by historical flood events in the last 15 years that were needed for calibration and verification of the model. Estimates were used from hydrological research institutes such as the VUV in the Czech Republic or from national statistical offices as well as from academic sphere. The historical flood loss data are listed in appendix section 5.1.6.

Two very important inputs to the possible flood loss model have been the flood hazard zones and the vulnerability functions. The flood hazard zones have been delineated using the Geomorphologic Regression approach that was originally developed by the Nat Cat Team of the Swiss Re reinsurance company and further developed by Intermap's developers. The vulnerability functions are based on the historical loss records of the insurance companies in the Czech Republic that were calibrated and verified with the loss records during some of the recent extreme flood events in the V-4 region. Thanks to the cultural proximity and similar historical development of the V-4 countries the vulnerability functions are well transferable to the other three countries of the group. The methodology of modeling of the flood hazard zones is described in section 3.7 and the results are shown in appendix section 5.1.8. Section 3.8 describes the construction of the vulnerability functions.

1. Definitions

1.1. Territorial Scope

The analysis explores the possible losses caused by floods in the Czech Republic, Poland, Hungary, and the Slovak Republic. The respective territories of these V-4 countries are administratively divided into three principal hierarchical levels, that is, provinces, districts, and municipalities.[4] The provinces correspond to NUTS-3 level[5] in the Nomenclature of Units for Territorial Statistics (NUTS)[6] that is used for comparisons within the EU, while the districts correspond to LAU-1[7] and municipalities to LAU-2[8] level. For the purposes of the analysis, the districts are used as the smallest territorial unit.

1.2. Thematic Scope

The main aim of this analysis is to map possible extreme losses on both public services[9] and public commercial enterprises.[10] Private properties are mapped as well. Based on the experience from recent extreme floods, the governments have been providing substantial amounts of resources covering the losses on private property, especially those for residential buildings and their contents.

Due to efficient application of modeling, the assets have been divided into few classes using a three-dimensional classification used by national accounting in the respective countries that have been standardized to a certain level for all the EU member states. The three-dimensional classification contains the following dimensions: Industry Branch,[11] Asset Category,[12] and Institutional Sector.[13]

1.3. Value Definitions

1.3.1. REPRODUCTION (REPLACEMENT) VERSUS HISTORICAL PRICES

The *Reproduction price* stands for the price, for which the property would be purchased in the current year, that is, the current market price of the property. The *Historical price* represents the value of the property expressed either in the prices of a fixed historical year (for example, 2000) or in those of the year of purchase. When the analysis estimates real losses, the reproduction prices of the property are applied.

1.3.2. TIME DIMENSION

The property values as well as estimated loss values are related to year-end 2007 values.[14]

1.3.3. Gross versus Net Asset Value

The *Gross value* represents the price of the property without depreciation, that is, the value of the new property when purchasing. The *Net value* is the depreciated gross value (with depreciation amortization subtracted). For the loss modeling as well as property structure classification, the net value (in reproduction prices) is used.

1.3.4. Transnational Estimates

For the transnational cross-country comparison, the loss values were denominated in EUR. Pertinent conversions used either *Exchange Rates* or *Purchasing Power Parity* (PPP) measures. As the structure of the property considered in the model may significantly differ from the basket of goods used for PPP estimates, the Exchange Rate is used for transnational comparisons rather than PPP. The average exchange rates to convert from national currencies to EUR were used according to the European Central Bank (ECB) data for the period between July 1, 2008 and June 30, 2009.[15]

1.4. Flood Definition

The analysis focuses on the effects of the extreme events of river/fluvial flood. The river network considered streams with catchments greater than 20 square kilometers in the headwater areas. Pluvial/flash floods were considered only to the extent that they contributed to the losses caused by the river network (that is, when collecting the water from the thunderstorm or collapse of a human structure such as a dam). Losses were not considered when caused by surface water in areas with no permanent rivers/streams. Furthermore, tidal/coastal floods/storm surge were not considered.

2. Input Data and Providers

2.1. Property Value Data

The national statistical authorities are the main sources of information on the property values classified in a three-dimensional split as defined in section 3.2. These asset classifications are published for individual countries on a yearly basis. Territorial Distribution of the assets is available only to a limited extent. The data sources of property value and structure in the particular countries are described in sections 3.2.10 and 3.2.11.

To obtain information on household property, which is not registered by the national statistical authorities, data from the insurance industry were collected. The procedure for household property estimation is explained in section 3.2.4. The particular value distributions are listed in appendix section 5.1.5 for national level and in appendix section 5.1.12 for the regional level.

2.2. Property Location Data

The national statistical offices provide fixed asset value or formation data regionalized to the NUTS-2 or NUTS-3 level. Data split into lower level administrative units, that is, districts (LAU-1 level) are not available and have been modeled. The property location data sources for the particular countries as well as the regionalization procedure are described in sections 3.4.1, and 3.4.2. The distribution of the property into the hazard zones is described in section 3.5.

Individual property location data from public registers were not used due to unavailability for most countries including property categories.

2.3. Population and Income Data (Regional Distribution)

Both the population distribution and the income distribution data down to the second level administrative units, that is, districts (LAU-1 level) were provided by the national statistical offices. The data population and income data sources as well as their application are described in section 3.4.2 while the data are listed in appendix section 5.1.13.

2.4. Flood Loss Data

Historical flood loss data as well as their data sources are listed in appendix section 5.1.6. Application of the flood loss data for the vulnerability calculation is described in section 2.9.

2.5. Land Cover Data

Coordination of Information on the Environment (CORINE) Land Cover data with a 100 meter resolution grid have been used.[16] For GIS analyses, the raster data have been vectorized. Application of the land cover data is described in section 2.5. For the complete list of CORINE categories, see appendix section 5.1.11.

2.6. Hydrological Network Data

The river network used for flood hazard zone modeling corresponds to national topographical maps in scales of around 1:25,000 to 1:50,000:

- **Czech Republic**. The hydrology network of a 1:25 000 Digital Model of the Territory (Digitální model území 1:25 000) vector data has been used (see [9]).
- **The Slovak Republic**. The hydrology network of the Digital Vector Map of the Slovak Republic with 1:50,000 of Mapa Slovakia Plus[17] has been used.
- **Hungary**. The hydrology network of the Digital Vector Map of Hungary with 1:10,000 of HISZI-Map[18] has been used.
- **Poland**. Due to lack of data, the CCM River and Catchment Database, version 2.1 (CCM2, see [1]) was used and which corresponds to the SRTM elevation model[19] with a 100 meter grid and validated with Landsat TM panchromatic satellite data.[20]

2.7. Digital Elevation Model

The best available digital terrain models (DTM) were used in the particular countries. The flood protection that is recognizable in the terrain model was considered directly in the model.

- **Czech Republic.** In the Czech Republic, the DTM is based on contour lines and elevation spots of the 1:25,000 scale national topographic dataset.[21]
- **The Slovak Republic.** In the Slovak Republic, the DTM is based on contour lines and elevation spots of the 1:50,000 scale national dataset.[22]
- **Hungary.** In Hungary, the MONA Pro Europe[23] dataset derived from topographic maps of 1:50,000 scale maps (DMA series) has been used in combination with SRTM (Shuttle Radar Topography Mission) dataset.[24]
- **Poland.** In Poland, the MONA Pro Europe dataset derived from topographic maps of 1:50,000 scale maps (DMA series) has been used in combination with SRTM (Shuttle Radar Topography Mission) dataset.

2.8. Flood Hazard Data

Flood hazard zones based on the return period were delineated using an in-house built flood modeling approach that is a modification of the Geomorphologic Regression (GMR)[25] method of the Swiss Re[26] re-insurer (figure 2.1). The rivers and other streams were modeled if their catchment exceeded 20 square kilometers.[27]

A flood zoning revision was performed using 1:50,000 and 1:25,000 scale topographic maps in order to consider flood protection that is not recorded in the terrain model:

- **Czech Republic**. The flood hazard zones were modeled in 2003–05 for usage by the Czech insurance market. After modeling by the Swiss Re using the GMR method, a revision based on topographic maps was done by Multimedia Computer.[28]
- **The Slovak Republic**. The flood hazard zones were modeled in 2005 for usage by the Slovak insurance market. After modeling by the Swiss Re using the GMR method, a revision based on topographic maps was done by Multimedia Computer.
- **Hungary**. The flood hazard zones were modeled in 2009 for the purpose of this analysis. The flood hazard zones modeled by the VITUKI[29] were used for calibration[30] of the model. No revision was done.
- **Poland**. The flood hazard zones were modeled in 2009 for the purpose of this analysis. No revision was done.

2.9. Flood Vulnerability Data

The source for flood vulnerability data are Intermap's previous in-house analyses[31] based on the flood loss data of various Czech insurers and historical flood loss data, which are listed in appendix section 5.1.6.

3. Methodology

3.1. Flood Exposure Determination

The key input to the model is the three-dimensional split of the property values as described in section 3.2, plus the assets re-classified into simplified classes as defined in sections 3.2.2, 3.2.4, and 3.2.6. The spatial distribution of the three-dimensional asset values into the provinces[32] is described in section 3.4.1 while the refinement of the spatial distribution to the district level is explained in section 3.4.2. Property values are redistributed into the flood hazard zones within each district as described in section 3.5.

As discussed in section 3.8, vulnerability functions are calibrated according to historical loss data separately for each property class shown in section 3.4.3. The above provides basis for construction of a virtual portfolio of districts vs. hazard zones vs. property types. Based on the information on property distribution throughout districts, and the hazard zones and geographically defined scenarios (as mentioned in section 3.6), the potential losses are estimated with proper vulnerability functions.

As mentioned in section 3.11, the Loss Exceedance Probabilities are predicted for different scenarios whereas potential losses for distinct return periods of the flood loss are represented on the resulting dependence trend of the loss exceedance curve. Moreover, the Survival Function is also constructed—this function represents the percent probability that a certain loss will be exceeded. The above two functions represent the main outcomes of the analysis.

Figure 2.1. Overall Exposure Modeling Workflow

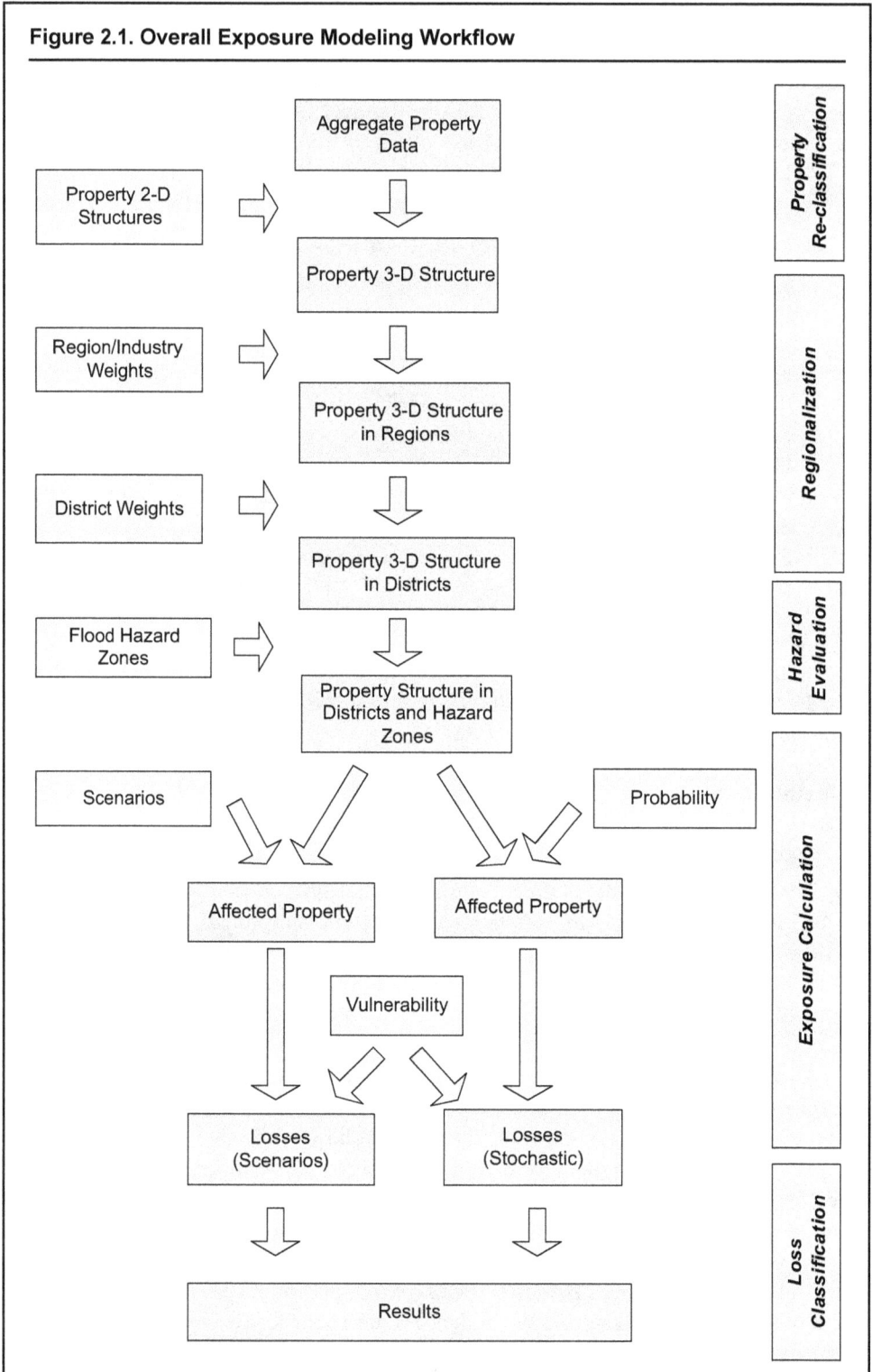

Source: Intermap Technologies.

In order to evaluate the possible loss of the individual countries as well as the V-4 Group, the loss exceedance curves are calculated for each country and the V-4 Group by using extrapolation of the stochastic method, as described in the section 3.10. The detailed classification of the losses for each scenario for a certain return period in the three-dimensional split and spatial distribution of the losses to the province level, is modeled as described in section 3.11.4.

3.2. Property Value and Classification

3.2.1. INDUSTRY BRANCH

The first dimension is the classification by Industrial Branches based on the "Classification of Economic Activities in the European Community" (NACE), revision 1.1. The NACE classification, which is used by the EU member states, is a modified version of the "International Standard Industrial Classification of all Economic Activities" (ISIC) that is supported by the United Nations (UN).[33] The NACE categories are defined in a hierarchical structure of 4 levels.[34] The main categories of the highest level—Sections—as grouped in this work are listed in table 2.1. The property structure in 1D split by Industry Branch is listed in appendix section 5.1.5.

Table 2.1. Industry Branch Classes as Used in the Study

Class	Industry
A&B	Agriculture, hunting, forestry and fishing[a]
C	Mining and quarrying
D	Manufacturing
E	Electricity, gas and water supply
F	Construction
G	Wholesale and retail trade; repair
H	Hotels and restaurant
I	Transportation, storage and communication
J	Financial intermediation
K	Real estate, renting, research and business activities
L	Public administration and defense; compulsory social security
M	Education
N	Health and social work
O	Other community, social and personal services (recreation, culture and sport; membership organizations; sewage and sanitation)

Source: Intermap Technologies.
a. Assets 12 (inventories) are not considered.

3.2.2. RECLASSIFICATION OF INDUSTRY BRANCHES

To compare asset value data with the regional distribution and with loss data, the Industry Branches were aggregated into three super-classes: *"industrial," "residential,"* and *"network"* property types. Spatial distribution of the Industrial Branches as defined in section 3.2.1 is available for the province level only.[35] In the model, the simplified prop-

Table 2.2. Industry Branch Classes as Reclassified into Three Property Types

Class	Industry
"Industrial" property type	
C	Manufacturing
D	Mining and quarrying
F[a]	Construction[a]

a. 50% of the total assets are included (the rest included in "Residential" type).

"Network" property type	
I[a]	Transportation, storage and communication[a]

a. Only assets category AN.1112 (Other buildings and structures) is included (the remaining asset categories are included in the "Residential" type).

"Residential" property type	
A[a]	Agriculture[a]
B[a]	Hunting, forestry and fishing[a]
E	Electricity, gas and water supply
F[b]	Construction[b]
G	Trade and repair
H	Hotels and restaurants
I[c]	Transportation, storage and communication[c]
J	Financial intermediation
K	Real estate, renting and business activities
L	Public administration and defense; compulsory social security
M	Education
N	Health and social work
O	Other services (recreation, culture and sport; membership organizations; sewage and sanitation)

a. Assets 12 (inventories) are not considered (see also paragraph 0).
b. 50% of the total assets are included (the rest included in "Industrial" type).
c. Except for the assets category AN.1112 (Other buildings and structures), which is included in the "Network" property type.

Source: Intermap Technologies.

erty types as defined in table 2.2 are used for weighting property values during regionalization, to districts,[36] for value distribution to flood hazard zones,[37] and for vulnerability calculations.[38]

3.2.3. Asset Category

The second dimension is the classification by Asset Categories based on the "European System of Accounts" revision of 1995 (ESA'95) that is an adaptation of the "United Nations System of National Accounts" (SNA) used for the purposes of the EU. This classification represents physical property structure. For more details about ESA see [5]. For the Asset Category classification, see table 2.3. For the Asset Categories not considered in the study, see table 2.4. The property structure in 1-D split by Asset Category is listed in appendix section 5.1.5.

Table 2.3. Classification by Asset Categories Considered in the Study

Code	Asset Category
AN	Non-financial assets
AN.1	Produced assets
AN.11	Fixed assets
AN.111	Tangible fixed assets
AN.1111	**Dwellings**
AN.1112	**Other buildings and structures**
AN.11121	Nonresidential buildings
AN.11122	Other structures
AN.1113	**Machinery and equipment**
AN.11131	Transport equipment
AN.11132	Other machinery and equipment
AN.12	**Inventories**
AN.121	Materials and supplies
AN.123	Finished goods
AN.124	Goods for resale

Source: Intermap Technologies.
Note: The categories used for the property and loss classification in the study are printed in bold.

Table 2.4. Classification by Asset Categories Not Considered in the Study

Code	Asset Category
AN.1114	Cultivated assets (such as livestock, vineyards, orchards, and so forth.)
AN.112	Intangible fixed assets (such as artistic originals, computer software, and so forth.)
AN.122	Work in progress
AN.13	Valuables (such as precious metals, antiques, and so forth.)
AN.2	Non-produced assets
AN.21	Tangible non-produced assets (such as land, sub-soil, non-cultivated biological, water, and so forth.)
AN.22	Intangible non-produced assets (such as patents, goodwill, and so forth.)
AF	Financial assets

Source: Intermap Technologies.

3.2.4. RECLASSIFICATION OF ASSET CATEGORIES

In this analysis, the asset categories as defined in section 3.2.3, are aggregated into two super-classes, that is, *"building"* and *"content"* (Asset Category). In addition to the classes listed in table 2.3, the *Household Equipment* class, which is not registered by the national statistical authorities, is defined. It is included in the *content* super-class. The value of *Household Equipment* is calculated by an expert estimate based on (1) insurance data, (2) population data, and (3) GDP per capita data. The algorithm of the Household Equipment value calculation is described in appendix section 5.1.4.

Table 2.5. Structure of Asset Category Classes ("Building" and "Content") and Their Definitions as Used in the Study

Building	
AN.1111	Dwellings
AN.1112	Other buildings and structures

Content	
AN.1113	Machinery and equipment
AN.12	Inventories
—	Household equipment

Source: Intermap Technologies.
Note: For comparison see table 2.3.

3.2.5. INSTITUTIONAL SECTOR

The third dimension is the classification by Institutional Sectors also based on the ESA'95.[39] The ESA sectors/units included in the "public" class are listed in table 2.6.

Table 2.6. ESA Sectors/Units Included in the Public Class

Sector	Subsector	Unit
S.11 Non-financial corporations		S.11001 Public Non-financial corporations
S.12 Financial corporations[a]	S.121 Central bank	
	S.122 Other monetary financial institutions	S.12201 Public Other monetary financial institutions
	S.123 Other financial intermediaries	S.12301 Public Other financial intermediaries
	S.124 Financial auxiliaries	S.12401 Public Financial auxiliaries
	S.125 Insurance corporations and pension funds	S.12501 Public Insurance corporations and pension funds
S.13 General government	All subsectors	
S.15 Non-profit institutions serving households		
S.2 Rest of the world		

Source: Intermap Technologies.
a. Although the sector *S.12 Financial corporations* contains most of the subsectors, most of the property value is included in the sector *S.11 Non-financial corporations*.

3.2.6. RECLASSIFICATION OF INSTITUTIONAL SECTORS

The third dimension is the classification by Institutional Sectors also based on the ESA'95. The ESA sectors/units are re-classified into the following 3 sectors: (1) private, (2) public and (3) households. The reclassification is listed in table 2.7. The property structure in 1-D split by Institutional Sector is listed in appendix section 5.1.5.

Table 2.7. Reclassification of the ESA Sectors/Units

Original sector classification			Reclassification
Sector	Subsector	Unit	
S.11 Non-financial corporations		S.11001 Public Non-financial corporations	Public
		all other units	Private
S.12 Financial corporationsª	S.121 Central bank		Public
	S.122 Other monetary financial institutions	S.12201 Public Other monetary financial institutions	Public
		all other units	Private
	S.123 Other financial intermediaries	S.12301 Public Other financial intermediaries	Public
		all other units	Private
	S.124 Financial auxiliaries	S.12401 Public Financial auxiliaries	Public
		all other units	Private
	S.125 Insurance corporations and pension funds	S.12501 Public Insurance corporations and pension funds	Public
		all other units	Private
S.13 General government	all subsectors	all units	Public
S.14 Households	all subsectors	all units	Households
S.15 Non-profit institutions serving households			Public
S.2 Rest of the world	all subsectors		Private

Source: Intermap Technologies.
a. Although the sector *S.12 Financial corporations* contains most of the subsectors, most of the property value is included in the sector *S.11 Non-financial corporations*.

3.2.7. ELIMINATION OF SOME PROPERTY CATEGORIES CONSIDERED IN THE STUDY

In the analysis, all asset categories listed in table 2.3 (section 3.2.4) are considered, except for the inventories in the industry branches A (Agriculture) and B (Hunting, forestry and fishing).[40] Moreover, the following kinds of losses are not considered:

- Ecological losses
- Losses on subways, tunnels, and underground collectors.

3.2.8. PROPERTY RECLASSIFICATION SUMMARY

The summary of the property reclassification is listed in table 2.8.

Table 2.8. Property Reclassification Summary

Dimension	Chapter	Table	Split	Summary
Industry Branch	3.2.2	3.2	Residential	C, D, (F)
			Industrial	A, B, E, (F), G, H, I, J, K, L, M, N, O
Asset Category	3.2.4	3.5	Building	AN.1111 & AN.1112
			Content	AN.1113 & AN.12 & House-Equip.
Institutional Sector	3.2.6	3.7	Public	S.11001, S.121, S.12X01, S.13, S.15
			Households	S.14
			Private	Others

Source: Intermap Technologies.

3.2.9. Sector/Purpose reclassification of the Property

For identification of losses not only on public property but also on public services in particular (that is, excluding public enterprises), a supplementary reclassification of the property to *infrastructure/enterprise* classes was used. The *infrastructure* class includes the industry branches which can be considered as social or technical infrastructure while the *enterprise* class includes other activities. For the property and loss classification, the categories infrastructure/enterprise were used in a combination with the institutional sector classification.[41] The sector/purpose reclassification was defined as described in table 2.9.

Table 2.9. Sector/Purpose Reclassification of the Property

| Purpose | Institutional Sector | |
	Public	Non-Public
Infrastructure	Infrastructure Public[42] (property in the industry branches E, I, L, M, N, and O in the "public" institutional sector)	Infrastructure Non-public[43] (property in the industry branches E, L, M, N, and O in the "private" or "households" institutional sectors)
Enterprise	Enterprise Public[44] (property in the industry branches A, B, C, D, F, G, H, J and K in the "public" institutional sector)	Enterprise Non-public[45] (property in the industry branches A, B, C, D, F, G, H, I, J and K in the "private" or "households" institutional sectors)

Source: Intermap Technologies.

The property structure in the mentioned supplementary split is listed in appendix section 5.1.5 and the loss split in this structure is listed in appendix sections 5.2.3, 5.2.5, and 5.3.

Note that *the industry branch I* (Transportation, storage and communication) is included in the *"Infrastructure Public"* for public assets but included in *"Enterprise Non-public"* for the private assets. The reason is that publicly owned property in this branch mostly represents infrastructure and public transportation, while privately owned ones represent mostly enterprise related property, such as storage, cargo transportation, and so forth.

3.2.10. Data Sources on Property Value

The following data sources for the property value and one-dimensional[46] classification were used:

- ▧ **The Czech Republic**
  - The fixed asset[47] as well as inventories[48] values and structures data were provided by the Czech Statistical Office
- ▧ **The Slovak Republic**
  - The fixed asset data[49] were provided by the Statistical Office of the Slovak Republic. However, as the total value of the public sector property provided by the Statistical Office of the Slovak Republic relates only to industry branches L-N, the proportion of the public property in the remaining industry branches was calculated based on the structure of the Czech Republic. Therefore, the proportion of the public property value considered for the model is higher than the one reported by the Slovak Republic's Statistical Office.
  - As inventories data (asset category AN.12) are not available for the Slovak Republic, the value and structure of the inventories was calculated as a propor-

tion of the asset value within each industry branch according to classification of the inventories to industry branches in the Czech Republic.

- **Hungary**
  - The fixed assets as well as inventories values and structure data[50] were provided by the Hungarian Central Statistical Office.
- **Poland**
  - The fixed asset values and structure data provided by the Central Statistical Office of Poland,[51] were used, with the following two adjustments:
    - As the sector classification used by the Central Statistical Office of Poland contains only public and private sectors (that is, the value of the *households* sector is included in the *private* sector), the *household* property value for each industry branch in Poland was estimated as a percentage of the *private*[52] sector according to proportion of the *household* property value within the combined *household* + *private* sectors property value in the Czech Republic.
    - As the fixed asset values reported by the Central Statistical Office of Poland compared to the fixed asset values reported by any other of V-4 national statistical authorities differed substantially from the relation to GDP of the remaining countries,[53] the total fixed asset value considered for modeling purposes was adjusted in order to provide results comparable with the remaining V-4 countries. In particular, the total property value reported by the Central Statistical Office of Poland was adjusted by the relative GDP index of the Czech Republic vs. Poland.
  - As inventories data are not available for Poland, the value and structure of the inventories was calculated as a proportion of the asset value within each industry according to classification of the inventories into the industry branches in the Czech Republic.

3.2.11. ACHIEVING THE THREE-DIMENSIONAL PROPERTY CLASSIFICATION

For purposes of loss modeling, the property is classified in the 3-dimensional[54] structure. The 3-D property structure was generated in the following manner:

- **The Czech Republic**
  - The 3-D property structure of the fixed assets was provided by the Czech Republic's Statistical Office,[55]
  - Inventories (asset category AN.12) were distributed into the 3-D structure based on the 1-dimensional classification of the inventories to industry branches and the 2-dimensional classification of industry branches v. institutional sectors.[56]
- **The Slovak Republic**
  - The 3-D property structure of the fixed assets was generated by using 2-D property structure matrices of industry branch vs. asset category[57] provided by the Statistical Office of the Slovak Republic and 2-D property structure of the institutional sector vs. industry branch used for the Czech Republic.[58]
  - Inventories were distributed into the 3-D structure based on the 1-dimensional classification of the inventories to industry branches calculated according to section 3.2.10 b).

▥ **Hungary**
  - The 3-D property structure of the fixed assets was generated by using 2-D property structure matrices of industry branch vs. asset category[59] and institutional sector vs. industry branch[60] provided by the Hungarian Central Statistical Office.
  - The structure of the inventories (asset category AN.12) was generated from the 1-dimensional classification of the inventories into industry branches[61] and the 2-D classification of the institutional sector vs. industry branch.[59]

▥ Poland
  - The 3-D property structure of the fixed assets was generated by using the 2-D property structure matrices of industry branch vs. asset category and institutional sector vs. industry branch[62] provided by the Central Statistical Office of Poland.
  - Inventories were distributed into the 3-D structure based on 1-dimensional classification of the inventories to industry branches calculated according to section 3.2.10 d) and the 2-D classification of institutional sector vs. industry branch.[61]

3.3. Time Dimension

The total property values as well as estimated loss values were related to year-end 2007. As the property structures provided by the national statistical authorities were related to year-end 2006,[63] the property values used in the model were obtained by multiplying the 2006 data by indexes representing the fixed asset value growth between the years 2006 and 2007 in the particular country. The fixed asset values in THE years 2006 and 2007 and the indexes calculated as well as the data sources are in Appendix section 5.1.3.

3.4. Regional Distribution of Assets

The regional distribution of the property value data, separately for each industry branch, is available at the province/region level (that is, NUTS-3/NUTS-2) only. To estimate the territorial distribution of the property at lower administrative levels, namely in individual districts (that is, LAU-1, formerly marked as NUTS-4), a regionalization approach has been used. The administrative divisions of the countries are in appendix section 5.1.1.

3.4.1. PROPERTY DISTRIBUTION INTO PROVINCES

The weights for the regional distributions of the assets into provinces (that is, NUTS-3[64] or NUTS-2[65] level) are obtained either from the *Regional Gross Fixed Asset Balance Data* for each industry provided by the national statistical institutes (Poland[66] and the Czech Republic[67]) or the *Regional Gross Fixed Asset Formation Data* (Hungary[68] and the Slovak Republic,[69] for which the *Regional Gross Fixed Asset Balance Data* is not available). The property distribution into provinces is in appendix section 5.1.12.

3.4.2. PROPERTY DISTRIBUTION INTO DISTRICTS

The distribution of the property into the districts was processed separately for (1) residential and industrial and (2) "network" property types.[70]

1. Residential and Industrial Property Types

The property distribution from provinces (NUTS-2/3) into districts (LAU-1) level is not provided[71] by the national statistical offices. Therefore, the distribution has been estimated as a proportion of the property value in the superior province (NUTS-3)[72] or region (NUTS-2).[73] The weights were used as follows:

- For the **Czech Republic,** the historical data of fixed asset formation[74] (aggregated for all industries) were used for distribution of the property into the LAU-1 units within the NUTS-3 unit.
- For **Poland**[75] and the **Slovak Republic,**[76] total income within in the LAU-1 unit estimated as income multiplied by the population was used for distribution of the property into the LAU-1 units within the NUTS-2 unit (Poland) or within the NUTS-3 unit (the Slovak Republic).
- For **Hungary,**[77] total income was used for distribution of the property into the LAU-1 units within the NUTS-2 unit.

The weights for the districts are listed in appendix section 5.1.13. Note that in the Pilot Study, the property distribution into the LAU-1 units was estimated separately for the "industrial" and "residential" property types.[69] While the weights for the *"residential"* types for the Czech Republic were estimated by using income and population data, the weights for the *"industrial"* types have been estimated based on territorial representation of the "industrial" land cover class.[78]

Before applying the industrial weights in the final analysis, a comparison of the residential and industrial weights was processed in order to estimate which of them is a better approximation of the weights based on the real fixed asset formation data[73] for the Czech Republic, which was used as a sample (figure 2.2). The comparison showed that the industrial weights provide a much worse[79] approximation than the residential weights. The reason is probably the low precision of the CORINE land cover data. Therefore, the industrial weights based on the CORINE land cover data were not used in the final report and the residential weights were applied instead.

Figure 2.2. Sample Estimation of the Weights of the Districts

a. Spatial distribution of the population—percent share of the districts from the national total

b. Spatial distribution of the income—percent ratio of the districts to the national average

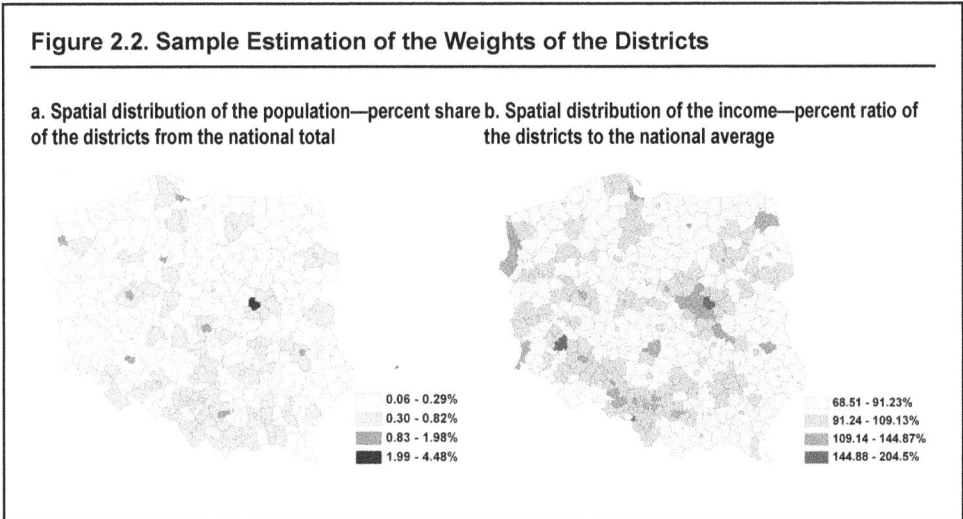

0.06 - 0.29%	68.51 - 91.23%
0.30 - 0.82%	91.24 - 109.13%
0.83 - 1.98%	109.14 - 144.87%
1.99 - 4.48%	144.88 - 204.5%

(Figure continues on next page)

Figure 2.2 (continued)

c. Weights of the districts within their respective province for the residential and industrial categories

d. Weights of the districts within their respective province for the network category

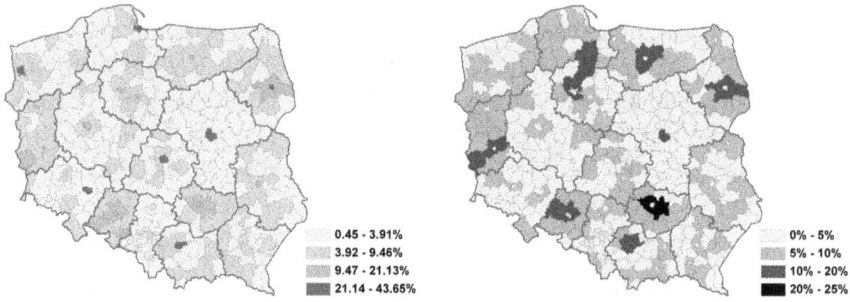

| 0.45 - 3.91% |
| 3.92 - 9.46% |
| 9.47 - 21.13% |
| 21.14 - 43.65% |

| 0% - 5% |
| 5% - 10% |
| 10% - 20% |
| 20% - 25% |

Source: Intermap Technologies.
Note: For graphical as well as tabular outputs for all V-4 countries, see section 5.1.13.

2. Network Property Type

The network[80] property type distribution from provinces (NUTS-2/3) into the district (LAU-1) level has been estimated according to distribution of the transportation network length into the districts, based on the transportation network reference data.[81] The transportation network categories according to the structure of the reference data are listed in appendix section 5.1.10.

First, the length of the network within each district was calculated separately for each network category. Second, the relative value of the network within each district was calculated as a weighted sum of the length of each transportation network category within the district, whereas the weights that the category represents pertains to the relative value of 1 km of the network.

The relative values of 1 km of the network were estimated based on data of the Road and Motorway Directorate of the Czech Republic,[82] Railway Infrastructure Administration of the Czech Republic,[83] and the Czech Ministry of Transport,[84] and are listed in appendix section 5.1.10.

3.4.3. DEFINITION OF THE VULNERABILITY CLASSES

As a result of property reclassification, five distinct regionalization classes have been constructed, namely: *Industrial-Building, Industrial-Content, Residential-Building, Residential-Content* and *Network*. These five classes represent distinct combinations of the three Industry Branch super-classes[85] and the two Asset Category super-classes[86] (see table 2.10).

Table 2.10. Five Vulnerability Classes as Combinations of the Super-classes of the Industry Branch versus Asset Category

Vulnerability Class		Asset Category	
		Building	Content
Industry Branch	Industrial	*Industrial-Building*	*Industrial-Content*
	Residential	*Residential-Building*	*Residential-Content*
	Network	*Network*	

Source: Intermap Technologies.

3.4.4. LAND COVER CLASSES USED IN THE MODEL

For the land cover analysis, the CORINE Land Cover data[87] with 100 m resolution grid was used. For GIS analyses, the raster data have been vectorized. In this study, the "*industrial*" land cover category is represented by the class 121 (industrial or commercial units) of the CORINE classification. Unlike the pilot study, the "*residential*" CORINE land cover category was not used due to a low resolution of the CORINE data.[88]

3.5. Property Distribution into Hazard Zones

Individual property locations were not available. Therefore, for the "*industrial*" property type,[89] the property distribution into flood hazard zones within each district was estimated according to the proportion of each hazard zone area in the "industrial land" CORINE cover class.

The distribution of the "residential" property type was estimated according to the distribution of all reference address points (for the *Czech Republic*,[90] *the Slovak Republic*,[91] and *Hungary*[92]) into the flood hazard zones within the district. For *Poland*, the address points were not available. Therefore, the distribution of the settlement residential area polygons[93] into the hazard zones was used instead.

The distribution of the "*network*" property type into the flood hazard zones has been estimated according to the distribution of the network relative values into the flood hazard zones within each district, an analogy to the procedure used for the network property distribution into the districts, as described in section 3.4.2 (2).

3.6. Flood Scenario Determination

Four types of extreme flood scenarios were determined, as shown below.[94]

   ▨ Areas of large catchments:
   - 7 catchments in the **Czech Republic** (see appendix section 5.1.9 a/i): Elbe/Labe, Moldau/Vltava, Berounka, Ohre, Morava, Dyje, and Oder/Odra
   - 5 catchments in **the Slovak Republic** (see appendix section 5.1.9 b/i): Danube/Dunaj, Vah, Hron & Ipel, Hornad & Slana, and Tisa & Bodrog
   - 7 catchments in **Hungary** (see appendix section 5.1.9 c/i): Danube/Duna, Raba, Sio & Balaton, Drava, Tisza & Bodrog, Hernad & Sajo, and Koros/Crisul
   - 12 catchments in **Poland** (see appendix section 5.1.9 d/i): Upper Oder/Odra, Lower Oder/Odra, Warta, Notec, Nysa & Bobr, Upper Vistula/Wisla, Middle Vistula/Wisla, Lower Vistula/Wisla, San, Bug, Western Baltics, and Eastern Baltics

■ Areas covered by recent major flood events (see appendix sections 5.1.9 a/ii and 5.1.9 d/ii):
  • the scenario of the August 2002 Flood (applied for the Czech Republic);
  • the scenario of the July 1997 flood (applied for Poland and the Czech Republic).
■ Large complex geographical units:
  • for the Czech Republic, two scenarios based on large geographical units were used: the historical territories of **Bohemia** and **Moravia** (see appendix section 5.1.9 a/iii);
  • for the Slovak Republic, two aggregate scenarios were used: **Danube**/Dunaj (including Vah, Nitra, Hron, and Ipel) and **Tisza**/Tisa (including Bodrog, Hornad, and Slana) (see appendix section 5.1.9 b/ii);
  • for Hungary, two aggregate scenarios were used: **Danube**/Duna (including Drava, Sio & Balaton, Raba, and Ipoly) and **Tisza** (including Bodrog, Hernad, Sajo, and Koros/Crisul) (see appendix section 5.1.9 c/ii);
  • for Poland, two aggregate scenarios were used: **Oder**/Odra (including Warta, Notec, Nysa and Bobr) and **Vistula**/Wisła (including Bug and San) (see appendix section 5.1.9 d/iii).
■ Large cross-border scenario (see appendix section 5.1.9 e):
  • **Oder**/Odra (affected countries: Poland and the Czech Republic);
  • **Danube**/Duna/Dunaj (affected countries: the Slovak Republic and Hungary);
  • **Tisza**/Tisa (affected countries: the Slovak Republic and Hungary).

3.7. Flood Hazard Zoning Construction

Intermap's flood zoning model yields nationwide events covering 50, 100, 250, and 500 year flood events (figure 2.3).

The underlying assumptions of the Geomorphologic Regression model are as follows:

■ First, naturally flowing rivers shape their channel and flood plains according to basin-inherent forces and characteristics that can be described by flood water volume and catchment descriptors like catchment area, slope, and so forth., whereby

Figure 2.3a Example of the Digital Terrain Model (DTM) with 5:1 Vertical Exaggeration

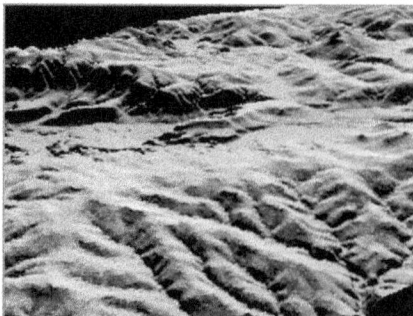

Figure 2.3b. Example of the Flood Hazard Zones in the Czech Republic

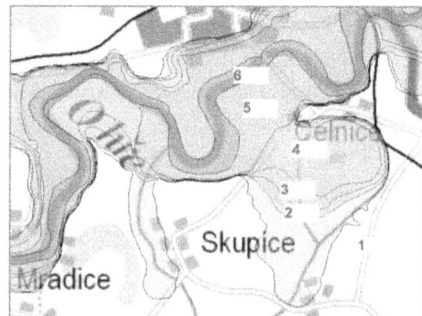

Source: Intermap Technologies.

flood water volume can also be described by catchment attributes including climate or rainfall information.

▨ Second, the extent of actual flood water strongly depends on the shape of the flood plain that can be defined by the vertical and horizontal distance to the relevant river. The regression model was calibrated and validated using a method of multiple non-linear regression analysis (MARS).[95] The flood hazard zones are described in appendix section 5.1.8.

3.8. Flood Vulnerabilities

During this analysis, the vulnerability ratio (damage to corresponding Total Value) is a discrete function of the property damage versus the extent of the flood (see figure 2.4) expressed as vulnerability coefficients within a vulnerability matrix. The matrix explains the relationship of the flood event return period[96] versus the return period of the flood hazard zone (that is, the likelihood of a flood occurring in that particular zone, see figure 2.4, inset).[97]

Due to limited access to loss data broken up by the desired classes, five distinct vulnerability matrices were used and they are shown in table 2.10,[98] namely: *Industrial-Building, Industrial-Content, Residential-Building, Residential-Content* and *Network*.

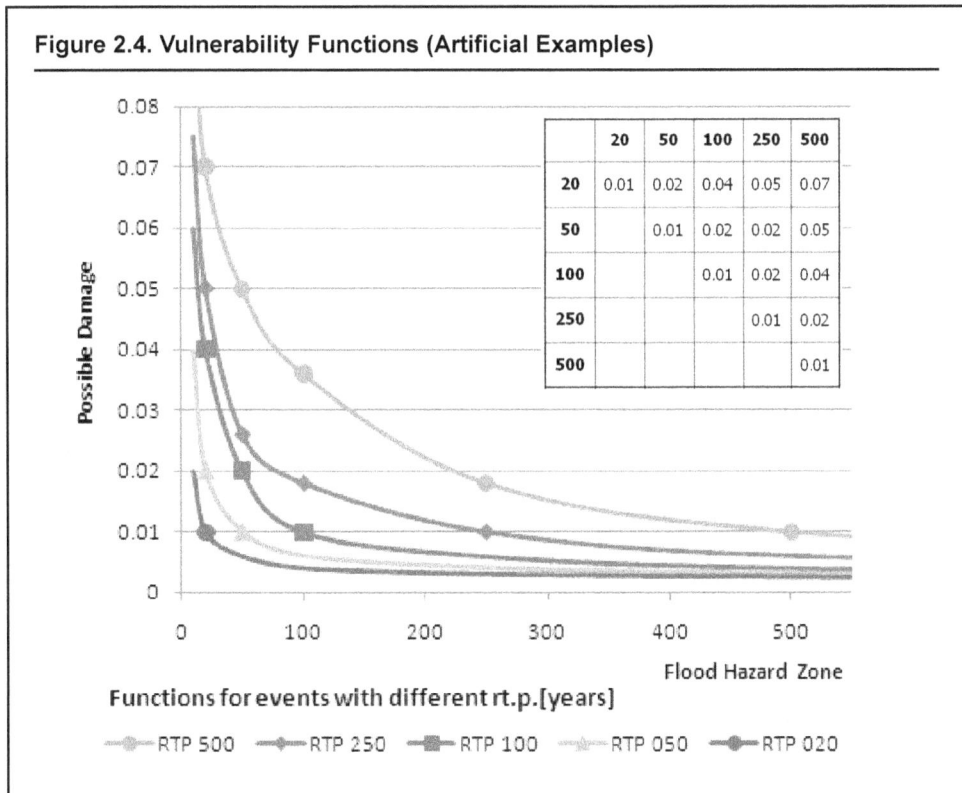

Figure 2.4. Vulnerability Functions (Artificial Examples)

	20	50	100	250	500
20	0.01	0.02	0.04	0.05	0.07
50		0.01	0.02	0.02	0.05
100			0.01	0.02	0.04
250				0.01	0.02
500					0.01

Functions for events with different rt.p.[years]

— RTP 500 — RTP 250 — RTP 100 — RTP 050 — RTP 020

Source: Intermap Technologies.
Note: Graph—example of the discrete vulnerability functions (damage vs. flood hazard zone) for different flood events (the markers correspond to the discrete vulnerability coefficients in the vulnerability matrix). Inset—example of the vulnerability matrix (damage coefficients for various hazard zones vs. flood event).

The vulnerabilities were estimated from the historical loss data of the major insurance companies in the Czech Republic. The coefficients were then verified and calibrated according to aggregate real loss data[99] during the August 2002 event and verified based on the loss data of the July 1997 event of the Czech Republic and Poland.

During the calibration procedure, the loss for the scenario was modeled by using an initial form of the vulnerability matrix and the results were then compared to the actual loss data.[100] Based on this comparison, the vulnerability matrices were multiplied by a correction coefficient and the loss was recalculated. This iterative procedure was repeated until the modeled loss value was equal to the real loss value.

For verification, the obtained vulnerability matrices were then applied to the July 1997 scenarios (both for Poland and the Czech Republic) and the modeled losses were compared to the real losses. For both Poland and the Czech Republic, the modeled losses were only slightly higher than the real losses and, therefore, the vulnerability matrices did not have to be recalculated. This procedure ensures that, for real-event based scenarios, the losses calculated by the model are equal to or slightly higher than the actual losses, and therefore in accordance with the safe-side principle.

3.9. Scenario Method of Loss Exceedance Curve (LEC) Calculation

The scenario method assumes that the flood event occurs with a constant intensity (that is, flood return period or probability) within the whole area covered by the scenario.[101] The losses are calculated for selected return periods of the flood (20, 50, 100, 250, and 500 years). The algorithm of the loss calculation for the scenario method is shown in figure 2.5.

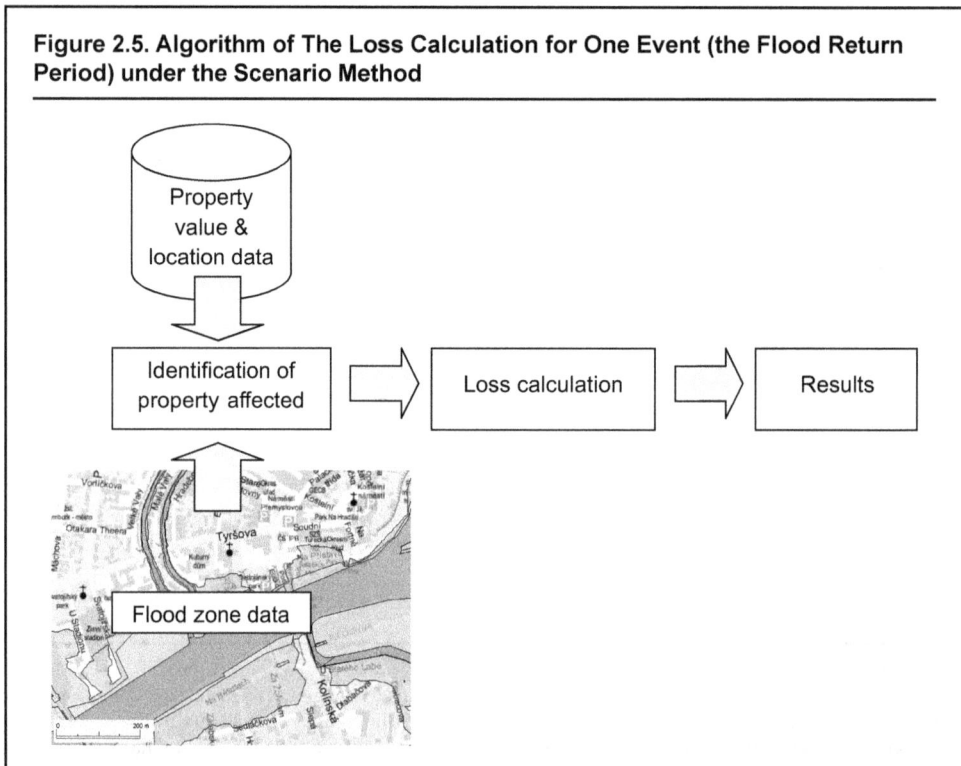

Figure 2.5. Algorithm of The Loss Calculation for One Event (the Flood Return Period) under the Scenario Method

Source: Intermap Technologies.

3.10. Extrapolated Stochastic Method of LEC Calculation

For each country, LECs were calculated for several scenarios. However, the main aim of this work was to find an LEC that characterizes the probable losses of the individual countries as well as of the whole V-4 Group. The various scenario-based LECs indicate the range in which the probable loss occurs. Below, the method that enables one to find the appropriate mean value of the LEC for each country is described. This method is based on extrapolation of the stochastic method, taking into consideration the behavior of the probable loss as a function of distinct characteristics of a territory, such as property value, area, and property distribution in the flood hazard zones.

The stochastic method calculates the loss based on a large number of randomly generated scenarios. As the input data, especially the historical n-years discharges and discharge correlations, were available only for the Czech Republic, an extrapolation of the Czech Republic results was used in order to calculate the LEC in the remaining countries as well as the whole V-4 Group. The stochastic method is described in sections 3.10.1, 3.10.2, and 3.10.3. The extrapolation of the Czech Republic results toward the remaining countries is described in section 3.10.4.

3.10.1. GENERAL CONCEPT OF THE STOCHASTIC METHOD[102]

Under the stochastic method, the loss exceedance curve (LEC) is calculated based on the hypothetical events generated by the Monte-Carlo method. Each event specifies the area affected by the flood and the flood intensity in each spatial unit. The events are generated by the Monte Carlo method and consider the historical information[103] about the discharges in the gauging stations[104] and the correlations of the discharges within each pair of stations.

As the input data for the Monte Carlo method wee available only for the Czech Republic, extrapolation was used for calculation of the LEC in the remaining countries.[105] The overall procedure of the Monte-Carlo method of LEC calculation is described in the following paragraphs.

3.10.2. ASSUMPTIONS OF THE METHOD

- **Spatial Units.** For the purposes of the Monte Carlo method, a country area is divided into spatial units, for which the constant flood return period is assumed within each event. In particular, the spatial units for the Czech Republic are determined by the 4x4 km square grid.[106]
- **One Event Represented by Monthly Maximum Discharges.** Each event is represented by maximum monthly discharges at each gauging station. The length of one month was selected as an optimum value, as (a) given the size of the catchments in the V-4 countries, there is a high probability that any flood event occurs within this period, and (b) occurrence of more significant floods within this period is very unlikely.[107] In total, 120,000 synthetic events representing 120,000 fictive months in 10,000 fictive years were generated.

3.10.3. STOCHASTIC METHOD PROCEDURE

- **Discharge Simulation.** The discharge values for all the 120,000 events and the 145 gauging stations were generated by using the Monte Carlo simulation. The input values were (a) historical N-years of discharges[108] at the gauging stations and (b) correlation matrices of the monthly maximum discharges[109] within each pair of stations. The results were 120,000 events representing maximum discharges at all 145 stations. The method assumes a log-normal distribution of the discharges.[110]

▪ **Discharge Interpolation.** In this step, the discharge values calculated for all 145 gauging stations were extended to the flood return period in all 5,481 spatial units. First, the discharge values in the gauging stations were standardized.[111] Second, the information of the standardized discharge values was extended to all spatial units by using the Kriging[112] 2D spatial interpolation method. Finally, the standardized values in the spatial units were transformed to flood return period values. The result of this step is a set of 120,000 events (that is, maps), where each event represents a particular return period of a synthetic flood in each spatial unit. For sample of the events, see figure 2.6.

▪ **Event-set Generation Overview** (see figure 2.7).

▪ **Loss Calculation.** For each event generated, the loss is calculated by the same algorithm as applied in the scenario method (see figure 2.5). Finally, the loss return periods[113] are assigned the loss values which were calculated for each event.

Figure 2.6. Samples of the Scenarios Generated by the Stochastic Method

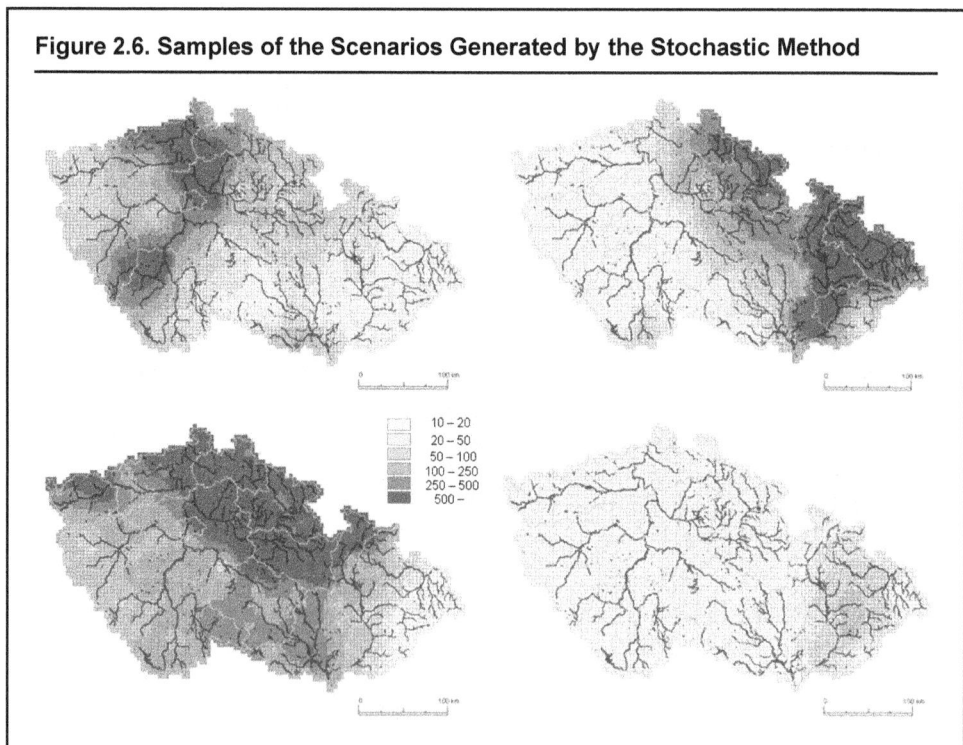

Source: Intermap Technologies.
Note: Colors represent flood intensity in each spatial unit measured by flood return period in years.

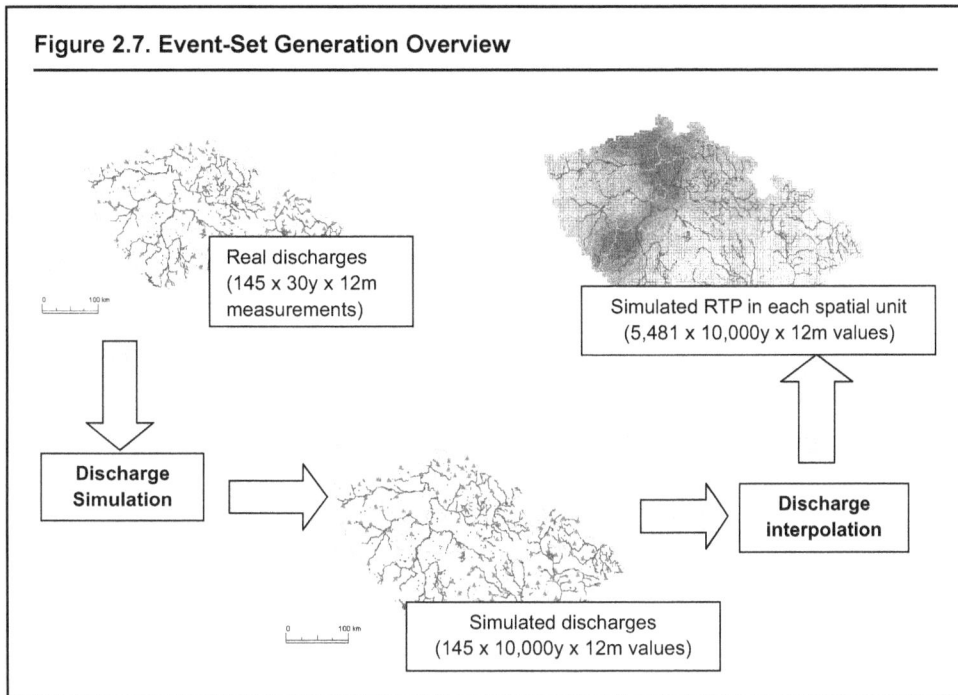

Figure 2.7. Event-Set Generation Overview

Real discharges
(145 x 30y x 12m
measurements)

Discharge
Simulation

Simulated discharges
(145 x 10,000y x 12m values)

Discharge
interpolation

Simulated RTP in each spatial unit
(5,481 x 10,000y x 12m values)

Source: Intermap Technologies.
Note: Colors represent flood intensity in each spatial unit measured by flood return period in years.

3.10.4. EXTRAPOLATION OF THE RESULTS TO THE REMAINING COUNTRIES

As the input data necessary for the stochastic method were available for the Czech Republic only, the results for the remaining countries were calculated by using extrapolation of the results obtained for the Czech Republic. The extrapolation considers three factors:

a. **Difference in the property value** in the particular country in comparison with the Czech Republic. This factor was calculated as a proportion of the total property of the respective countries.
b. **Differences in property distribution in the flood hazard zones** in the particular country in comparison with the Czech Republic. This factor was calculated by using proportion of the property in distinct flood zones in the respective countries.
c. **Differences in the country area** in comparison to the Czech Republic. This factor considers the difference between the return period of the flood and return period of the loss.[113] The larger the area observed, the bigger is the difference between when the return period occurs. For example, a 100-year loss in a small area, such as district, may represent 100-year flood in the whole area, while in a larger area such as province, it would represent an average return period of the flood that is lower than 100 years. Moreover, in a very large area, such as a country or a group of countries, a considerable area would remain unaffected by the flood at all. This factor was derived on the Czech Republic data, separately for each return period

Figure 2.8. A Sample of the Function Used for the Modeling of the Factors

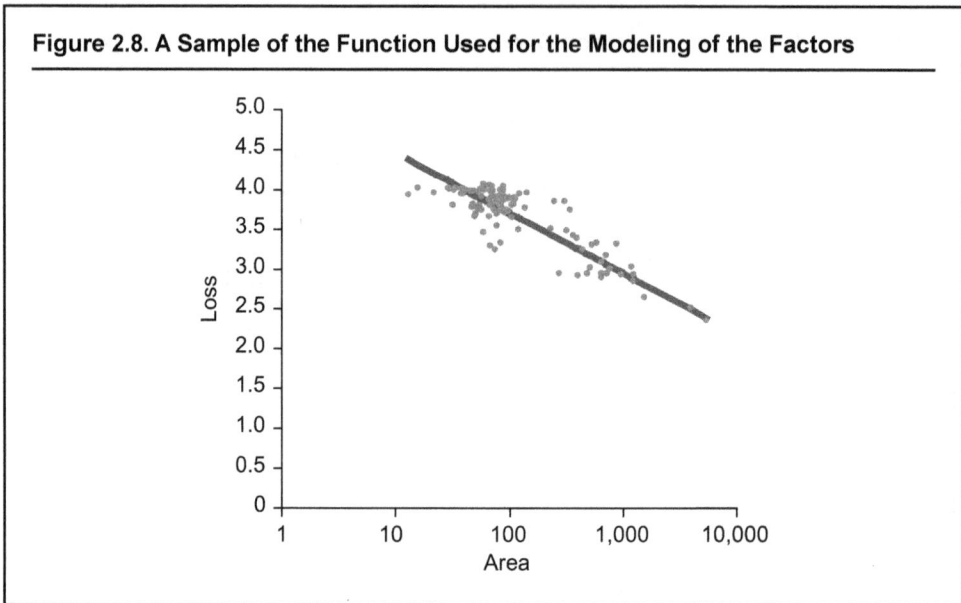

Source: Intermap Technologies.
Note: Figure shows area differences based on empirical data, as a function of the territory area (that is, country, NUTS-4, NUTS-3, LAU-1, scenario) vs. probable loss.

of the loss, by calculation of the LEC for the whole country, the lower administrative units (NUTS-4, NUTS-3, LAU-1) and the territories defined by the flood scenarios (see figure 2.8).[114]

The final formula for calculation of the loss for a particular country and flood return period is thus:

$$Loss(C, n) = Loss(CZ, n) * PF * FzF * AF(n),$$

where n = the flood loss return period,
PF = factor considering for property value difference (see the bullet (a) above),
FzF = factor considering for flood hazard zones difference (see the bullet (b) above),
AF = factor considering area difference for the given n (see the bullet (c) above),
$Loss(C, n)$ = n-years loss in a country C.

3.11. Outputs

3.11.1. Loss Exceedance Curve and Survival Function

The main output of this analysis is an estimate of the flood loss probability distribution for selected scenarios expressed by the loss exceedance curve (LEC—see figure 2.9), which returns the probable loss (vertical axis) corresponding to a certain return period (horizontal axis). The primary concern for the modeling are losses with extremely high return periods, that is, with return periods between 20 and 500 years.

Alternatively, the probability distribution can be expressed as a *survival function*, which returns a probability (vertical axis), against a loss (on horizontal axis) that will be exceeded (see figure 2.10).

Figure 2.9. Sample of LEC as a Function of the Property Loss versus the Return Period (RTP) of the Flood Loss Event

Figure 2.10. Sample of Survival Function as a Function of the Probability of the Flood Loss Event (in Percent) versus the Property Loss

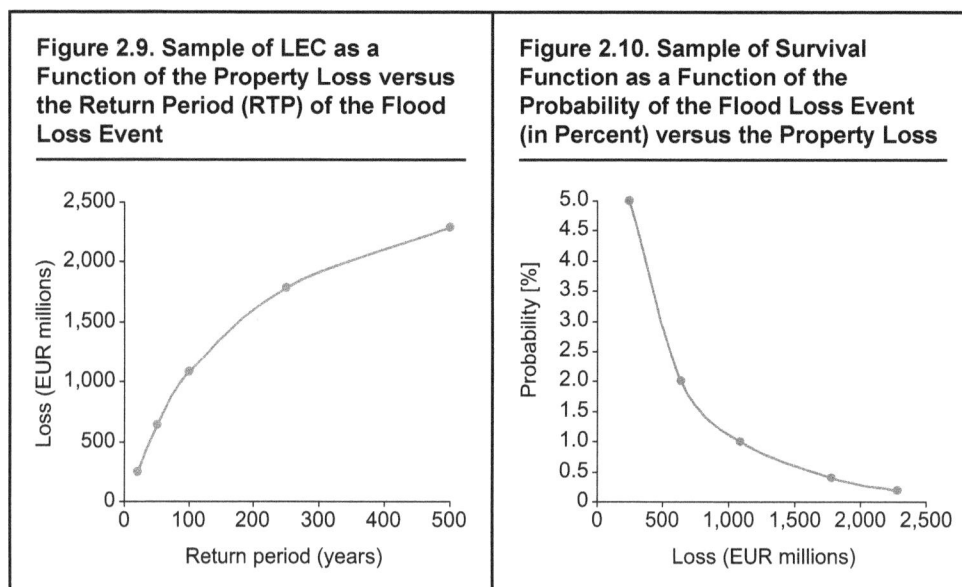

Source: Intermap Technologies.

3.11.2. LEC OF THE POOL OF COUNTRIES VS. INDIVIDUAL COUNTRIES

As described in section 3.10.4, the Loss Exceedance Curve (LEC) of a pool of countries is not an additive function of the LEC of individual countries. A sum of the LEC of the individual countries is shown in section 4.2.1 and appendix section 5.2.1 for a comparison with the LEC of the whole V-4 Group (that is, pooled).

3.11.3. LEC CONFIDENCE INTERVALS

As the variance and possible error of the inputs have very complex magnitudes,[115] it is not possible to estimate the standard probability-based confidence intervals of the calculated loss exceedance curves,[116] that is, the final loss exceedance curve should be interpreted as a point estimate or estimate of the mean value (or the most probable value) of the loss for a given flood return period and scenario (see figure 2.11).

However, the confidence limits of the LEC can be set by an expert estimate, based on analysis of the LEC obtained by using the scenario method in the particular countries (see section 4.2.1). The confidence intervals were thus set in the following way:

- For the loss return period 20 years, as a symmetric interval LEC of +/− 60 percent
- For the loss return period 50 years, as a symmetric interval LEC of +/− 50 percent
- For the loss return period 100 years and higher, as a symmetric interval of LEC +/− 40 percent.

3.11.4. REGIONAL DISTRIBUTION OF THE ESTIMATED LOSS

In order to estimate the loss structure and regional distribution in the case of an extreme flood event, the return period of 250 years was used as standard for the outputs in this study. For each scenario, the spatial distribution of the losses into the regions for the 250 year flood was calculated (a) as a proportion of the total loss (see figure 2.12) and (b) as a loss intensity (a proportion of the province's loss to the province's total property; see figure 2.13).

Figure 2.11. Sample of the LEC with the Confidence Limits

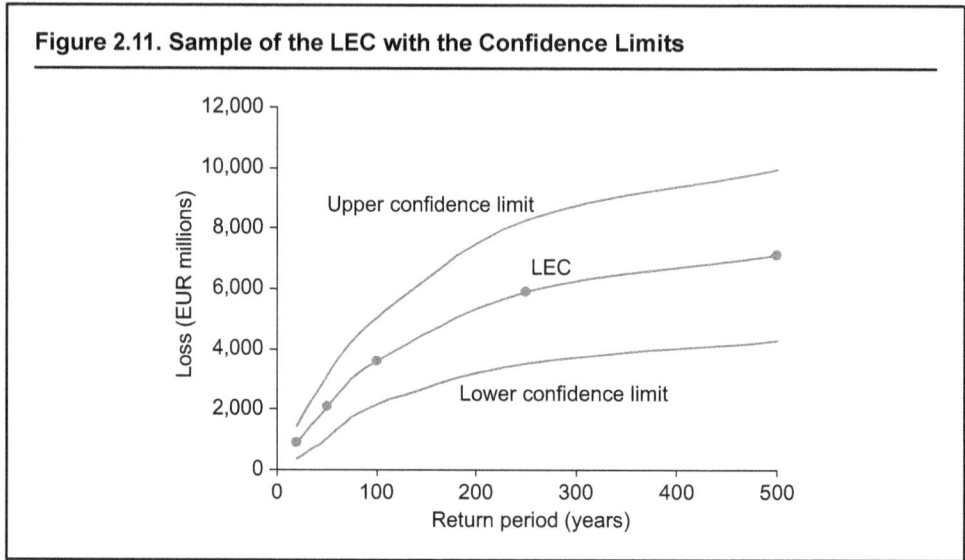

Source: Intermap Technologies.

Figure 2.12. Sample of the Regional Loss Structure (% of the Total Loss)

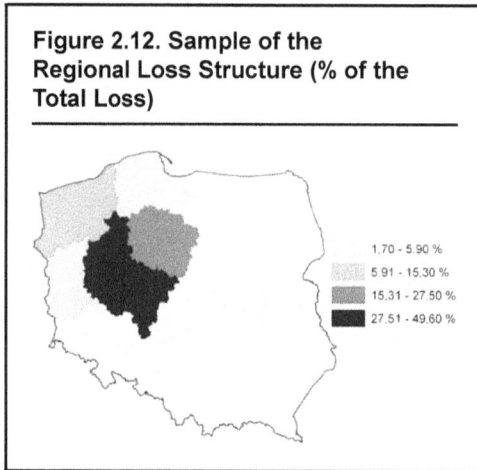

	1.70 - 5.90 %
	5.91 - 15.30 %
	15.31 - 27.50 %
	27.51 - 49.60 %

Figure 2.13. Sample of the Regional Loss Structure (% of the Province Property)

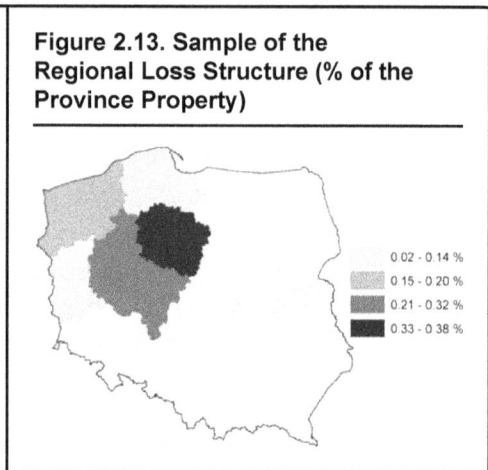

	0.02 - 0.14 %
	0.15 - 0.20 %
	0.21 - 0.32 %
	0.33 - 0.38 %

Source: Intermap Technologies.

3.11.5. LOSS STRUCTURE

For each scenario, the 1-dimensional as well as the 2-dimensional classification of the losses was calculated as well as the loss regional distribution. For the outputs, see appendix section 5.3.

3.11.6. AVERAGE LOSS STRUCTURE AND REGIONAL DISTRIBUTION

For each country, the theoretical scenario assuming the 250-year flood within the whole country is calculated. Based on this scenario, the average loss structure as well as regional distribution is estimated. For the average loss regional distribution, see section 5.2.4. For the average loss structure,[117] see appendix section 5.2.5

4. Outputs

4.1. Property Structure

4.1.1. REGIONAL PROPERTY DISTRIBUTION INTO PROVINCES

In this section, regional property distributions to NUTS-3 units, that is, provinces (NUTS-2 in Poland) for each of V-4 countries is shown. For tabular data as well as a regional split into industry branches,[118] asset categories[119] and institutional sectors,[120] see appendix section 5.1.12.

a. Regional Property Distribution in the Czech Republic[121]

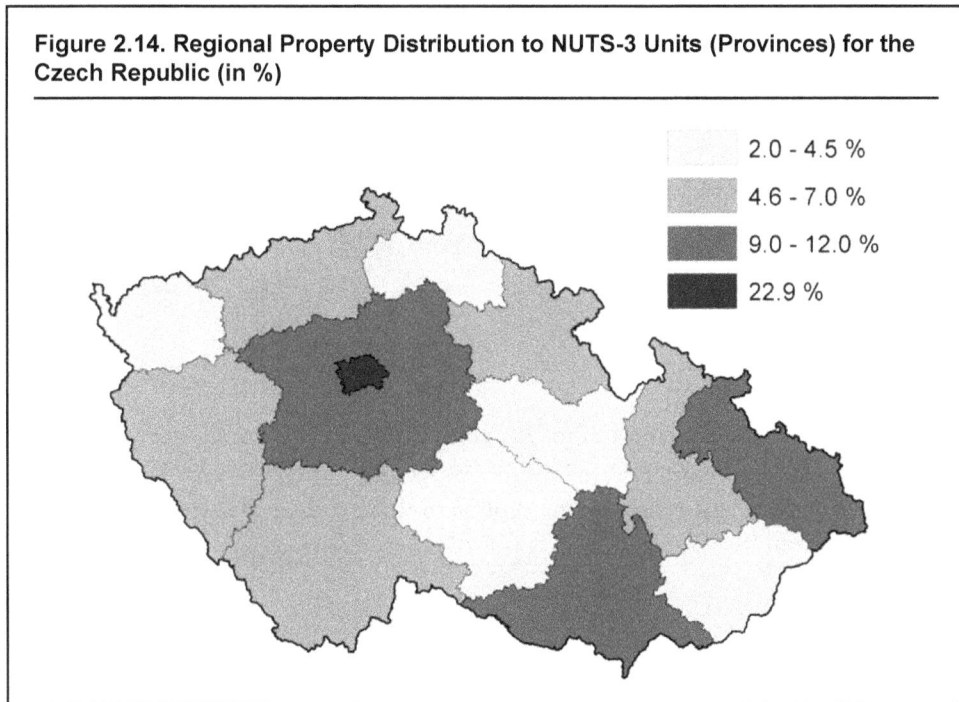

Figure 2.14. Regional Property Distribution to NUTS-3 Units (Provinces) for the Czech Republic (in %)

2.0 - 4.5 %
4.6 - 7.0 %
9.0 - 12.0 %
22.9 %

Source: Intermap Technologies.

b. Regional Property Distribution in the Slovak Republic[122]

Figure 2.15. Regional Property Distribution to NUTS-3 units (Provinces) for the Slovak Republic (in %)

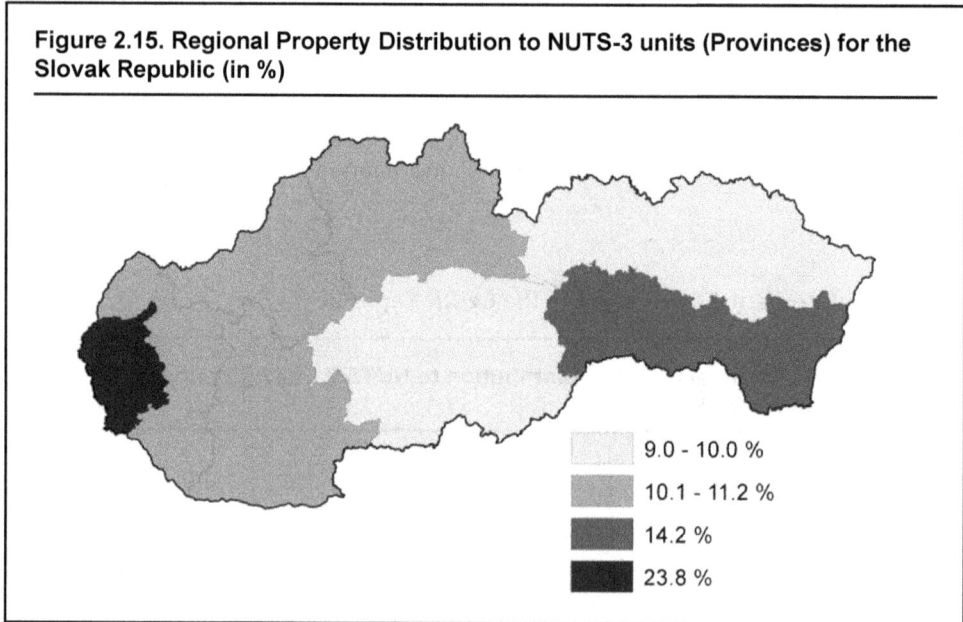

- 9.0 - 10.0 %
- 10.1 - 11.2 %
- 14.2 %
- 23.8 %

Source: Intermap Technologies.

c. Regional Property Distribution in Hungary[123]

Figure 2.16. Regional Property Distribution to NUTS-3 Units (Provinces) for Hungary (in %)

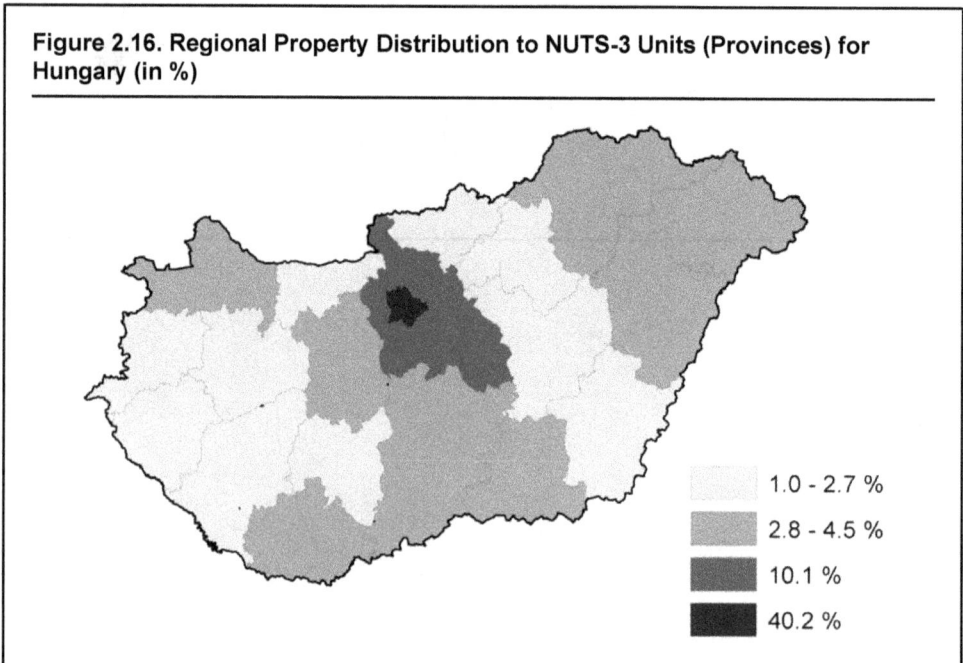

- 1.0 - 2.7 %
- 2.8 - 4.5 %
- 10.1 %
- 40.2 %

Source: Intermap Technologies.

d. Regional Property Distribution in Poland[124]

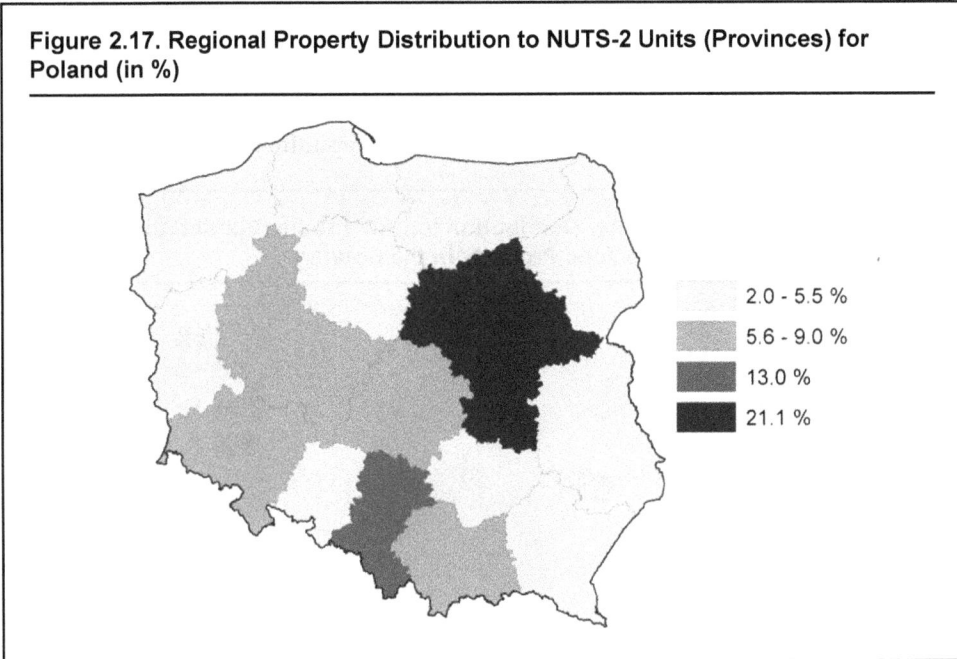

Figure 2.17. Regional Property Distribution to NUTS-2 Units (Provinces) for Poland (in %)

Source: Intermap Technologies.

4.1.2. REGIONAL PROPERTY DISTRIBUTION INTO DISTRICTS

In this section, the regional property distribution to LAU 1 unit (districts) within each of V-4 countries is shown. For tabular data as well as population and salary regional distribution, see appendix section 5.1.13.

a. Property Distribution into Districts in the Czech Republic[125]

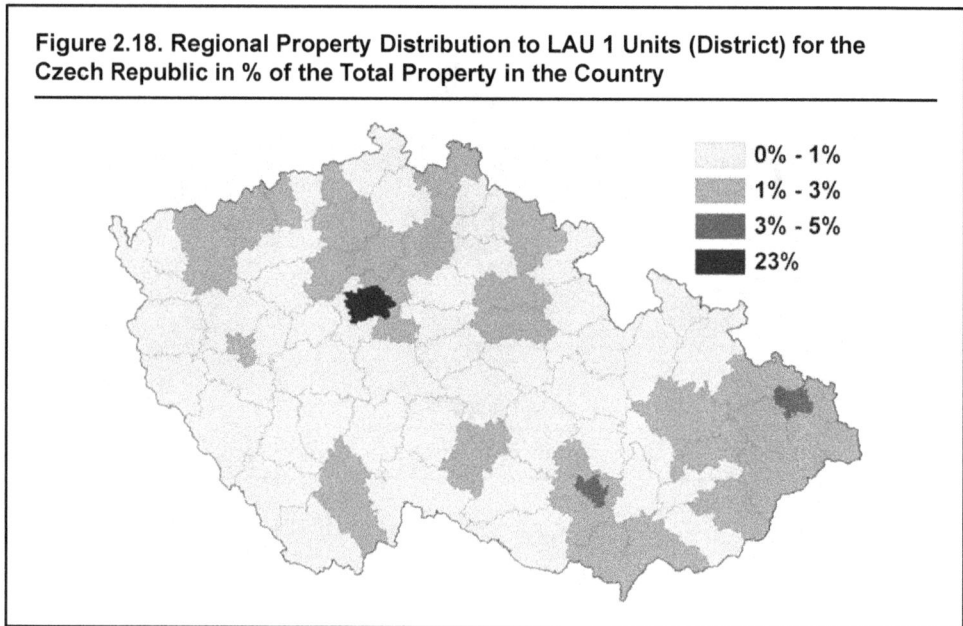

Figure 2.18. Regional Property Distribution to LAU 1 Units (District) for the Czech Republic in % of the Total Property in the Country

Source: Intermap Technologies.

b. Property Distribution to Districts in the Slovak Republic[126]

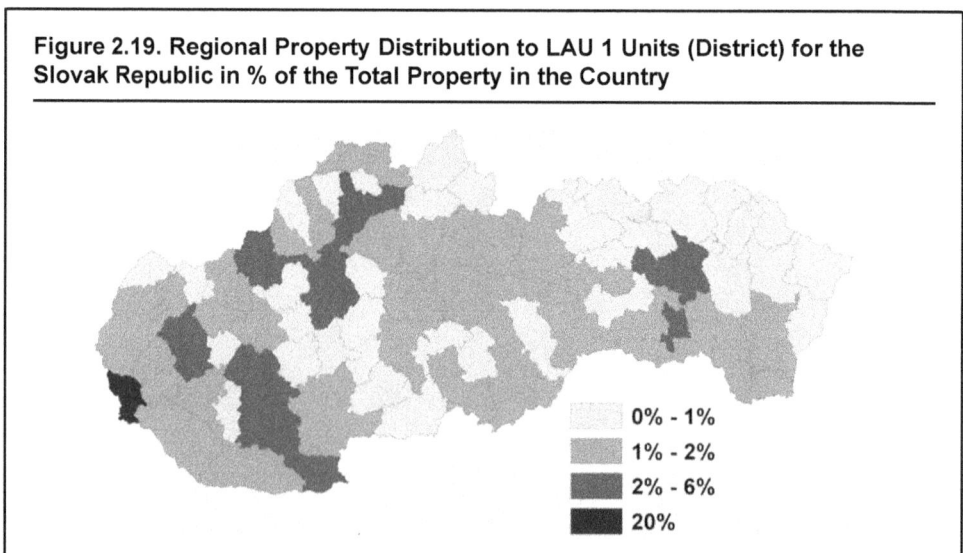

Figure 2.19. Regional Property Distribution to LAU 1 Units (District) for the Slovak Republic in % of the Total Property in the Country

Source: Intermap Technologies.

c. Property Distribution to Districts in Hungary[127]

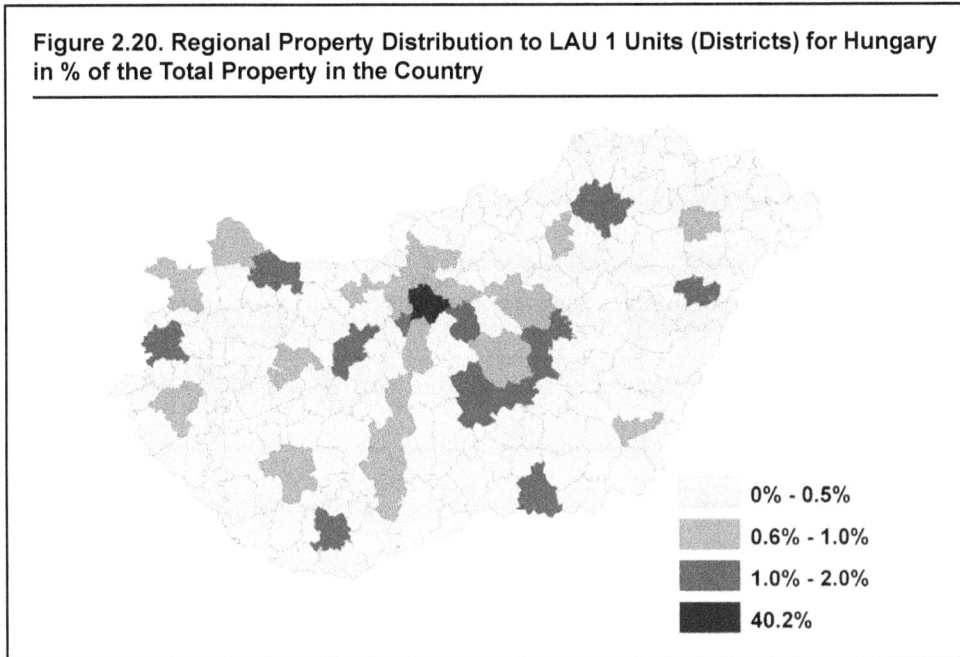

Figure 2.20. Regional Property Distribution to LAU 1 Units (Districts) for Hungary in % of the Total Property in the Country

Legend:
- 0% - 0.5%
- 0.6% - 1.0%
- 1.0% - 2.0%
- 40.2%

Source: Intermap Technologies.

d. Property Distribution to Districts in Poland[128]

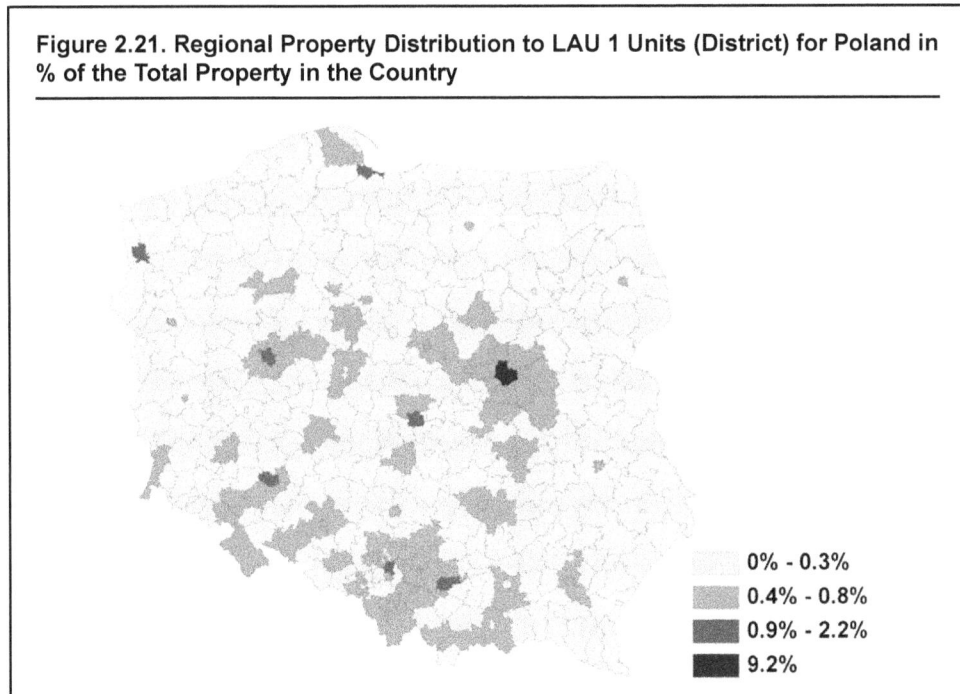

Figure 2.21. Regional Property Distribution to LAU 1 Units (District) for Poland in % of the Total Property in the Country

Legend:
- 0% - 0.3%
- 0.4% - 0.8%
- 0.9% - 2.2%
- 9.2%

Source: Intermap Technologies.

4.2. Loss Calculation Results

4.2.1. Loss Exceedance Curves

In this section, the loss exceedance curves calculated for each country are summarized for each country separately, for total property and public property. For the detailed overview of the results, see the data appendix.

Figure 2.22. Summary of the Exceedance Curves for the Czech Republic for Losses on Total Property

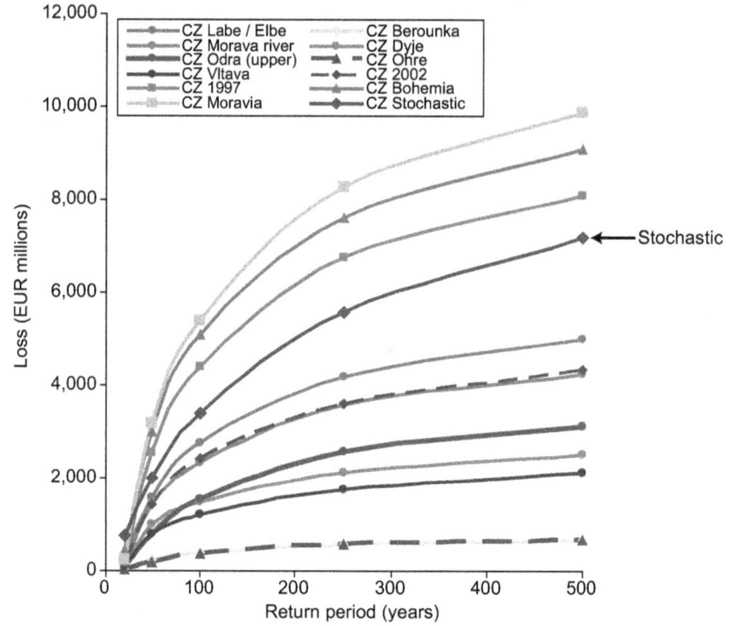

Source: Intermap Technologies.

Figure 2.23. Summary of the Exceedance Curves for the Czech Republic for Losses on Public Property

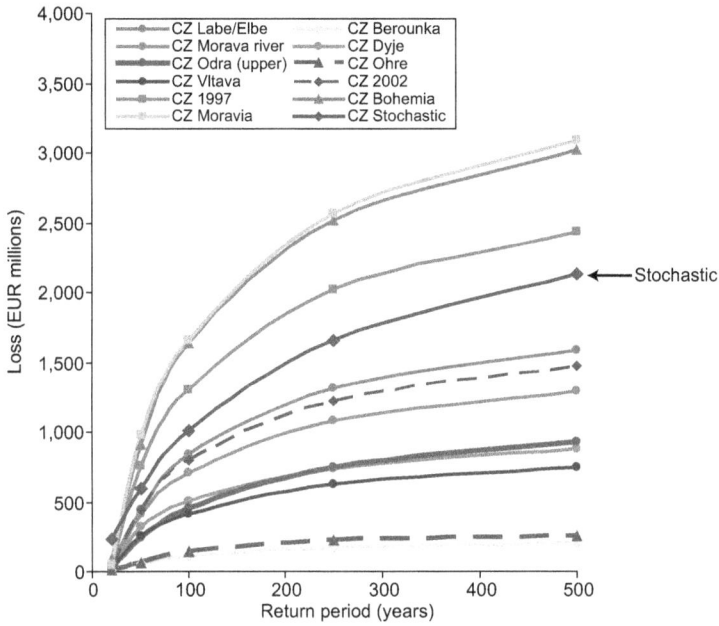

Source: Intermap Technologies.

Figure 2.24. Summary of the Exceedance Curves for the Slovak Republic for Losses on the Total Property

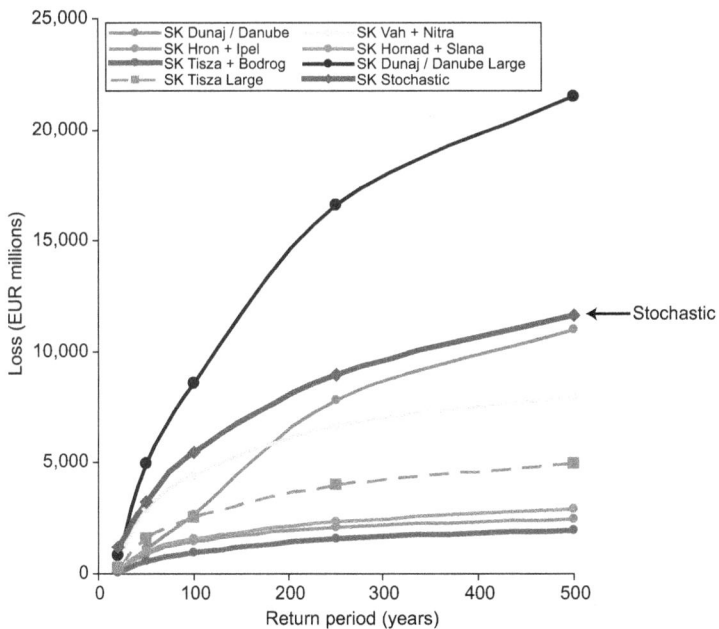

Source: Intermap Technologies.

Figure 2.25. Summary of the Exceedance Curves for the Slovak Republic for Losses on Public Property

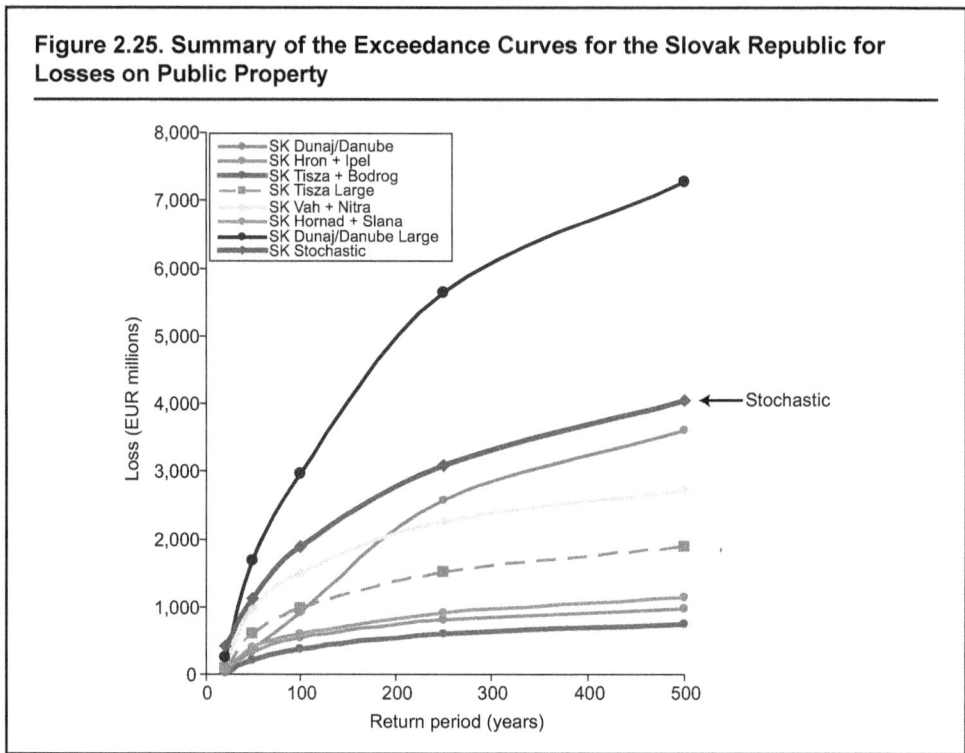

Legend:
- SK Dunaj/Danube
- SK Hron + Ipel
- SK Tisza + Bodrog
- SK Tisza Large
- SK Vah + Nitra
- SK Hornad + Slana
- SK Dunaj/Danube Large
- SK Stochastic

Stochastic

Source: Intermap Technologies.

Figure 2.26. Summary of Exceedance Curves for Hungary for Losses on Total Property

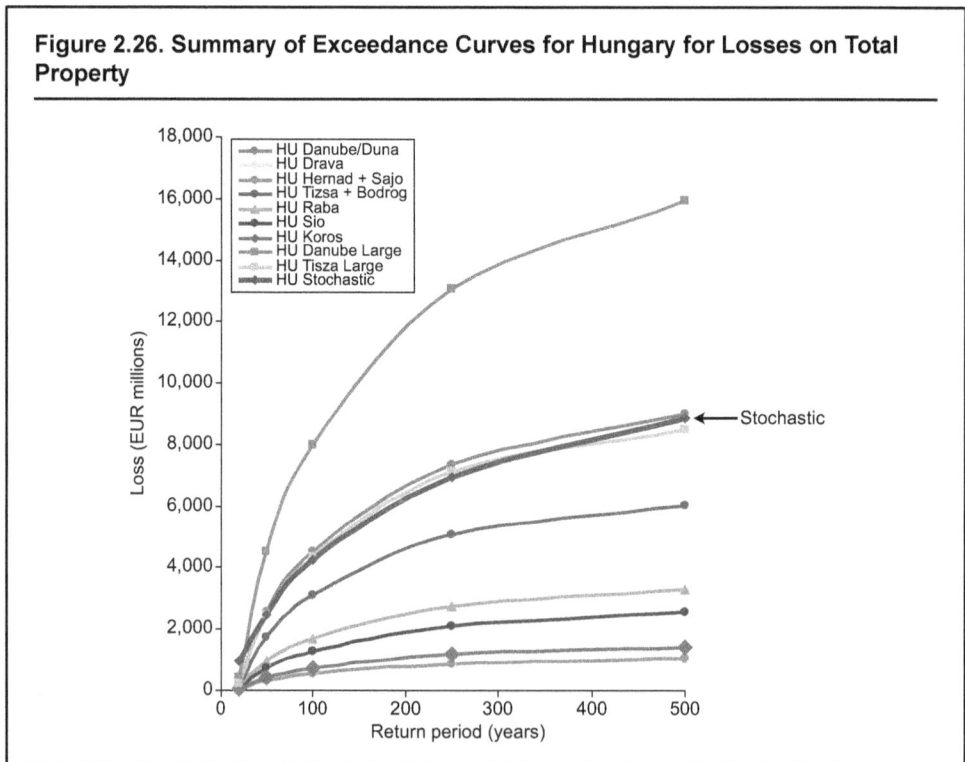

Legend:
- HU Danube/Duna
- HU Drava
- HU Hernad + Sajo
- HU Tizsa + Bodrog
- HU Raba
- HU Sio
- HU Koros
- HU Danube Large
- HU Tisza Large
- HU Stochastic

Stochastic

Source: Intermap Technologies.

Figure 2.27. Summary of Exceedance Curves for Hungary for Losses on Public Property

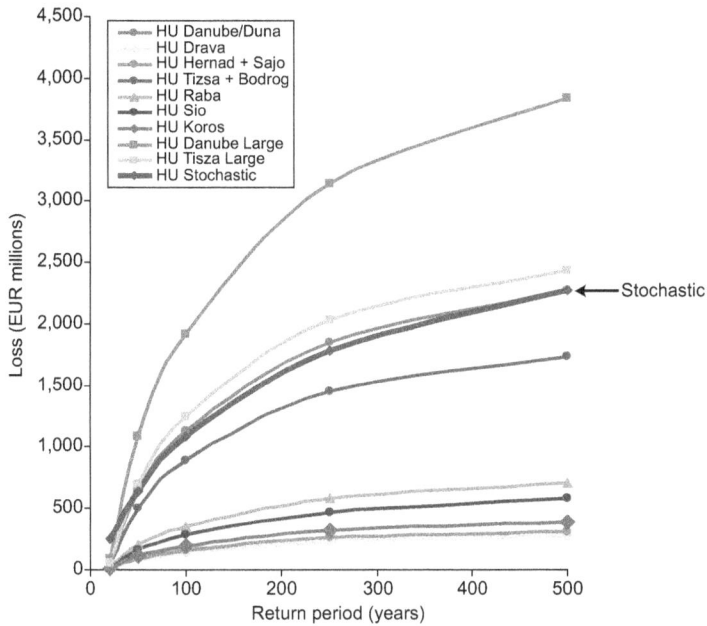

Legend:
- HU Danube/Duna
- HU Drava
- HU Hernad + Sajo
- HU Tizsa + Bodrog
- HU Raba
- HU Sio
- HU Koros
- HU Danube Large
- HU Tisza Large
- HU Stochastic

Y-axis: Loss (EUR millions)
X-axis: Return period (years)

← Stochastic

Source: Intermap Technologies.

Figure 2.28. Summary of the Exceedance Curves for the Poland for Losses on Total Property

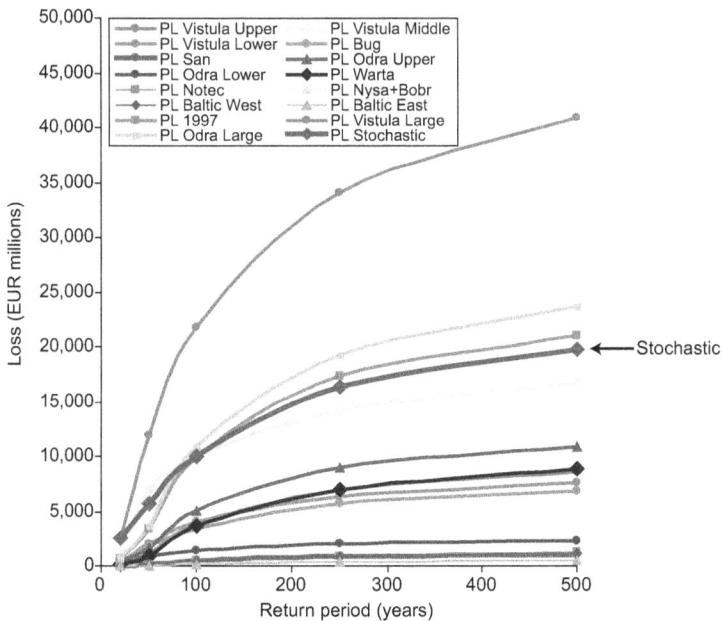

Legend:
- PL Vistula Upper
- PL Vistula Lower
- PL San
- PL Odra Lower
- PL Notec
- PL Baltic West
- PL 1997
- PL Odra Large
- PL Vistula Middle
- PL Bug
- PL Odra Upper
- PL Warta
- PL Nysa+Bobr
- PL Baltic East
- PL Vistula Large
- PL Stochastic

Y-axis: Loss (EUR millions)
X-axis: Return period (years)

← Stochastic

Source: Intermap Technologies.

Figure 2.29. Summary of the Exceedance Curves for the Poland for Losses on Public Property

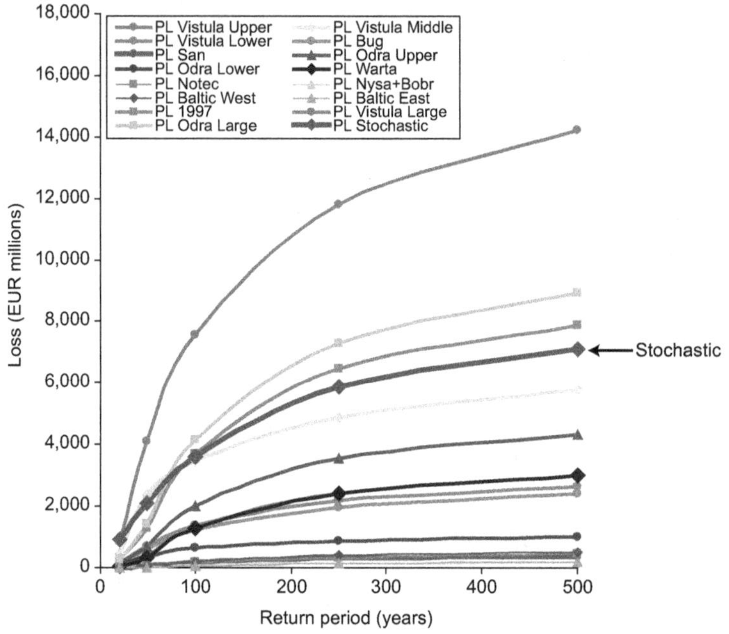

Source: Intermap Technologies.

Figure 2.30. LEC for Loss on Total Property for Each Country and the V-4 Group

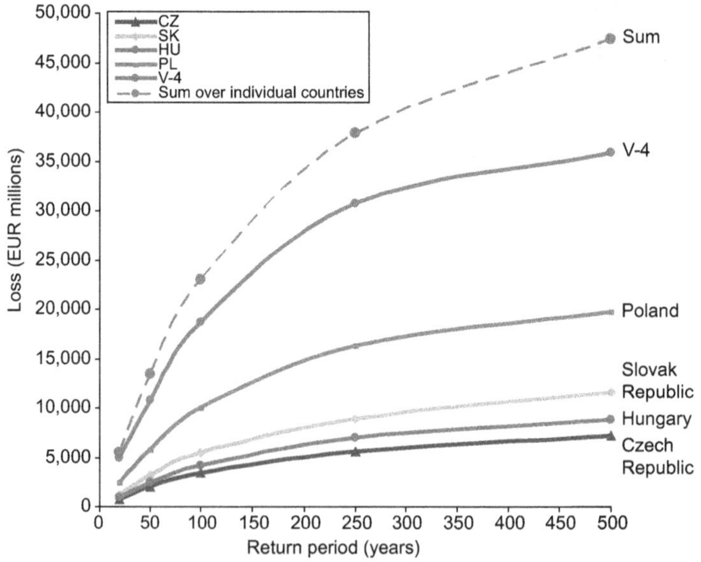

Source: Intermap Technologies.
Note: Dashed line represents the sum of LEC of individual countries) and results of the extrapolated stochastic method.

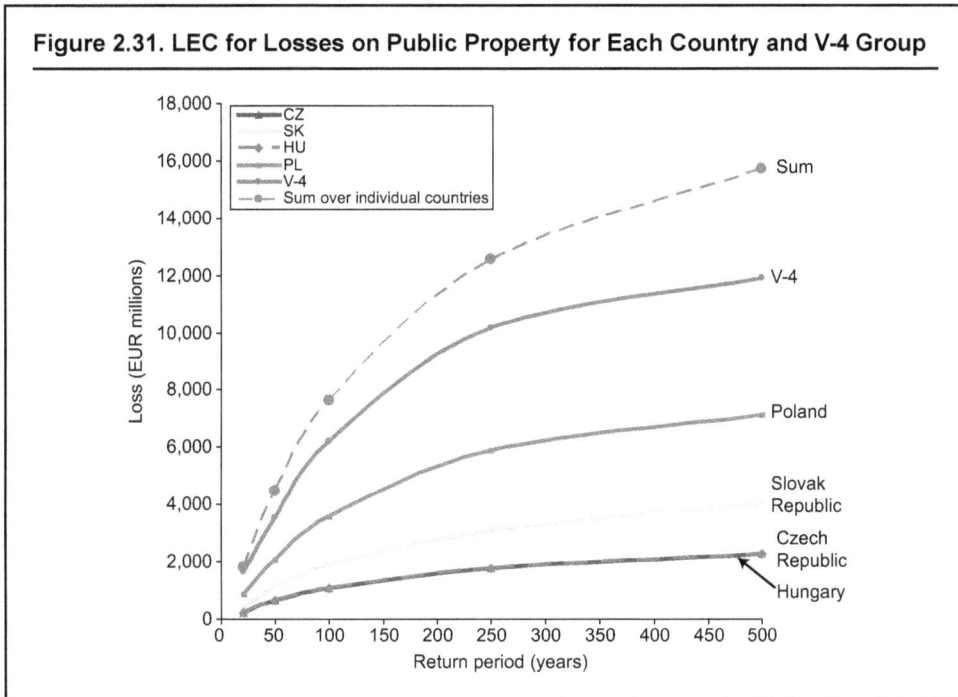

Figure 2.31. LEC for Losses on Public Property for Each Country and V-4 Group

Source: Intermap Technologies.
Note: Dashed line represents the sum of LEC of individual countries) and results of the extrapolated stochastic method.

Conclusion

Estimation of possible losses is a complex task and at times a convoluted exercise with many limitations in access to input data. The model is based on the assumption that the modeled event in the future should have similar impacts as those that occurred in the past. Extreme events occur very rarely, and the history of detailed measurements of flood characteristics is rather short, while the history of mapping the loss records is even shorter. Any estimation of the outcome of an event in the future is biased given insufficient historical records, large changes in property distributions and characteristics and therefore the modeling is based only on a limited comparable experience. This causes a relatively high ratio of residuals in such models.

A typical issue is in the construction of the vulnerability functions. Even if the property, its values and locations can be precisely mapped, it is usually very hard to compare them with the historical loss data that is rarely classified, precisely due to the specific conditions when quick help to the flooded population and property is necessary and there is a lack of time and resources for accurate loss localization and evaluation. For this reason, simplifications must be introduced to asset classifications in order to obtain comparable total value and loss classes for vulnerability estimations.

Another issue is the proper localization of properties. Usually, poor data on geographic location of the property is available at both the state authority level and the insurance market. When a country-wide modeling is carried out, only a sample of properties can be localized and then consequences are derived based on those samples.

Therefore, the proxy distribution of property to distinct hazard zones as well as to regional geographic units, such as river catchments, districts, or zip code areas, is applied despite the fact that those geographic units may be internally non-homogeneous in respect to the distribution of the potential flood behavior in such space. The approach in this analysis has been based on several simplifications and the accuracy of the territorial distribution of property depends on the extent to which ancillary variables and the assumptions reflect the real distribution.

As well, mapping of the hazard is quite challenging. The more precise the modeling is executed, the more resources, effort, and time are required as well as as expensive input data such as gauging station records. In the case of accurate hazard zone delimitation, the geographic location of the property may be insufficient, and if accurate flood depth parameters are derived, there may be a lack of data on building heights or the storey on which the properties are located. Other issues pertain to the insufficiency of flood protection characteristics, the behavior of the population and the authorities before and during critical events, the sum of their experiences from the past, all of which reflect unknown parameters, just to mention a few.

Based on the limitations mentioned above, several assumptions were made in this analysis. Some of the assets such as automobiles were not considered in this phase due to lack of data. The asset classifications were simplified to five classes, each having distinct vulnerability functions.

The precise spatial distribution of the property was replaced with regionalization to districts based on the assumptions that spatial distribution of proxy variables such as population and income distribution, land cover classes, and regional distribution of networks, are the leading parameters for these considerations. The hazard zones were computed based on the return period, as the value of delineation of flood depth is very ambiguous due to lack of digital elevation models with sufficient vertical resolution.

The key input of the model is the property value data in the 3-dimensional split, the main sources of which are data of the national statistical authorities.[129] The property values were re-classified and spatially re-distributed (regionalized) into the provinces and then into the districts.[130] The property values were then re-distributed into the flood hazard zones within each district.[131]

The regionalized and re-classified property data show that the total property value in the whole V-4 Group is EUR 2,506 billion [132] of which 36 percent is public property, 37 percent property of private corporations[133] and 27 percent property of households.[134] According to the asset category[135] classification, dwellings, buildings and structures represent 72 percent, machinery and equipment 16 percent, and inventories and household equipment 12 percent of total property. As for the regional distribution of the property into the four countries, 50 percent of the total property value is located in Poland, 23 percent in the Czech Republic, 16 percent in Hungary, and 11 percent in the Slovak Republic.

As for the property distribution into the flood hazard zones within the whole V-4 Group, 8 percent of the property value is located in floodplains with annual probability of flooding of at least 2 percent (that is, in the flood hazard zones with a return period of 20 and 50 years), 22 percent in floodplains with annual probability of flooding 0.2-2.0 percent (in flood hazard zones with a return period of 100, 250, and 500 years) while 70 percent of the property is located outside the flood prone areas.[136]

The property distribution into the flood hazard zones within the individual countries is as follows: The proportion of the property value in all flood hazard zones (that is, in areas with at least 0.2 percent annual probability of flooding) is the highest in the Slovak Republic (54 percent), medium in Hungary and Poland (33 percent and 29 percent, respectively) and the lowest in the Czech Republic (20 percent).[136]

Based on the re-classified and regionalized property data redistributed into the flood hazard zones, plus the vulnerability functions[137] calibrated according to historical loss data separately for each property class, the loss exceedance probabilities were predicted for different flood scenarios. Potential losses for distinct return periods of the flood loss were represented on the resulting dependence—the loss exceedance curve (LEC).

In total, the LECs were calculated by using a scenario method[138] for 45 distinct flood scenarios of 4 types, in particular: 31 scenarios based on large catchments, 3 scenarios based on recent major flood events, 8 scenarios based on the large complex geographical units, and 3 large cross-border scenarios.[139] As well, 11 scenarios were defined for the Czech Republic, 7 for the Slovak Republic, 9 for Hungary, 15 for Poland, and 3 for cross-border events. Moreover, in order to evaluate the possible loss of the whole countries as well as the V-4 Group, the loss exceedance curves were calculated for each country and the V-4 Group by using extrapolation of the stochastic method.[140]

According to the probable loss estimated by the extrapolated stochastic method characterizing the probable losses in the whole V-4 Group or in a particular country, the estimated probable loss on the total property for the V-4 Group is approximately EU 19 billion for the return period of 100 years (that is, the annual loss occurrence probability of 1 percent) and EUR 31 billion for the return period 250 years (annual occurrence probability of 0.4 percent). A loss of EUR 11 billion occurs with the probability of 2 percent (a return period of 50 years) and a loss of EUR 5 billion with a 5 percent probability (a return period of 20 years).

Classification of the average loss structure based on the scenario method results shows[141] that the loss in the public institutional sector represents 31 percent,[142] the loss in the private sector[133] represents 42 percent, and the loss in the household sector represents 25 percent of the total probable loss.

As for the asset category[135] classification, the average probable loss on dwellings, buildings and structures represents 68 percent, the loss on machinery and equipment 20 percent, and the loss on inventories and household equipment represents 12 percent of the total loss. These results represent an average structure of the loss distribution for the extreme flood events within the whole V-4 Group, however, the estimated loss structure slightly differs depending on the flood scenario.[143]

The probable loss[144] on the total property in the particular countries related to the probable loss in the whole V-4 Group, is approximately 53 percent for Poland, 29 percent for the Slovak Republic, 23 percent for Hungary, and 18 percent for the Czech Republic. As the probable loss of the pool of countries calculated by the extrapolated stochastic method is not an additive function of probable losses in the individual countries,[145] the probable loss (for a given return period) for the whole V-4 Group is lower than the sum of probable losses of the individual countries. For example, the probable loss on public property for the return period of 250 years for the V-4 Group is approximately EU 11 billion while the sum of probable losses in the individual countries is approximately EUR 12.5 billion.

In absolute values, for the return period of 250 years (0.4 percent occurrence proba-bility) the probable losses on total property in the particular countries are approximately EUR 16 billion EUR for Poland, EUR 9 billion for the Slovak Republic, EUR 7 billion for Hungary, and EUR 5.5 billion for the Czech Republic. The probable loss on public property[146] in the particular countries for the return period of 250 years (0.4 occurrence probability) is approximately EUR 5.9 billion for Poland, EUR 3.1 billion for the Slovak Republic, and EUR 1.8 billion for Hungary as well as for the Czech Republic.

All of the probable loss values mentioned above represent the mean values of the es-timates for a given flood return period and country. In addition, the confidence intervals of the probable loss were estimated.[147] The estimated upper confidence limit of the prob-able loss on the total property in the whole V-4 Group is approximately 26 EUR billion for the return period of 100 years and EUR 43 billion for the return period of 250 years. For losses on public property, the estimated upper confidence limit is EUR 9 billion for the return period of 100 years and EUR 14 billion for the return period of 250 years.

The estimated upper confidence limits for the probable loss on total property in the particular countries for the return period of 250 years are approximately EUR 23 billion for Poland, EUR 12.5 billion for the Slovak Republic, EUR 10 billion for Hungary, and EUR 8 billion EUR for the Czech Republic. For the probable loss on public property, the upper estimated limits are EUR 8 billion for Poland, EUR 4 billion for the Slovak Repub-lic, and EUR 2.5 billion for Hungary as well as for the Czech Republic.

The detailed results of the loss modeling for all 45 scenarios are in appendix sec-tion 5.3. As an example, for the cross-border scenario for Odra, the probable loss for the return period of 100 years is approximately EUR 8.0 billion on total property (EUR 3.1 billion on public property) and for the return period of 250 years it is approximately EUR 13.5 billion on total property (EUR 5.2 billion on public property). Losses in the asset category of dwellings, buildings and structures are 65 percent, losses in the machinery and equipment are 22 percent, and losses in the inventories and household equipment represent 13 percent of total losses.

The provinces with the highest loss values are Dolnośląskie (Poland, 36 percent of total loss), Moravskoslezský kraj (Czech Republic, 18 percent), Opolskie (Poland, 11 percent), Śląskie and Lubuskie (Poland, each of them 10 percent of the total loss). T he provinces with the highest loss intensity[148] are Dolnośląskie (5 percent), Lubuskie (4.7 percent), Moravskoslezský kraj (4.5 percent), and Opolskie (4.2 percent of the province's property).

Possible improvements of the model for obtaining more precise results in the future could include: (a) use of the probabilistic method for all countries, which would enable a more precise flood loss evaluation for each of the countries or the V-4 Group (this approach would require historical discharge data for all countries); (b) use of a more detailed digital elevation model for obtaining more precise flood hazard zones (digital elevation data of the NEXTMap Europe are currently available for the Czech Republic and will be available for the other V-4 countries in the near future); and (c) creation of public sector-owned property registers, which would enable more precise flood hazard evaluation of public property.

As well, additional model improvements might include: (d) use of flood depth in-stead of flood hazard zones, which would refine the vulnerability functions (so far, the rough vertical resolution of the existing digital elevation models has not enabled generating credible flood depth maps); and (e) consideration of the pluvial flood in addition to the river flood—better resolution of digital elevation data, extensive precipitation gauge data as well as maps of soils and land-use with reasonable scales will be necessary for pluvial flood modeling.

Notes

1. Antecedent Precipitation Index (API_n) is an index derived from rainfall depth for the antecedent n days (or hours); see bibliographic reference # [43].
2. The team working on the Study included, first of all, the main contributor Jiří Vohlídal who led the collection of the asset data, probable flood loss modeling, producing the charts and tables, and the compilation of the final text. Other leading team members included Vladislav Hančil who did most of the revisions of the texts in various phases of the study as well as contributed to several parts of the methodology; Jan Roubalík was responsible for flood hazard modeling; Lukáš Makovička leading the effort for creating the maps in the text. The team was coordinated by Ladislav Garassy and the overall activity was managed by Ivo Bánovský.
3. The appendix is not included in this published World Bank Study. It can be accessed at http://documents.worldbank.org/curated/en/2012/01/16242871.
4. For more details, see Appendix section 5.1.1
5. Except of Poland where they correspond to the NUTS-2 level
6. For more details about NUTS and LAU classification see [3]
7. Formerly NUTS-4
8. Formerly NUTS-5
9. Administration, education, health, culture, transportation networks, and so forth.
10. Industry, financial, and so forth.
11. See sections 3.2.1 and 3.2.2
12. See sections 3.2.3 and 3.2.4
13. See sections 3.2.5 and 3.2.6
14. For more details, see section 3.3
15. For more details, see Appendix section 5.1.2
16. See [4]
17. See [8].
18. Hiszi-Map, Corvin u. 3, Gyula, Hungary. Internet access: http://www.hiszi-map.hu; see [7].
19. See [10].
20. See [4].
21. Vertical RMS of 2 meters in flat region and 5 meters in hilly landscape; see [10].
22. Vertical RMS of 3.5 meters in flat region and 7.5 meters in hilly landscape; see [10].
23. Vertical RMS of 5 meters in flat region and 10 meters in hilly landscape; see [11].
24. Vertical RMS of 20 meters; see [10].
25. See [15]; for information about FRAT 1.0—joint venture application of GMR in CE Europe see [12].
26. Swiss Reinsurance Company, Mythenquai 50/60, 8022 Zurich, Switzerland. Internet access: http://www.swissre.com.
27. See appendix section 5.1.8.
28. Currently Prague Office of the Intermap Technologies.
29. Environmental Protection and Water Management Research Institute (VITUKI—Környezetvédelmi és Vízgazdálkodási Kutató Intézet), Kvassay Jenő út 1, Budapest, Hungary. Internet access: http://www.vituki.hu.
30. See [16]. The data set contains flood zones with return periods of 100 and 1,000 years and flood protection dykes of only the 20 major rivers of Hungary.
31. See section 3.8.
32. See section 2.2.
33. For more details about difference between ISIC and NACE, see [14].
34. For complete list of all NACE codes see [2].

35. See figures 2.1–2.4.

36. See section 3.4.

37. See section 3.5.

38. See section 3.8.

39. For the complete ESA'95 institutional sectors classification See [5], Internet access: circa.europa. eu/irc/dsis/nfaccount/info/data/esa95/en/een00069.htm.

40. The reason for excluding the inventories in the industry branches A and B is that the losses on harvest and living stock, which is a major part of the inventories in these branches, are not considered in this study, as they are mostly covered by commercial insurance or other resources.

41. A simplified reclassification of institutional sectors on "public" and "non-public" was used, where the "non-public" class includes the "private" and "households" classes defined in section 3.2.6.

42. Examples of Infrastructure Public: public administration, education, healthcare, public transport infrastructure.

43. Examples of Infrastructure Non-public: non-public education, healthcare.

44. Examples of Enterprise Public: public industry, agriculture, real estate.

45. Examples of Enterprise Non-public: private industry, agriculture, real estate, transportation.

46. the property type dimensions are described in sections 3.2.1–3.2.6.

47. Data source of the fixed asset value and structure: [29], alternatively [30].

48. Data source of the inventories values and structure: [30].

49. Data source: [21], alternatively [23].

50. Data source: [32], [33].

51. Data source: [18], alternatively [35].

52. Reported by the Central Statistical Office of Poland (that is, private + households sectors according to the terminology used in this study).

53. For example, the reported fixed asset value in Poland is lower than the fixed asset value reported in the Czech Republic, although the GDP of Poland is approximately 230 percent of the GDP of the Czech Republic.

54. The property type dimensions are described in the sections 3.2.1–3.2.6.

55. Data source: [29].

56. Data source: [30].

57. Data source: [31].

58. The institutional sector versus industry structure for the Slovak Republic is not available; see also section 3.2.10 b).

59. Data source: [33].

60. Data source: [34].

61. Data Source: [32].

62. Data source: [18], alternatively [35], p. 662–669; the adjustments described in paragraph 3.2.10 d) were used.

63. The information about the 2007 property structure was not available yet while the total property value already was available.

64. The Czech Republic, the Slovak Republic, Hungary.

65. Poland.

66. Resource of the Regional gross fixed asset balance data at NUTS-2 level for Poland: [18], Gross value of fixed assets by national economy sectors.

67. Resource of the Regional gross fixed asset balance data for the Czech Republic at NUTS-3 level: [19].

68. Resource of the Regional gross fixed asset formation data for Hungary at NUTS-3 level: [20], table Gross fixed capital formation at NUTS level 3 (reg_e2gfcf).

69. Resource of the Regional gross fixed asset formation data for the Slovak Republic at NUTS-3 level: [21].

70. The residential, industrial, and network property types were defined in section 3.2.2.

71. Except for the Czech Republic—see [22].

72. The Czech Republic, the Slovak Republic.

73. Hungary, Poland. Even if the first level administrative units of Hungary (that is, provinces/"megye") correspond to NUTS-3 level, property distribution is available only for groups of provinces, that is, NUTS-2 level.

74. See [22].

75. Resource of salary and population data within the LAU-1 units in Poland: [18].

76. Resource of salary and population data within LAU-1 units in the Slovak Republic: [24], tables 3–7. Average monthly wage of employees by economic activities and 2-1. Mid-year population and population change.

77. Resource of 2001 salary data within LAU-1 units in Hungary: [41], p.5 (chart Egy állandó lakosra jutó szja-alapot képezô jövedelem 2001-ben (ezer Ft)).

78. For more about land cover classification, see [4] and paragraphs 3.4.4 and 5.1.11.

79. The lack of fit measured by the mean absolute error (MAE) for the industrial weights is approximately twice as higher than for the residential weights.

80. As defined in section 3.2.2

81. Sources of the transportation network reference data:
   - **The Czech Republic**. The transportation network of 1:25 000 Digital Model of the Territory (Digitální model území 1:25 000) vector data has been used (see [9]).
   - **The Slovak Republic**. The transportation network of the Digital Vector Map of the Slovak Republic 1:50,000 of Mapa the Slovak Republic Plus has been used (see [8]).
   - **Hungary**. The transportation network of the Digital Vector Map of Hungary 1:10,000 of HISZI-Map has been used (see [7]).
   - **Poland**. The transportation network of the map of Europe 1:200,000 of Mapa the Slovak Republic Plus has been used.

82. Roads and Motorways in the Czech Republic 2009, see [45]; Motorways and Speedways Backbone Network in the Czech Republic, see [46]; Annual Report 2008, see [47].

83. Annual Report 2008, see [48].

84. Railway Transport, see [49].

85. See section 3.2.2.

86. See section 3.2.4.

87. See [4]; for the complete CORINE classification, see Appendix section 5.1.11.

88. Based on the analysis of the reference address points CORINE classification, more than 20 percent of address points belong to the agriculture CORINE land cover category. Therefore the CORINE Land Cover data were not used for identification of the Residential property type.

89. For definition of "industrial" and "residential" property types, see paragraph 3.2.2.

90. Data source of the address points for the Czech Republic: [36] and [37].

91. Data source of the address points for the Slovak Republic: [38].

92. Data source of the address points for Hungary: [39].

93. Data source of the settlement residential area polygons for Poland: [40].

94. For more details see Appendix 5.1.9.

95. See [6].

96. That is, the return period of a real flood event at the location of a particular property.

97. That is, the flood hazard zone in which the particular property is located.

98. See appendix 3.4.3.

99. For the aggregated real loss data, see appendix section 5.1.6.

100. Before the calibration, all the real loss values were recalculated from the historical prices into the current prices, that is, end of the year 2007. See also Sections 1.3.2 and 3.3.

101. For the list of scenarios see table 5.29.

102. Also called as "probabilistic method."

103. Data source of the discharges for the Czech Republic: [27].

104. For the map of the gauging stations, see figure 5.22.

105. See section 3.10.4

106. In total, 5,481 grid cells are generated.

107. Moreover, sensitivity of the correlation structure on the period length was tested. According to results of this test, the correlation matrices calculated for 2-month maximums and quarterly maxi-

mums do not show significant differences from the correlation matrix calculated for the monthly maximum data.

108. Data source of the N-years discharges for the Czech Republic: [27].

109. Data source of the monthly maximum discharges: [26].

110. This assumption was tested by Kolmogorov—Smirnov test.

111. Standardized random variable has mean=0 and standard deviation = 1.

112. For kriging method description, see [28].

113. Note the difference between the flood return periods, which represent the return period of the discharge in the particular locations, and loss return period, which represents return period of the total loss within the whole territory.

114. For the flood scenarios see section 3.6.

115. The basic components of model which contribute to the total error are the following ones:

- *Loss reported during the historical events and subsequently calculated vulnerability:* The data are difficult to obtain from the national authorities, because either they are not registered or they are based partly on reported values and partly on estimates; for example, the loss reported by the district governments during the 1997 flood in the Czech Republic differs from the estimate of the total loss, according to national Water Research Institute.
- *Real allocation of the property into the flood hazard zones:* Modeled property allocation is based on assumption that it follows either the spatial distribution of the address points in the case of RES type properties or the allocation of industrial class of the CORINE land cover in the case of IND property type.
- *Regional distribution of the property value balance into the NUTS-2, NUTS-3 or LAU-1 units:* The distribution mentioned is available from the national statistical institute only for Poland and partly for the Czech Republic; for the other countries it is calculated by using the simplified approach using compatible input data, such as regional distribution of the fixed asset formation; the regional distributions of the property value balances as well as formation provided by the national statistical authorities that do not contain the confidence intervals.
- *Property value and classification estimated from national accounts:* The total property value as well as proportion of the individual property categories provided by the national statistical authorities do not contain any confidence intervals.

116. The final loss exceedance curve should be interpreted as a point estimate or estimate of the mean value (or the most probable value) of the loss for a given flood return period and scenario.

117. As the assumption of the 250-year flood is a non-realistic extreme event, only the loss structure as a percentage of the total loss is displayed in the outputs, and not the nominal values.

118. For industry branches definition and reclassification, see paragraphs 3.2.1 and 3.2.2.

119. For asset category definition, see paragraphs 3.2.3 and 3.2.4.

120. For asset institutional sectors definition, see paragraphs 3.2.5 and 3.2.6.

121. Regional distribution of Czech Republic property is tabulated in appendix section 5.1.12a) where the regional split into Industry Branches, Asset Categories, and Institutional Sectors is also listed.

122. Regional distribution the Slovak Republic property is tabulated in appendix section 5.1.12b) where regional split to Industry Branches, Asset Categories, and Institutional Sectors is also listed.

123. Regional distribution of the property in Hungary is tabulated in appendix section 5.1.12c) also regional split to Industry Branches, Asset Categories, and Institutional Sectors is also listed.

124. Regional distribution of the property in Poland is tabulated in appendix section 5.1.12d) where regional split to Industry Branches, Asset Categories, and Institutional Sectors is also listed.

125. Property distribution to districts in the Czech Republic is tabulated in appendix section 5.1.13a), particularly in table 5.44 and figure 5.58.

126. Property distribution to districts in the Slovak Republic is tabulated in appendix section 5.1.13b), particularly in table 5.45 and figure 5.63.

127. Property distribution to districts in the Slovak Republic is tabulated in appendix section 5.1.13c), particularly in table 5.46 and figure 5.68.

128. Property distribution to districts in the Slovak Republic is tabulated in appendix section 5.1.13d), particularly in table 5.47 and figure 5.73.

129. To obtain information on the household equipment value, which is not registered by the national statistical authorities, data from the insurance industry were collected.

130. Property data sources, reclassification and missing values handling are described in section 3.2.

131. Property redistribution into the flood hazard zones is described in section 3.5.

132. End of the year 2007.

133. For detailed specification of the public, private and household institutional sectors see sections 3.2.5 and 3.2.6.

134. For more detailed property structure within the countries, see appendix section 5.1.5. F or the regional split of property value, see appendix sections 5.1.12 and 5.1.13.

135. For the asset categories definition and reclassification see sections 3.2.3 and 3.2.4.

136. For the detailed property distribution into the flood hazard zones, see appendix section 5.1.8.

137. See section 3.8.

138. For the scenario method, see section 3.9.

139. See section 3.6 and appendix section 5.1.9.

140. For the description of the stochastic method, see section 3.10, for the detailed results, see appendix section 5.2.1.

141. For the detailed results, see appendix section 5.2.5. For the methodology, see section 3.11.6.

142. For the return period of 100 years (1 percent occurrence probability), the loss on the public property is approximately EUR 6 billion, for the return period of 250 years (0.4 percent occurrence probability).the loss in the public property is EUR 10 billion.

143. For the differences in the individual countries as well as scenarios, see appendix sections 5.2.5 and 5.3.

144. For more detailed results, see section 4.2.1 and appendix section 5.2.1.

145. See the extrapolated stochastic method description, section 3.10.

146. For more detailed results, see appendix section 5.2.5.

147. For methodology, see section 3.11.3. For the detailed results, see appendix section 5.2.1.

148. Loss intensity = loss in a territory as a percentage of the total property value in the territory; see also section 3.11.4.

Modeling for Losses Correlated to Flood Magnitude Triggers

This chapter presents a model for establishing a dependency structure between flood water discharges from various river catchments in the four CEE countries analyzed, and extreme losses. The purpose is to derive mutual correlations between the two, so as to formulate parametric triggers for payments under such flood events. Development of parametric triggers are beneficial for national authorities since under these, payment execution is simplified and based solely on measured physical events rather than site-by-site assessment of losses. In this regard parametric-based payments are more akin to financial options contracts rather than traditional indemnity based insurance contracts.

Data—Countries and River Catchments used in the Analysis

It is important to stress that flood loss models are highly complex and the overall result is an aggregate of detailed smaller components. When identifying parametric triggers, the scale of the problem needs to be kept at a reasonable level. Therefore, one needs to accept necessary trade-offs between the level of detail of the flood analysis with the level of complexity of the interdependence structure (that is, the dimensions in the correlation matrix). The V-4 countries were split into several main catchments in which measuring stations selected as representative of a whole catchment were used. This means that the dependency structures are being dealt with on a subregional scale. Catchments were selected to capture the main rivers, and stations were usually at the border of the catchment. Some of the Hungarian discharge data sets were not fully satisfactory, and therefore the last station in the neighboring country where sufficient data was present, was used as a proxy (for Hornad, Raab, and Leitha) (table 3.1).

Table 3.1. List of Stations/Countries

Station/Country	Czech Republic	Slovak Republic	Poland	Hungary
1	Bohumin—Odra	Bratislava—Dunaj	Gozdowice—Odra	Nagymaros—Dunaj
2	Straznice—Morava	Sala—Vah	Warszawa—Visla	Szeged—Tisza
3	Breclav—Dyje	Zdana—Hornad	Ostroleka—Narew	Felsoezsolca—Salo
4	Vranany—Vltava	Streda nad Bodrogom—Bodrog		Zdana (SK)—Hornad
5	Usti nad Labem—Labe			Balassagyarmat—Ipel
6				Feldbach (AT)—Raab
7				Deutsch Brodersdorf (AT)—Leitha

Source: Aon Benfield.

Historical Data on River Discharges

Maximum monthly discharges were used for the selected stations. Observations were considered since January 1951 (the starting date of measurement for most time series). Some time series have longer periods of observation, in particular bigger rivers like Labe or Dunaj, but for the purpose of measuring simultaneous dependencies it was desirable to have data present within all "cells" of the observation matrix. Time series were taken from official hydro-meteorological institutions of the studied countries. According to these institutions, data was already adjusted for the effects of human changes in the catchment area (for example, building dams, effect of flood regulation, and so forth).

Generation of Losses and Models Used

A brief description of loss generation follows. Loss in a given catchment is calculated by the aggregation of losses originating from the tributaries of the main river. Losses are generated per postcodes, where each postcode is divided into a rectangular shaped grid. As the height of the river increases, a greater area is flooded. Based on the calculated depth of water in a location and on vulnerability curves (curves translating depth of water to losses) losses are calculated accordingly. Models in the Czech Republic, the Slovak Republic, and Poland generate 10,000 events, with a probability of each event equal to 1/10,000. The loss is calculated for each event. The Hungarian model has fewer events with unequal probabilities.

The market portfolio (insured properties) was used for loss generation in all four countries. The portfolio was extrapolated up to 100 percent of the insurance market. Currently Aon Benfield models 86 percent of the Czech insurance market, 90 percent of the Slovak market, 71 percent of the Hungarian market and 93 percent of the Polish market, therefore the extrapolation/grossing up was minimal. The insurance penetration in the modeled countries is quite high (in the Czech Republic around 65 percent, the Slovak Republic around 60 percent, Hungary around 60 percent, PL 40 percent), so the insured losses quite accurately reflect the distribution of properties within the modeled countries.

In terms of properties insured, the Czech Republic has together with Poland the highest total insured value (2.5 times larger than Hungary and 4 times larger than the Slovak Republic) but the total insured value in the Czech Republic is more concentrated than in Poland. For the purpose of the analysis, 50,000 trials with event sets as outputs from the above-mentioned models were generated. Losses were kept in original currency after which exchange rates were applied (see tables 3.2 and 3.3, and figures 3.1 to 3.4).

Table 3.2. Exchange Rates Used

	CZK	SKK	HUF	PLN
per EUR 1	25.8	30.126	275	4.15

Source: Aon Benfield.

Table 3.3. Total Insured Value (TIV) per Type of Risk and Area (EUR Million)

Country	Catchment	Residential Building	Residential Content	Commercial	Industrial	Agro	Total
CZ	Odra	12,408	2,291	7,253	24,239		46,192
CZ	Morava	19,166	2,702	7,554	18,566		47,988
CZ	Dyje	17,292	2,455	5,871	18,994		44,613
CZ	Vltava	54,922	9,333	25,326	60,242		149,822
CZ	Labe	44,596	7,112	15,690	49,181		116,578
CZ Total		**148,385**	**23,893**	**61,694**	**171,222**	**N/A**	**405,194**
SK	Dunaj	14,140	2,889	9,480	16,919		43,428
SK	Vah	11,631	2,193	6,636	9,674		30,134
SK	Hornad	6,848	1,533	5,257	3,322		16,959
SK	Bodrog	3,800	750	1,710	1,324		7,585
SK Total		**36,418**	**7,365**	**23,083**	**31,239**	**N/A**	**98,105**
HU	Ipel	683	220	13	124	—	1,040
HU	Dunaj	59,905	17,518	1,394	14,924	177	93,918
HU	Salo	2,852	1,052	76	861	0.6	4,843
HU	Hornad	460	152	19	40	2.8	674
HU	Hornad-Salo	68	22	0.6	8.5	0.4	100
HU	Tisza	26,698	8,587	1,020	6,868	271	43,444
HU	Leitha	3,222	973	116	604	55	4,969
HU	Raab	5,663	1,677	206	1,334	49	8,929
HU	Raab-Leitha	544	146	28	567	1.0	1,287
HU Total		**100,096**	**30,348**	**2,874**	**25,330**	**557**	**159,204**
PL	Odra	57,860	5,243	60,394	40,358		163,856
PL	Wisla	83,211	6,766	64,706	59,309		213,991
PL	Narew	13,929	1,104	8,056	3,397		26,486
PL Total		**155,000**	**13,113**	**133,156**	**103,064**	**N/A**	**404,332**
CEE Total		**439,899**	**74,719**	**220,806**	**330,854**	**557**	**1,066,835**

Source: Aon Benfield.
Note: Hornad-Salo and Raab-Leitha are areas at confluences of these rivers where we could not appropriately assign TIV to a single river.

Figure 3.1. Catchments, the Czech Republic

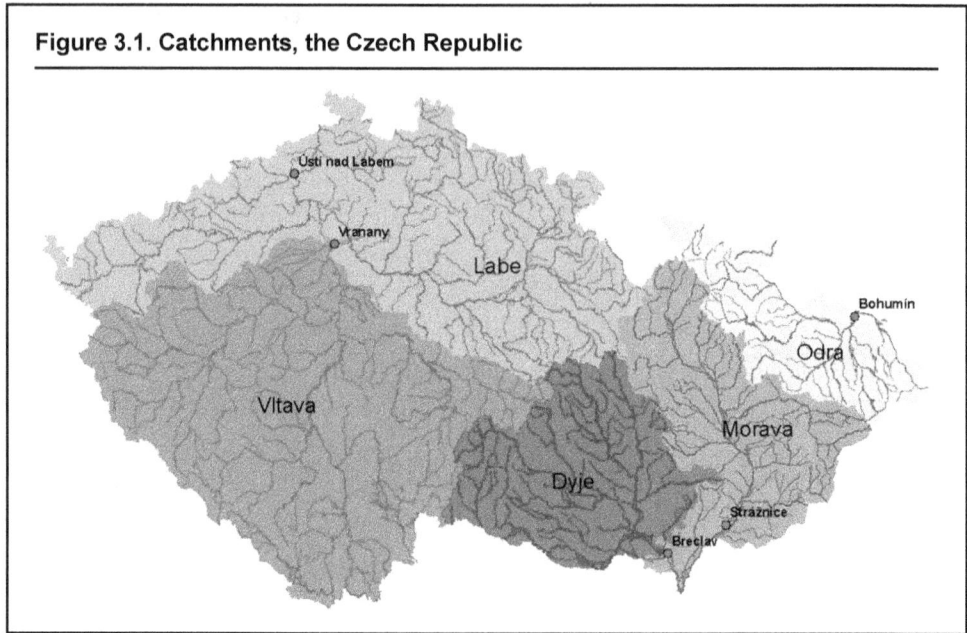

Source: Aon Benfield.

Figure 3.2. Catchments, the Slovak Republic

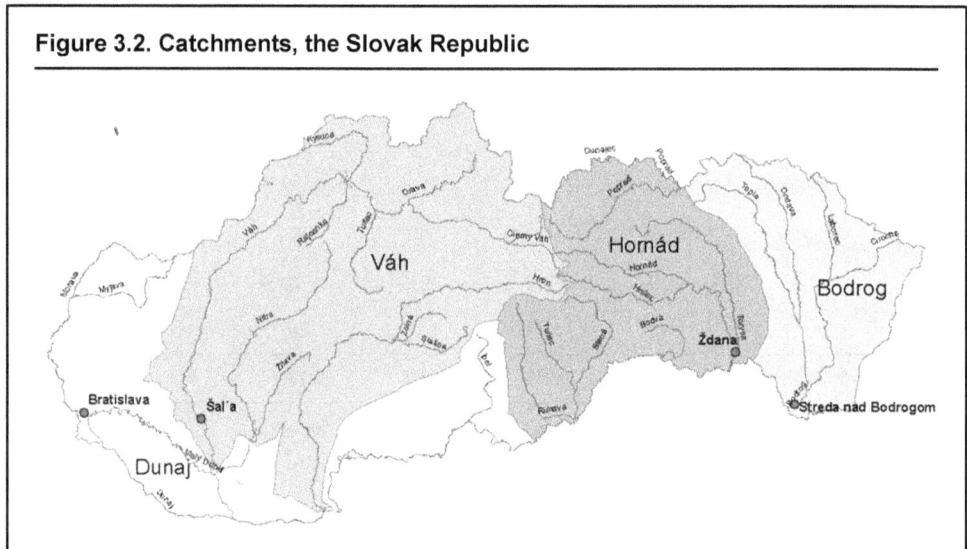

Source: Aon Benfield.

Correlation Matrices—Methodology

Monthly discharge maxima were considered for creating the correlation matrices for the following reasons: One can assume that the sources of correlations are atmospheric events which affect areas larger than a single catchment. Therefore, using yearly discharge maxima this would mix events originating at different times of the year. Using monthly data removes, to a large extent, this possible source of bias. It is still possible

Figure 3.3. Catchments, Poland

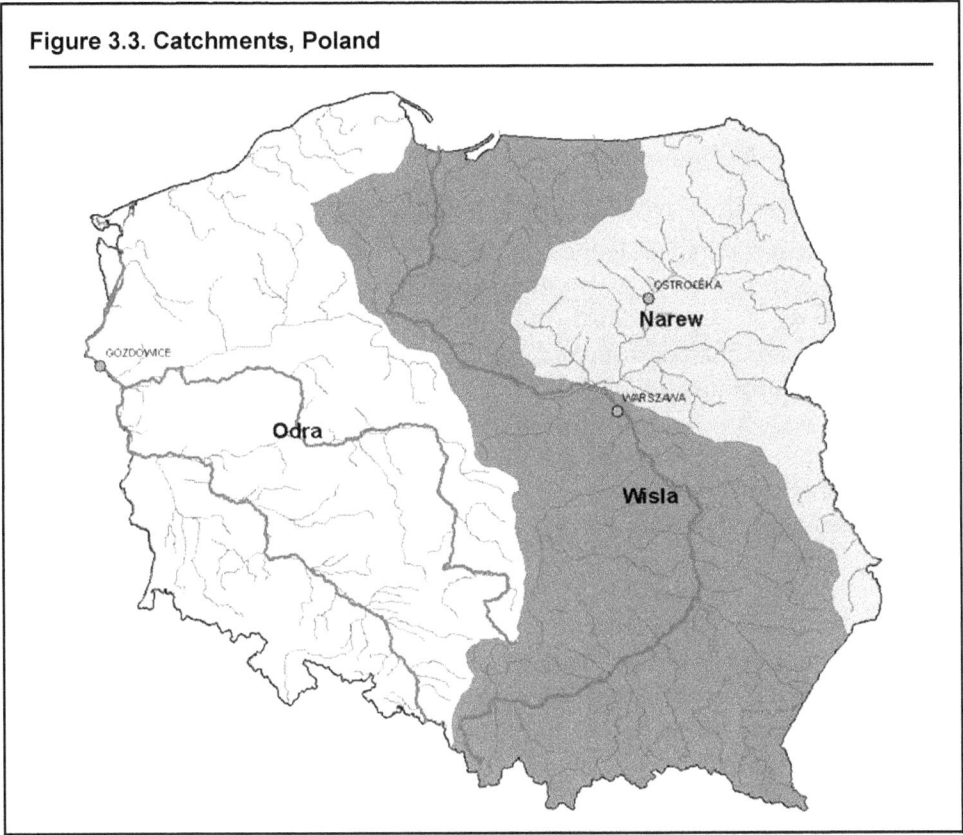

Source: Aon Benfield.

Figure 3.4. Catchments, Hungary

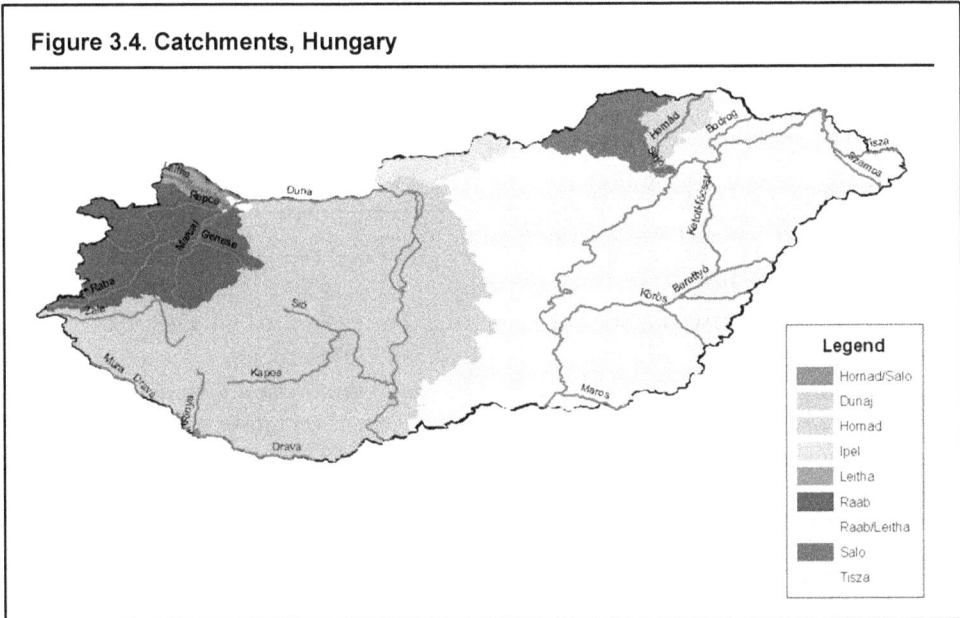

Source: Aon Benfield.

that two stations have large discharges and the discharges originate from two completely different events in a given month; however, this is highly unlikely.

River discharges in Central and Eastern Europe show seasonality. This seasonality would increase the correlation of the data set when taking the series of observations without any structuring. The same months of the year would be showing the same
relative increases (or decreases) across all stations. Therefore, it is more appropriate to
create twelve correlation matrices each representing one month of a year. The annex to
this chapter shows a graphical representation of monthly correlations between stations.
Correlation coefficients have medians and means close to each other (no high skewness),
thus the average is taken. In other words, the correlations are considered as pseudo repeated realizations of a stochastic variable.

It should be pointed out the word 'correlation' does not consider a standard Pearson's correlation (covariance of two variables divided by their standard errors) which
has some unpleasant characteristics. Pearson's correlation should be considered when
having normally distributed data, which is not the case for catastrophic events. Therefore, a Spearman's rank correlation which is defined as Pearson's correlation of the ranks
(or equivalently cumulative distribution functions) was used. Moreover, across catchments, the discharges rather than the losses were correlated, since loss correlation alone
could yield strange results when, for example, a loss occurred in one country in a given
period without a loss in another neighboring country. Subsequently, the correlated discharges were translated to losses using one-to-one mapping.

Complete observations were used for calculating the correlation matrix. In case of
missing data in one of the stations, all observations for that period were deleted. This
was later checked with pair wise correlations, that is, where the correlation is calculated
from pairs of variables and entered into the correlation matrix (each cell of the correlation matrix is thus based on a different data set). In a pair wise correlation matrix, if an
observation was missing in one station, the paired observation of the second variable
was deleted. As a result, only 3 percent of records in the correlation matrix differed in
absolute value between 0.01 and 0.03, and the remaining records differed absolutely by
less than 0.01. Therefore, it can be confirmed that both methods are nearly equivalent.

Results of Correlation Matrices

The average of the correlation matrices is shown in table 3.4. The pink color indicates
strong correlation (>=0.7), pale blue represents mild correlation (between 0.35 and 0.7)
and gray stands for weak correlation (<=0.35). Graphical representations are presented
in the annex to this chapter.

In general, the correlation between non neighboring regions is higher than originally expected around zero, and this can be attributed to atmospheric effects. For example
during a dry year, drought is highly likely to occur in the whole CEE region. Also, rainy
weather would affect several countries as the frontal system moves across the region. It
should be noted that records for Hornad in Hungary were crossed out because the same
data for Hornad in the Slovak Republic were used. The entry in the Hungarian part was
used only for the sake of completeness. Therefore, there is a black cell between Hornad
the Slovak Republic and Hornad Hungary as there is 100 percent correlation there.

Table 3.4. Average of Monthly Discharge Rank Correlation Matrices

Country	River	CZ Odra	CZ Morava	CZ Dyje	CZ Vltava	CZ Labe	SK Dunaj	SK Vah	SK Hornad	SK Bodrog	HU Ipel	HU Dunaj	HU Salo	HU(SK) Hornad	HU Tisza	HU(AT) Leitha	HU(AT) Raab	PL Odra	PL Wisla	PL Narew
CZ	Odra		0.86	0.68	0.47	0.54	0.48	0.67	0.49	0.42	0.44	0.50	0.47	0.49	0.40	0.35	0.25	0.56	0.57	0.32
CZ	Morava	0.86		0.77	0.55	0.65	0.52	0.74	0.48	0.44	0.43	0.56	0.42	0.48	0.39	0.38	0.27	0.59	0.55	0.35
CZ	Dyje	0.68	0.77		0.59	0.63	0.46	0.56	0.40	0.32	0.35	0.47	0.40	0.40	0.33	0.35	0.22	0.57	0.47	0.26
CZ	Vltava	0.47	0.55	0.59		0.90	0.65	0.42	0.31	0.29	0.27	0.66	0.38	0.34	0.35	0.36	0.18	0.64	0.39	0.36
CZ	Labe	0.54	0.65	0.63	0.90		0.68	0.50	0.32	0.34	0.28	0.67	0.35	0.32	0.39	0.34	0.13	0.71	0.45	0.43
SK	Dunaj	0.48	0.52	0.46	0.65	0.68		0.44	0.27	0.29	0.20	0.92	0.24	0.27	0.40	0.51	0.19	0.49	0.40	0.33
SK	Vah	0.67	0.74	0.56	0.42	0.50	0.44		0.51	0.50	0.41	0.52	0.43	0.54	0.40	0.32	0.24	0.49	0.61	0.32
SK	Hornad	0.49	0.48	0.40	0.31	0.32	0.27	0.51		0.68	0.66	0.36	0.79	0.49	0.49	0.30	0.33	0.37	0.61	0.28
SK	Bodrog	0.42	0.44	0.32	0.29	0.34	0.29	0.50	0.68		0.44	0.35	0.62	0.68	0.69	0.21	0.22	0.33	0.61	0.32
HU	Ipel	0.44	0.43	0.35	0.27	0.28	0.20	0.41	0.66	0.44		0.30	0.78	0.66	0.38	0.27	0.43	0.24	0.33	0.17
HU	Dunaj	0.50	0.56	0.47	0.66	0.67	0.92	0.52	0.36	0.35	0.30		0.35	0.36	0.43	0.56	0.25	0.52	0.48	0.35
HU	Salo	0.47	0.42	0.40	0.38	0.35	0.24	0.43	0.79	0.62	0.78	0.35		0.79	0.53	0.33	0.42	0.35	0.50	0.20
HU(SK)	Hornad	0.49	0.48	0.40	0.34	0.32	0.27	0.54	0.49	0.68	0.66	0.36	0.79		0.49	0.30	0.33	0.37	0.61	0.28
HU	Tisza	0.40	0.39	0.33	0.35	0.39	0.40	0.40	0.61	0.69	0.38	0.43	0.53	0.49		0.22	0.19	0.40	0.57	0.37
HU(AT)	Leitha	0.35	0.38	0.35	0.36	0.34	0.51	0.32	0.30	0.21	0.27	0.56	0.33	0.30	0.22		0.45	0.26	0.31	0.10
HU(AT)	Raab	0.25	0.27	0.22	0.18	0.13	0.19	0.24	0.33	0.22	0.43	0.25	0.42	0.33	0.19	0.45		0.08	0.18	-0.04
PL	Odra	0.56	0.59	0.57	0.64	0.71	0.49	0.49	0.37	0.33	0.24	0.52	0.35	0.37	0.40	0.26	0.08		0.55	0.57
PL	Wisla	0.57	0.55	0.47	0.39	0.45	0.40	0.61	0.61	0.61	0.33	0.48	0.50	0.61	0.57	0.31	0.18	0.55		0.46
PL	Narew	0.32	0.35	0.26	0.36	0.43	0.33	0.32	0.28	0.32	0.17	0.35	0.20	0.28	0.37	0.10	-0.04	0.57	0.46	

Source: Aon Benfield.

Note: Some of the river discharge measurements attributed to Hungary were taken where the river crossed the country's borders. In these cases, the actual measuring stations were located just across the border in the neighboring country (mentioned in parentheses).

Dependency structure of discharges—Methodology

Copulas were used to tie the random variables together. The only difference between a copula and a multivariate distribution is that the copula deals with percentiles and the multivariate distribution with original values of x. Thus:

$$\Pr(X_1 \le x_1, X_2 \le x_2,...,X_n \le x_n) = H(x_1,x_2,...,x_n)$$
$$= C(F_1(x_1),F_2(x_2),...,F_n(x_n)) = C(u_1,u_2,...,u_n),$$

where X is the original random variable and x is a specific value; H is the multivariate distribution and F is the cumulative distribution function for each random variable X. Thus, F(x) is the probability that a random variable X will be smaller or equal to x. C is the notation for a copula and u is a relevant percentile of x (again the probability that the random variable X will be smaller or equal to x), that is u = F(x).

To deal with a dependency structure, a t-Copula was used. t-Copula is a method to express a multidimensional dependency in a slightly different way than the ordinary correlation matrix does. The "ordinary" in this sense means that the correlation is based on an assumption of a multivariate normal distribution. This is done using Iman-Conover method which transfers the ranks into percentiles of a normal distribution and then data is drawn together according to the given correlation matrix. The dependence structure is thus implicitly, a so called, Gaussian Copula.

However, a Gaussian Copula has a property that yields asymptotically independent tails, that is, the joint probability of two extreme events is 0 which is somehow in contradiction with what is expected when dealing with flood events. Unlike the Gaussian Copula, the t-Copula does not have asymptotically independent tails and is similar to the Gaussian Copula (both use the same correlation matrix), (Embrechts 2002). Because of the above reasons, a t-Copula was used. The second parameter of the t-Copula, besides the correlation matrix, is the number of degrees of freedom. The more degrees of freedom, the more it resembles the Gaussian Copula.

In this case, number of degrees of freedom was again calculated for twelve correlation matrices using the maximum likelihood method, having a fixed correlation matrix. (See Demarta, McNeil 2004). A fixing correlation matrix was chosen in order to simplify the computational aspects and, as per the mentioned authors' studies, should lead to similar results. Degrees of freedom (df) for each month's correlation matrix were calculated, and the median of these df were taken (this was preferred to the average because of the skewness, that is, some months had a very high number of df which, however, differed from much smaller amount of df in terms of maximum likelihood, by less than one percent).

The correlation matrix that was used as a parameter was not the rank correlation but the linear correlation which can be obtained using following formula:

$$\rho_{Linear} = 2\sin\left(\frac{\pi\rho_{Spearman}}{6}\right).$$

Results of Dependency Structures of Discharges

The resulting number of degrees of freedom, expressed as median of df of individual monthly correlation matrices, was df = 7.5 which was rounded up to df = 8. The linear correlation matrix of the t-Copula was then obtained by transforming Spearman rank correlation to a Pearson's linear correlation using the formula above (table 3.5).

Table 3.5. Linear Correlation Matrix as Input in t-Copula

Country / River		CZ					SK				HU	HU	HU	HU(SK)	HU	HU(AT)	HU(AT)	PL		
		Odra	Morava	Dyje	Vltava	Labe	Dunaj	Vah	Hornad	Bodrog	Ipel	Dunaj	Salo	Hornad	Tisza	Leitha	Raab	Odra	Wisla	Narew
CZ	Odra	■	0.87	0.70	0.49	0.56	0.50	0.69	0.51	0.44	0.45	0.51	0.49	0.51	0.42	0.37	0.27	0.57	0.59	0.33
CZ	Morava	0.87	■	0.78	0.56	0.67	0.54	0.76	0.50	0.46	0.45	0.57	0.44	0.50	0.41	0.40	0.28	0.61	0.57	0.37
CZ	Dyje	0.70	0.78	■	0.61	0.65	0.48	0.58	0.42	0.33	0.36	0.48	0.42	0.42	0.34	0.36	0.23	0.58	0.48	0.27
CZ	Vltava	0.49	0.56	0.61	■	0.91	0.66	0.44	0.32	0.30	0.28	0.68	0.39	0.32	0.37	0.37	0.18	0.65	0.40	0.38
CZ	Labe	0.56	0.67	0.65	0.91	■	0.70	0.52	0.34	0.35	0.29	0.69	0.36	0.34	0.40	0.35	0.14	0.72	0.47	0.44
SK	Dunaj	0.50	0.54	0.48	0.66	0.70	■	0.46	0.28	0.30	0.21	0.93	0.25	0.28	0.41	0.53	0.20	0.51	0.42	0.34
SK	Vah	0.69	0.76	0.58	0.44	0.52	0.46	■	0.53	0.51	0.43	0.54	0.45	0.53	0.41	0.34	0.25	0.50	0.63	0.34
SK	Hornad	0.51	0.50	0.42	0.32	0.34	0.28	0.53	■	0.70	0.68	0.38	0.80	0.51	0.51	0.31	0.34	0.38	0.63	0.29
SK	Bodrog	0.44	0.46	0.33	0.30	0.35	0.30	0.51	0.70	■	0.46	0.37	0.64	0.70	0.70	0.22	0.23	0.34	0.63	0.34
HU	Ipel	0.45	0.45	0.36	0.28	0.29	0.21	0.43	0.68	0.46	■	0.31	0.80	0.68	0.40	0.28	0.45	0.25	0.35	0.18
HU	Dunaj	0.51	0.57	0.48	0.68	0.69	0.93	0.54	0.38	0.37	0.31	■	0.37	0.38	0.45	0.58	0.26	0.53	0.50	0.37
HU	Salo	0.49	0.44	0.42	0.39	0.36	0.25	0.45	0.80	0.64	0.80	0.37	■	0.80	0.54	0.35	0.43	0.36	0.52	0.21
HU(SK)	Hornad	0.51	0.50	0.42	0.32	0.34	0.28	0.53	0.51	0.70	0.68	0.38	0.80	■	0.54	0.34	0.34	0.38	0.63	0.29
HU	Tisza	0.42	0.41	0.34	0.37	0.40	0.41	0.41	0.51	0.70	0.40	0.45	0.54	0.54	■	0.23	0.19	0.41	0.58	0.39
HU(AT)	Leitha	0.37	0.40	0.36	0.37	0.35	0.53	0.34	0.31	0.22	0.28	0.58	0.35	0.34	0.23	■	0.47	0.28	0.32	0.11
HU(AT)	Raab	0.27	0.28	0.23	0.18	0.14	0.20	0.25	0.34	0.23	0.45	0.26	0.43	0.34	0.19	0.47	■	0.08	0.18	-0.04
PL	Odra	0.57	0.61	0.58	0.65	0.72	0.51	0.50	0.38	0.34	0.25	0.53	0.36	0.38	0.41	0.28	0.08	■	0.57	0.59
PL	Wisla	0.59	0.57	0.48	0.40	0.47	0.42	0.63	0.63	0.63	0.35	0.50	0.52	0.63	0.58	0.32	0.18	0.57	■	0.48
PL	Narew	0.33	0.37	0.27	0.38	0.44	0.34	0.34	0.29	0.34	0.18	0.37	0.21	0.29	0.39	0.11	-0.04	0.59	0.48	■

Source: Aon Benfield.
Note: Some of the river discharge measurements attributed to Hungary were taken where the river crossed the country's borders. In these cases, the actual measuring stations were located just across the border in the neighboring country (mentioned in parentheses).

Marginal distributions—Methodology

For the purpose of marginal distributions, maxima per year were also considered. This is because the model operates on a yearly basis, and the model design discharges (those obtained from a model, or estimates from the official institutions) are based as return periods in years. In the case of the Czech Republic and the Slovak Republic the discharges as per the model outputs were used. In the case of Poland, empirical data set up to approximate a 1in50 event (since we only have around 50 years of data) were used. The design discharge estimates by the official institutions were used above this return period. In the case of Hungary, a methodology similar to Poland was applied with the difference that top part (above approximately 1/50) of the distribution was estimated solely from the model, as no such observations were present in the data set. Fitting to the empirical values was not used and instead, an empirical cumulative distribution function (CDF; ogive) was applied.

Relationship between discharges and losses—Methodology for loss generation

The approach was to create a one-to-one link between the discharges and the losses. For the Czech Republic and the Slovak Republic, this is already provided in the event loss table. For Poland, the event loss table provides only the water level (stage) of the river at the station. Comonotonicity was assumed, that is, a 100 percent correlation between a percentile of water level and a discharge. In other words, the percentiles of water level provided in the event loss table were used and assumed that these percentiles exactly match the percentiles of the river discharge.

For HU, the event loss table with discharges were provided only for events which generated a loss. Therefore, large discharges without any loss were not captured. To overcome such an obstacle an empirical CDF was taken for the observed historical discharges and compared with the discharges resulting from the event loss table. Then, a dummy discharge was entered between successive events with a probability set, in a way that each of these two observed events (with a loss and discharge) had a percentile corresponding to the percentile of the empirical CDF. Of course this did not yield an exact match, however the error was optimized using a minimum mean squared error.

For example, Event 1 had a discharge of 400 (which corresponds to the 70th percentile of the empiric discharges) and event 2 had 410 (corresponding to the 72nd percentile). Event 1 had a probability of 1 percent. Therefore, a dummy event with discharge of 405 had to be entered with a probability of 1 percent so that the discharge of the second event matched the corresponding percentile of the empirical CDF. The only variable randomly generated was the percentile of the discharge which was then linked via the table on event loss, to an appropriate loss amount. Once the discharges per catchment were generated, the losses were assigned to them and aggregated on a country-wide basis for subsequent analysis.

Results on Relationship between Losses and Discharges

Modeling floods and related losses is highly complex and the resulting loss can be viewed as a sum of many nonidentical distributed random variables (that is, losses to individual insurance policies). Parametric functions transforming discharges to losses were not found to be very accurate; one of the reasons may be that using linear models in a highly nonlinear environment does not lead to the desired results. As can be seen from the following graphs, there is great variability of final losses even for events with nearly the same discharge level in a given station because one is dealing with a model on a subregional scale. Therefore, the relationship between discharges and losses was taken only from the empirical one, based on the models.

It should be remembered that a total loss for each catchment is observed; therefore, the variability in losses arises out of various conditions of the catchments covered by the representative station. Various conditions could be represented by different sizes of the catchment area from individual rivers (for example, having Labe catchment split into 20 areas and Vltava into 100), the regulation and mitigation actions around rivers (water dams, defences), the number of tributaries (streams, springs and small rivers), and other exogenous factors. These factors are, by their nature, unique to each of the catchments.

As a result, nearly the same discharges could have been generated by two completely different events. As an example, two tributaries where one is larger and the other smaller can be examined. When two events with the same discharge at the station after confluence of these two rivers occurs, this discharge could have arrived (under normal conditions) from the smaller river, for which it is would be a 1–in-500 event causing massive damages in the area of the smaller river. On the other hand, having a high discharge in a larger river can be nothing more than just an increased state of the water level, which may not causing any damage in the area of the bigger river.

Sudden breakpoints in the trend of losses (for example, small losses disappear and an approximately linear positive relationship holds) at a certain level of discharge, reflects a breach of flood defenses. This is best visible in case of Bratislava, city on Dunaj, that are heavily defended by a system of dams. Figures 3.5 to 3.8 show the relationship of losses within a catchment, related to discharges.

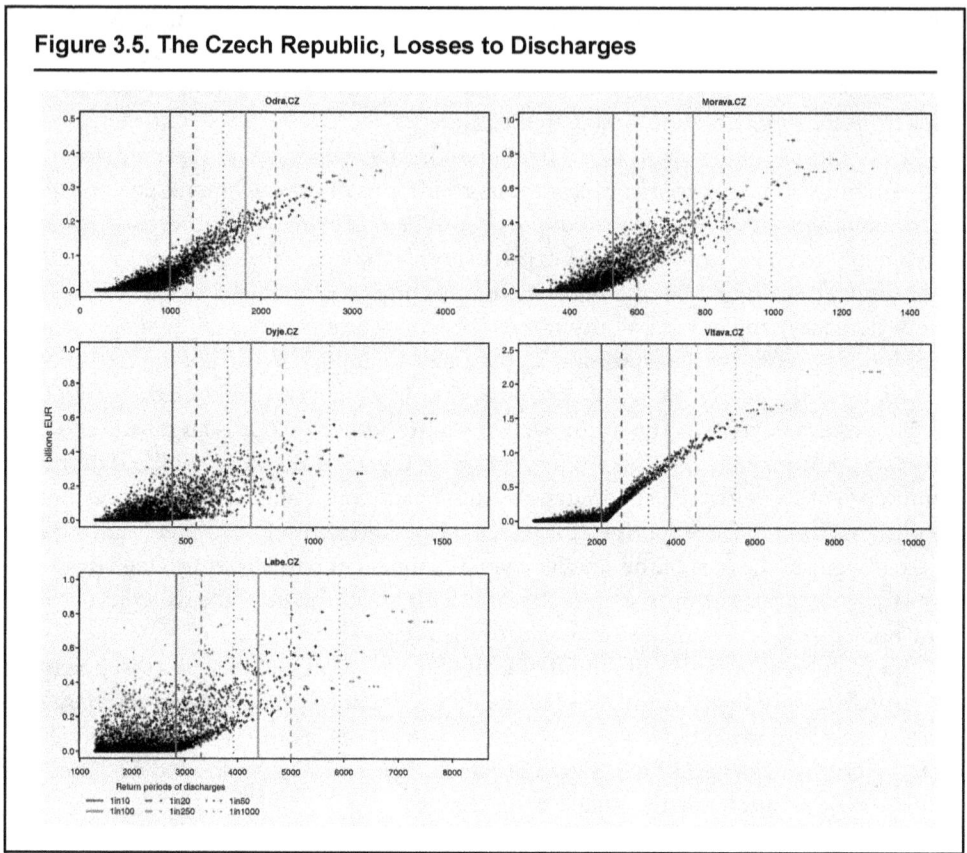

Figure 3.5. The Czech Republic, Losses to Discharges

Source: Aon Benfield.

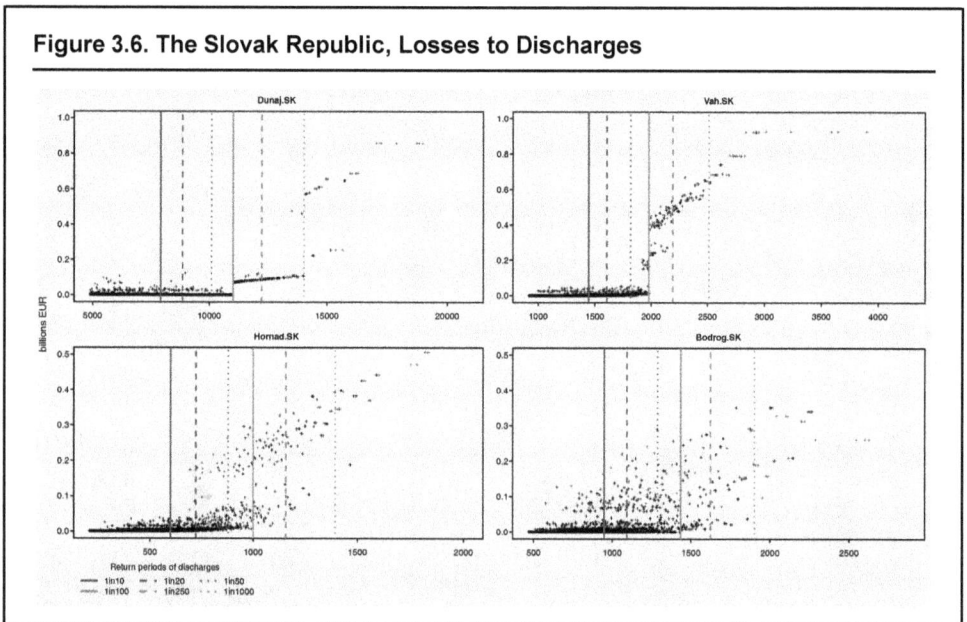

Figure 3.6. The Slovak Republic, Losses to Discharges

Source: Aon Benfield.

Figure 3.7. Hungary, Losses to Discharges

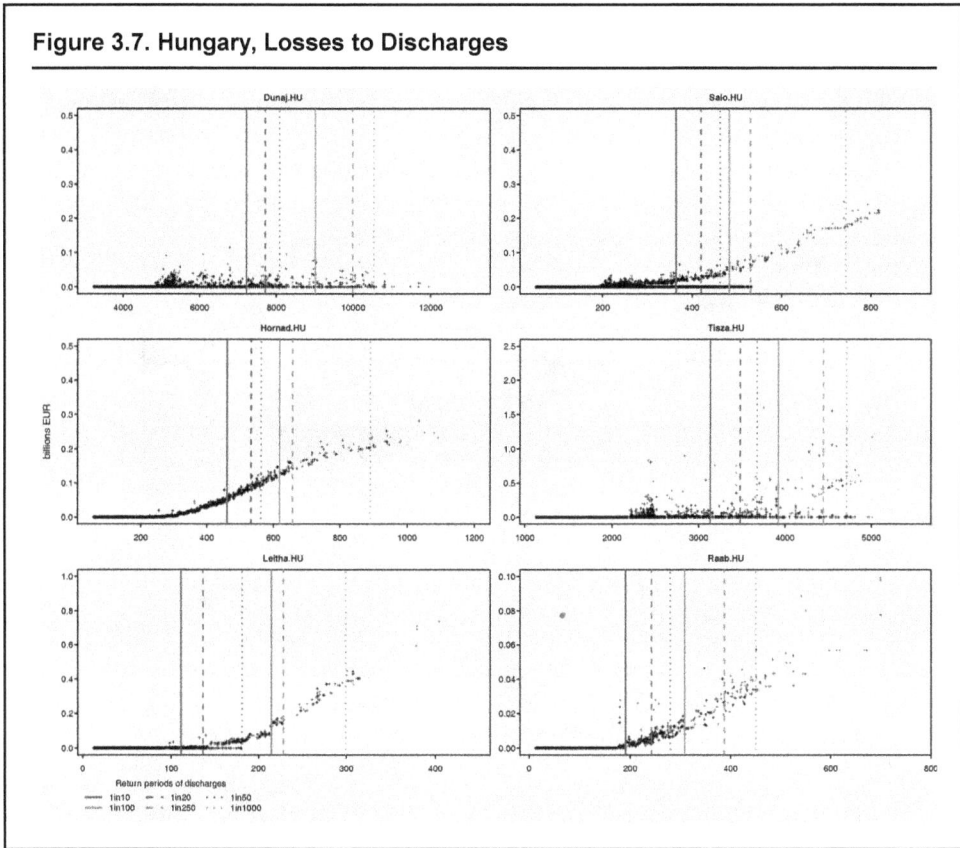

Source: Aon Benfield.

Figure 3.8. Poland, Losses to Discharges

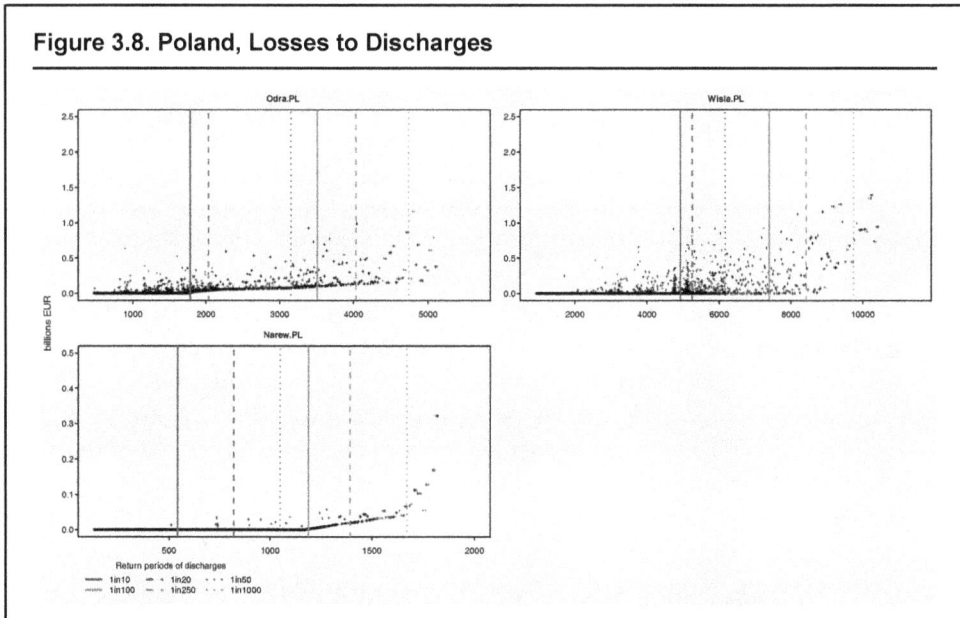

Source: Aon Benfield.

Outputs per Gross Loss

Return periods for each country were calculated as a simple empirical CDF of the simulated losses. Maxima per year were simulated; thus the distribution will be equal to the Occurrence Exceedance Probability (OEP) curve. Following that, the relative contribution of each country within the CEE loss was calculated in order to provide an answer to question as to which catchments were the key contributors to the CEE losses. The correlation of floods between losses is shown in table 3.6.

Table 3.6. Correlation of All Gross Losses between Countries

	CZ	SK	HU	PL
CZ		0.39	0.42	0.41
SK	0.39		0.59	0.30
HU	0.42	0.59		0.30
PL	0.41	0.30	0.30	

Source: Aon Benfield.

Outputs under Assumed Parametric Reinsurance Contracts

The features under a parametric contract for this analysis, is considered to work as follows: if a loss reaches or exceeds a pre-specified threshold, the contract recovers in full for that loss amount. However, if the loss is below the threshold, nothing is recovered. Scenarios which could be classified under two approaches were modeled:

- The same loss thresholds for each country were used (thresholds being defined in EUR billions in increments of EUR: 0.2 billion, 0.5 billion, 1.0 billion, 1.5 billion, 2.0 billion, 2.5 billion, 3.0 billion, and 4.0 billion), and also applied to the overall group CEE loss.
- Thresholds were also set probabilistically at 1 in 10 year losses (10 percent probability) and were used for each country as well.

For each of these scenarios probabilities of events under individual country settings were calculated (where a loss must exceed a given threshold in a country in order to be recovered) and under a pooled setting (where the overall loss exceeds the threshold after which one calculates the probability that a country contributes to such loss) were calculated. Table 3.7, showing the probabilities under pooled settings with derived parametric triggers, was then calculated.

For example, in the Czech Republic there may be a loss of 550 million, in the Slovak Republic 0, in Hungary 230, and in Poland 150, and the loss threshold is 500 million and above. On an individual basis, the Czech Republic loss would be recovered in full, thus the CEE unrecovered (retained) loss under the individual setting would be 380 = 550 + 0 + 230 + 150 − 550. Under the pooled setting the losses sum to 930 million which is above the CEE threshold of 500 million; thus, the loss in full would be recovered under pooled setting.

The variance and mean of retained and ceded losses were also measured. These statistics were then calculated for gross losses, losses under individual settings, losses under pooled settings and lastly under pooled settings with parametric triggers, which are derived later in the paper.

Table 3.7. Rank Correlation Matrix of Discharges when Overall CEE Loss Exceeds EUR 200 Million

		CZ	CZ	CZ	CZ	CZ	SK	SK	SK	SK	HU	HU	HU	HU(SK)	HU	HU(AT)	HU(AT)	PL	PL	PL
Country	River	Odra	Morava	Dyje	Vltava	Labe	Dunaj	Vah	Hornad	Bodrog	Ipel	Dunaj	Salo	Hornad	Tisza	Leitha	Raab	Odra	Wisla	Narew
CZ	Odra	■	0.75	0.47	0.09	0.17	0.22	0.51	0.28	0.22	0.28	0.23	0.26	0.28	0.19	0.18	0.16	0.28	0.37	0.13
CZ	Morava	0.75	■	0.58	0.17	0.31	0.26	0.61	0.22	0.22	0.26	0.29	0.17	0.22	0.14	0.21	0.18	0.31	0.31	0.16
CZ	Dyje	0.47	0.58	■	0.30	0.33	0.20	0.34	0.12	0.06	0.15	0.19	0.16	0.12	0.08	0.16	0.11	0.30	0.19	0.05
CZ	Vltava	0.09	0.17	0.30	■	0.84	0.50	0.09	-0.04	-0.03	0.01	0.50	0.09	-0.04	0.09	0.18	0.02	0.45	0.06	0.20
CZ	Labe	0.17	0.31	0.33	0.84	■	0.55	0.19	-0.05	0.03	0.00	0.52	0.03	-0.05	0.14	0.15	-0.04	0.54	0.14	0.28
SK	Dunaj	0.22	0.26	0.20	0.50	0.55	■	0.20	0.00	0.06	0.00	0.89	0.00	0.00	0.22	0.40	0.07	0.31	0.17	0.19
SK	Vah	0.51	0.61	0.34	0.09	0.19	0.20	■	0.34	0.35	0.28	0.30	0.25	0.34	0.22	0.17	0.16	0.24	0.46	0.18
SK	Hornad	0.28	0.22	0.12	-0.04	-0.05	0.00	0.34	■	0.62	0.62	0.12	0.75	0.75	0.38	0.17	0.29	0.09	0.48	0.12
SK	Bodrog	0.22	0.22	0.06	-0.03	0.03	0.06	0.35	0.62	■	0.35	0.13	0.54	0.62	0.62	0.08	0.17	0.09	0.51	0.21
HU	Ipel	0.28	0.26	0.15	0.01	0.00	0.00	0.28	0.62	0.35	■	0.11	0.75	0.62	0.27	0.16	0.40	0.02	0.20	0.03
HU	Dunaj	0.23	0.29	0.19	0.50	0.52	0.89	0.30	0.12	0.13	0.11	■	0.13	0.12	0.26	0.46	0.14	0.33	0.26	0.21
HU	Salo	0.26	0.17	0.16	0.09	0.03	0.00	0.25	0.75	0.54	0.75	0.13	■	0.75	0.41	0.21	0.39	0.09	0.35	0.05
HU(SK)	Hornad	0.28	0.22	0.12	-0.04	-0.05	0.00	0.34	0.75	0.62	0.62	0.12	0.75	■	0.38	0.17	0.29	0.09	0.48	0.12
HU	Tisza	0.19	0.14	0.08	0.09	0.14	0.22	0.22	0.38	0.62	0.27	0.26	0.41	0.38	■	0.09	0.10	0.19	0.45	0.27
HU(AT)	Leitha	0.18	0.21	0.16	0.18	0.15	0.40	0.17	0.17	0.08	0.16	0.46	0.21	0.17	0.09	■	0.40	0.09	0.16	-0.03
HU(AT)	Raab	0.16	0.18	0.11	0.02	-0.04	0.07	0.16	0.29	0.17	0.40	0.14	0.39	0.29	0.10	0.40	■	-0.07	0.08	-0.13
PL	Odra	0.28	0.31	0.30	0.45	0.54	0.31	0.24	0.09	0.09	0.02	0.33	0.09	0.09	0.19	0.09	-0.07	■	0.34	0.50
PL	Wisla	0.37	0.31	0.19	0.06	0.14	0.17	0.46	0.48	0.51	0.20	0.26	0.35	0.48	0.45	0.16	0.08	0.34	■	0.35
PL	Narew	0.13	0.16	0.05	0.20	0.28	0.19	0.18	0.12	0.21	0.03	0.21	0.05	0.12	0.27	-0.03	-0.13	0.50	0.35	■

Source: Aon Benfield.

Note: Some of the river discharge measurements attributed to Hungary were taken where the river crossed the country's borders. In these cases, the actual measuring stations were located just across the border in the neighboring country (mentioned in parentheses).

In addition to the previous approaches, in cases with the same threshold, the rank correlation of losses between countries was calculated when the overall loss exceeded the CEE group threshold. This is the only way a correlation can be calculated as in such a case equal sample sizes are present. The correlation of losses exceeding thresholds on a per country basis is not possible as this involves matching different return periods, thus pair wise samples cannot be generated.

Scenario with threshold of EUR 500 million

Tables 3.8, 3.9, and 3.10 show the results of setting the loss level at EUR 500 million. Later in the report, this scenario is linked to flood discharge levels in order to establish the physical parameters associated with this level of loss per country.

Table 3.8. Selected Options and Probabilities, Given a Loss Exceeding the EUR 500 million Threshold on an Individual Basis; and Given That the Overall CEE Loss Exceeds EUR 500 Million

CZ	SK	HU	PL	Individual Setting			Pooled Setting			Pooled—optimal trigger solution		
				Prob. (%)	RTP	RTP merged	Prob. (%)	RTP	RTP merged	Prob. (%)	RTP	RTP merged
0	0	0	0	90.50			87.73			89.33		
0	0	0	1	0.35	287		0			0		
0	0	1	0	0.17	581		0			0		
0	0	1	1	0.02	5,000		0			0		
0	1	0	0	0.09	1,087	149	0			0		
0	1	0	1	0.01	7,143		0			0		
0	1	1	0	0.02	5,000		0			0		
0	1	1	1	0.00	25,000		0			0		
1	0	0	0	7.67	13	13	0.12	820		0.16	633	
1	0	0	1	0.41	243		0.15	658		0.13	781	
1	0	1	0	0.14	725		0.39	256	66	0.42	240	71
1	0	1	1	0.01	12,500		0.49	202		0.40	253	
1	1	0	0	0.34	292	87	0.15	658		0.15	649	
1	1	0	1	0.15	685		0.20	510		0.16	641	
1	1	1	0	0.05	1,923		3.16	32	32	2.86	35	35
1	1	1	1	0.06	1,786		7.60	13	13	6.41	16	16
12.27%	11.11%	11.64%	8.44%	Pooled Setting—probability of recovering in each country								

Source: Aon Benfield.
Note: 1 represents an event happening and 0 an event not happening; thus 1,0,0,0 means that only in CZ a loss was greater than the threshold (Individual Setting) or CZ loss was the only contributor to a CEE loss exceeding the threshold (Pooled Setting).

Table 3.9. Rank Correlation of Losses between Countries—CEE Loss Exceeds EUR 500 Million

	CZ	SK	HU	PL
CZ		0.05	-0.07	0.09
SK	0.05		0.55	0.19
HU	-0.07	0.55		0.14
PL	0.09	0.19	0.14	

Source: Aon Benfield.

Table 3.10. Ceded and Retained Losses under Pooled and Individual Setting

	Retained Losses			Ceded Losses		
	StDev of retained	Mean retained	Coefficient of variation	StDev of ceded	Mean ceded	Coefficient of variation
CEE Gross Losses	465,482,171	231,145,920	2.01	—	—	—
CEE Individual	155,395,307	123,188,011	1.26	414,886,059	107,957,909	3.84
CEE Pooled	112,060,442	86,667,163	1.29	478,706,316	144,478,757	3.31
CEE Pooled—optimal trigger solution	149,139,341	101,647,125	1.47	469,848,907	129,498,794	3.63

Source: Aon Benfield.
Note: — = not applicable.

Scenario with Threshold of EUR 1.5 billion

A more dramatic scenario, for the purposes of displaying exceedance probabilities, is run for losses of EUR 1.5 billion and above (tables 3.11–3.13). In this case, the trigger probabilities are lower and thus any pricing would be reduced given the lower likelihood of triggering or "attachment."

Results

The previous tables showed that in all scenarios it is in general convenient for all countries to be a part of a pool as it greatly increases their chances for a recovery. There is clear shift from the most probable event of only one country recovering under individual settings, to recovering in all countries. Moreover, the tables show the fact, already visible. Under all scenarios the pooling effect greatly reduces the mean and volatility of retained losses. The pooled setting under optimized triggers always performs slightly worse than in an ideal option. This reflects that the efficiency of the optimized triggers is not 100 percent, analogous to deciding whether to accept Type I or Type II errors.

Trigger Methodology

In the process of defining the triggers two approaches were used. The first of them is relevant when looking at the losses on a CEE group basis. The other is similar; however, it looks at each country separately. Both used the logical OR between discharges in various catchments, and the trigger was defined as a threshold that was exceeded based on aggregate annual country catchment triggering. Thresholds were translated from percentiles in each catchment. In other words, the algorithm used only percentiles which were then described in terms of discharges in cubic meters per second (m^3s^{-1}).

Table 3.11. Selected Options and Probabilities, Given Loss Exceeding EUR 1.5 Billion Threshold on an Individual Basis; and Given that the Overall CEE Loss Exceeds EUR 1.5 Billion

CZ	SK	HU	PL	Individual Setting Prob. (%)	RTP	RTP merged	Pooled Setting Prob. (%)	RTP	RTP merged	Pooled—optimal trigger solution Prob. (%)	RTP	RTP merged
0	0	0	0	98.50			97.31			97.53		
0	0	0	1	0.01	16,667		0			0		
0	0	1	0	0.01	12,500		0			0		
0	0	1	1	0			0			0		
0	1	0	0	0.01	16,667	5,000	0			0		
0	1	0	1	0			0			0		
0	1	1	0	0			0			0		
0	1	1	1	0			0			0		
1	0	0	0	1.44	69	69	0.004	25,000		0.01	10,000	
1	0	0	1	0.01	7,143		0.02	6,250		0.02	5,556	
1	0	1	0	0.01	16,667		0.02	4,545	658	0.05	2,083	424
1	0	1	1	0			0.07	1,351		0.10	1,000	
1	1	0	0	0.02	6,250	2,381	0.01	12,500		0.02	5,000	
1	1	0	1	0.00	25,000		0.03	3,571		0.04	2,500	
1	1	1	0	0.00	50,000		0.24	424	424	0.31	325	325
1	1	1	1	0			2.30	43	43	1.92	52	52
2.69%	2.58%	2.64%	2.42%	Pooled Setting - probability of recovering in each country								

Source: Aon Benfield.

Note: 1 represents the event occurring and 0 for the event not occurring; thus 1,0,0,0 means that only in CZ a loss was greater than the threshold (Individual Setting) or CZ loss was the only contributor to a CEE loss exceeding the threshold (Pooled Setting).

Table 3.12. Rank Correlation of Losses between Countries—CEE Loss Exceeds EUR 1.5 Billion

	CZ	SK	HU	PL
CZ		-0.10	-0.15	-0.10
SK	-0.10		0.45	0.23
HU	-0.15	0.45		0.16
PL	-0.10	0.23	0.16	

Source: Aon Benfield.

Table 3.13. Ceded and Retained Losses under Pooled and Individual Settings

	Retained Losses StDev of Retained	Mean Retained	Coefficient of Variation	Ceded Losses StDev of Ceded	Mean Ceded	Coefficient of Variation
CEE Gross Losses	465,482,171	231,145,920	2.01	—	—	—
CEE Individual	337,138,977	199,908,462	1.69	266,283,926	31,237,458	8.52
CEE Pooled	259,297,741	167,514,465	1.55	413,227,706	63,631,455	6.49
CEE Pooled—optimal trigger solution	290,663,617	175,497,179	1.66	389,513,924	55,648,741	7.00

Source: Aon Benfield.
Note: — = not applicable.

The Logical OR was necessary since having a trigger in one catchment for the whole CEE group would not allow capture of the majority of significant losses.

▨ CEE approach: As there are 19 catchments, the parametric trigger will look like a polygon. Thus one requires an optimization criterion. The weight was set to 1 for correctly triggered losses and -1 for incorrectly triggered ones (Type I). Under this configuration a weight of -1 was assigned to Type II events (not triggered but should have been triggered) (figure 3.9). This, in the insurance context refers to the "basis risk" described in chapter 1. If a loss moves from a correctly triggered to a Type II, it results in decreasing the optimization criterion (table 3.8).

▨ It was decided not to use other layouts as setting 1 for correctly triggered losses and -1 for Type II events as this would ultimately lead to triggers which would start at minimum discharges (as they would tend to capture all the losses above the CEE threshold, even those with very small discharges in all catchments).

▨ Also, it was decided not to set any weight to correctly non triggering events (bottom left) as a number of these events would outweigh those correctly triggered. There is also the possibility of assigning a broader weight set than just {-1, 1}. One could, for example, set weights according to the size of the loss or relative importance of each participating country.

▨ Individual country treatment: the threshold was set for each country separately and then the optimization was run in the same manner as in the CEE approach.

Figures 3.10 to 3.13 represent the overall CEE aggregate losses given discharges in each catchment. Figures 3.14 to 3.17 capture losses in a particular country (for example, for Czech catchments these show only the total Czech loss) given discharges in each catchment.

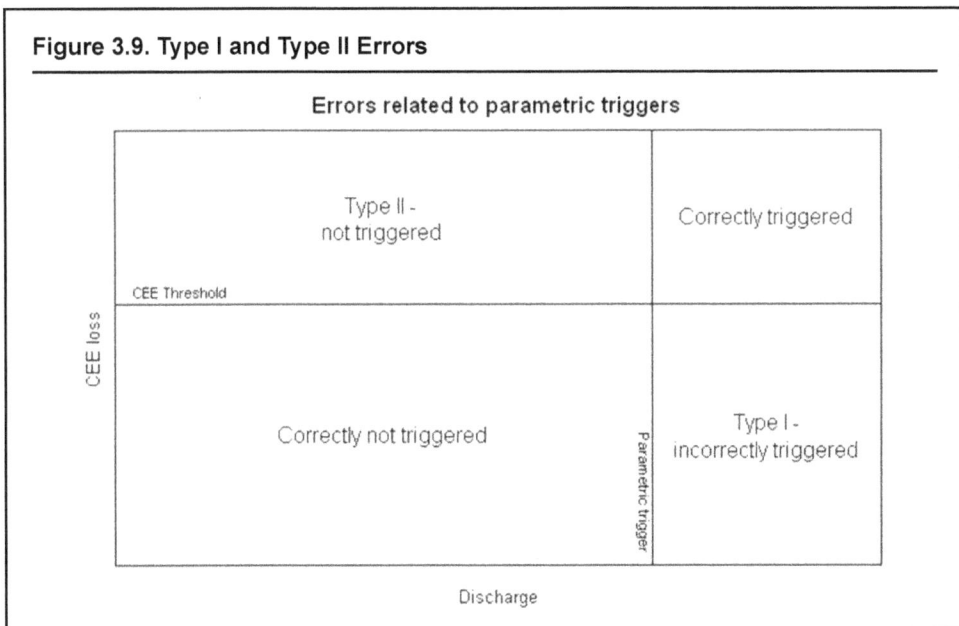

Figure 3.9. Type I and Type II Errors

Source: Aon Benfield.

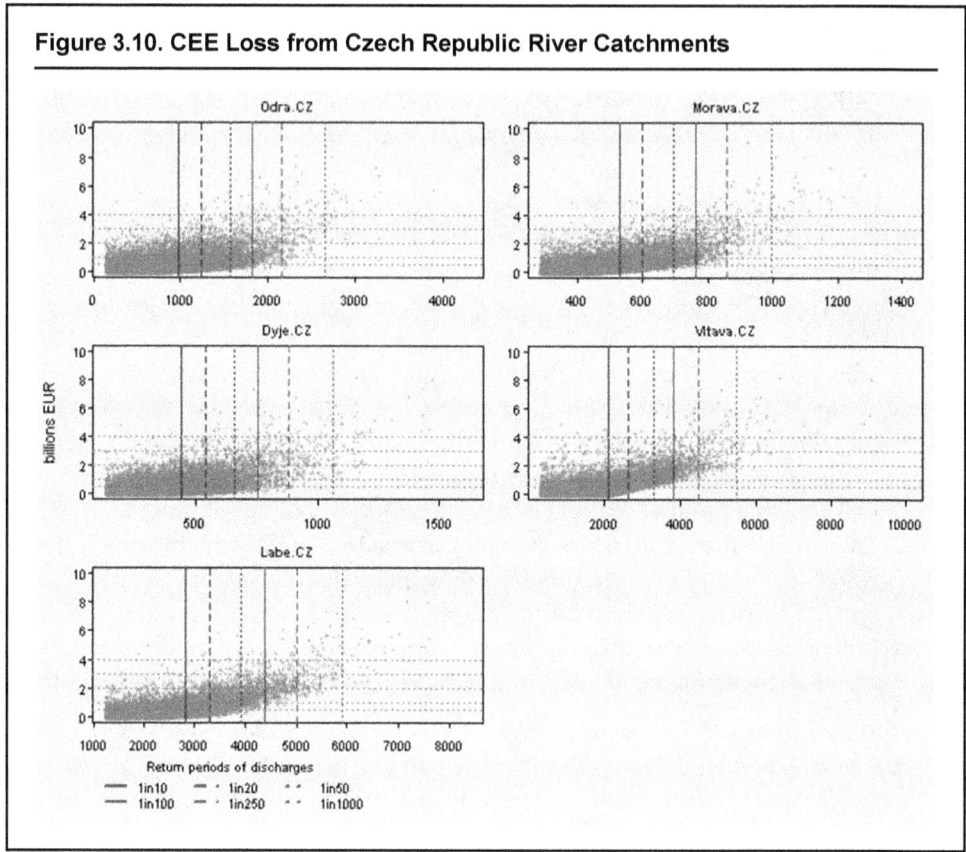

Figure 3.10. CEE Loss from Czech Republic River Catchments

Source: Aon Benfield.

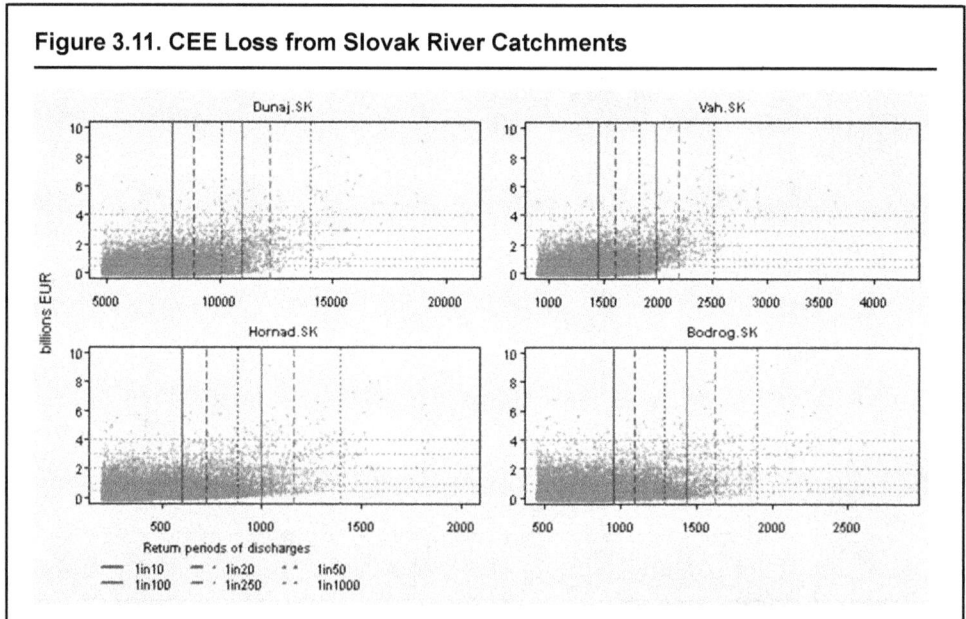

Figure 3.11. CEE Loss from Slovak River Catchments

Source: Aon Benfield.

Figure 3.12. CEE Loss from Hungarian River Catchments

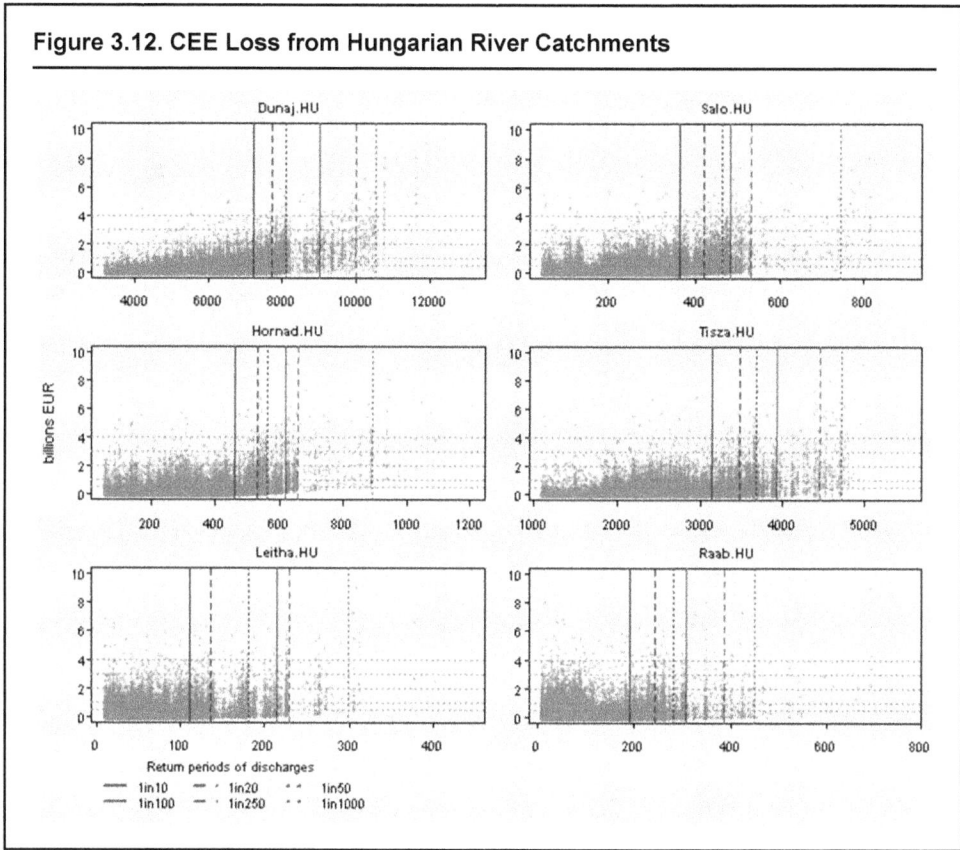

Source: Aon Benfield.

Figure 3.13. CEE Loss from Polish River Catchments

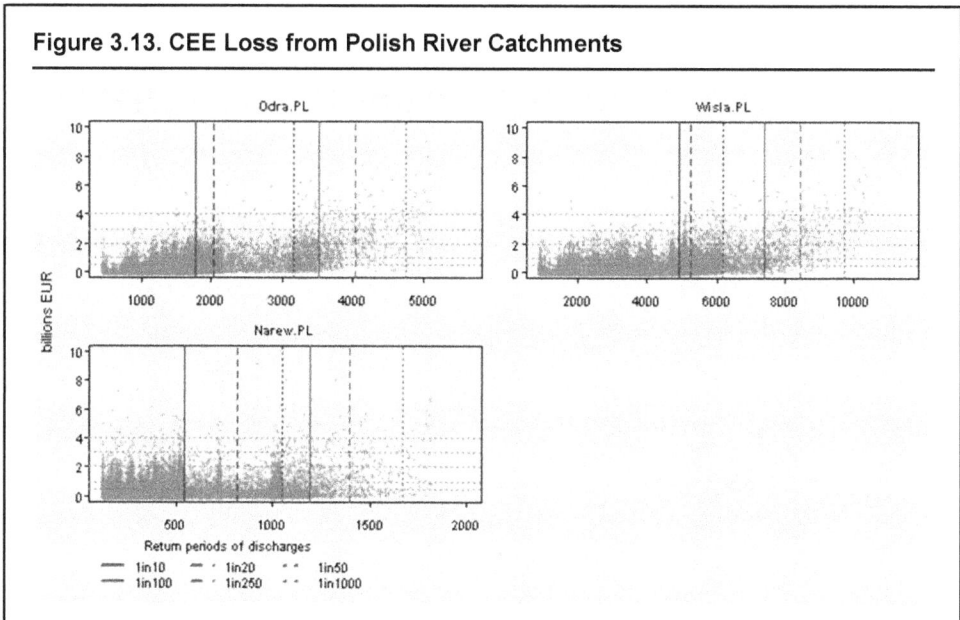

Source: Aon Benfield.

Figure 3.14. Czech Republic—Per Country Loss

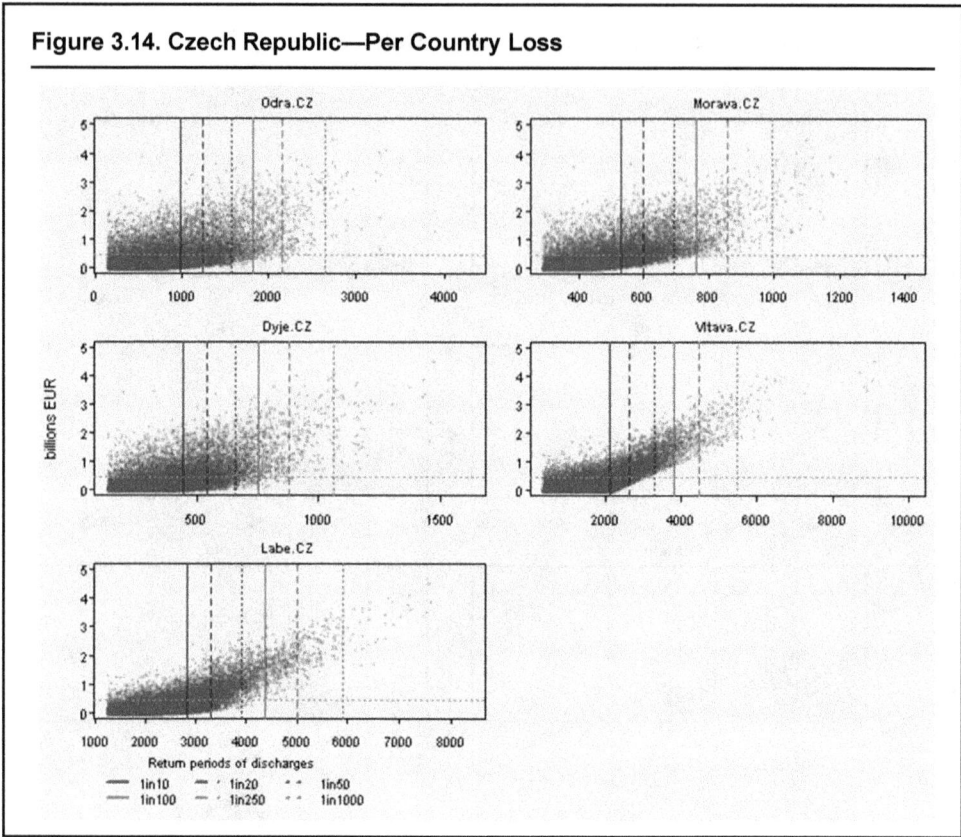

Source: Aon Benfield.
Note: Horizontal line corresponds to 1 in 10 RTP.

Figure 3.15. Slovak Republic—Per Country Loss

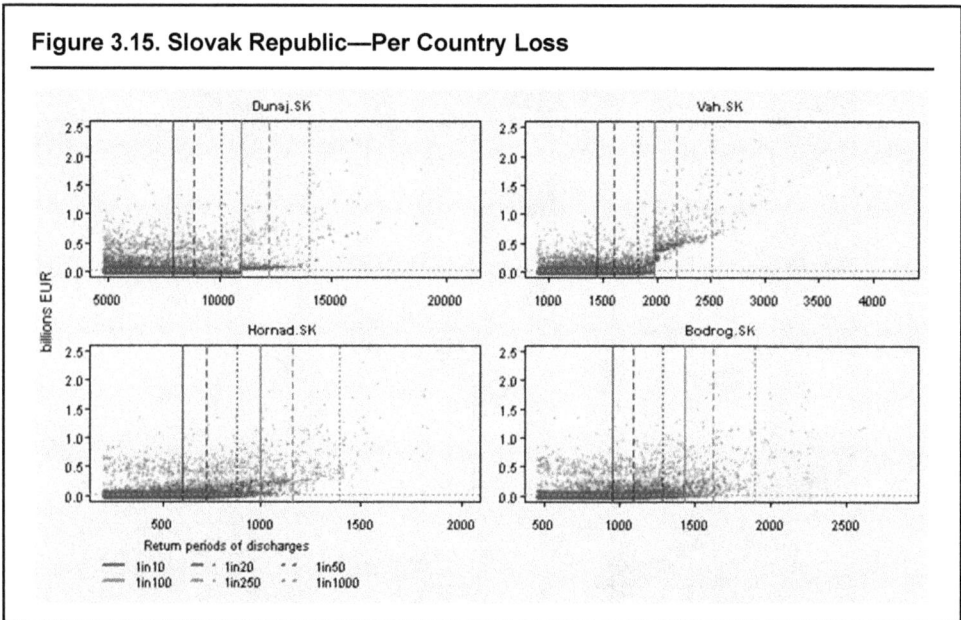

Source: Aon Benfield.
Note: Horizontal line corresponds to 1 in 10 RTP.

Figure 3.16. Hungary—Per Country Loss

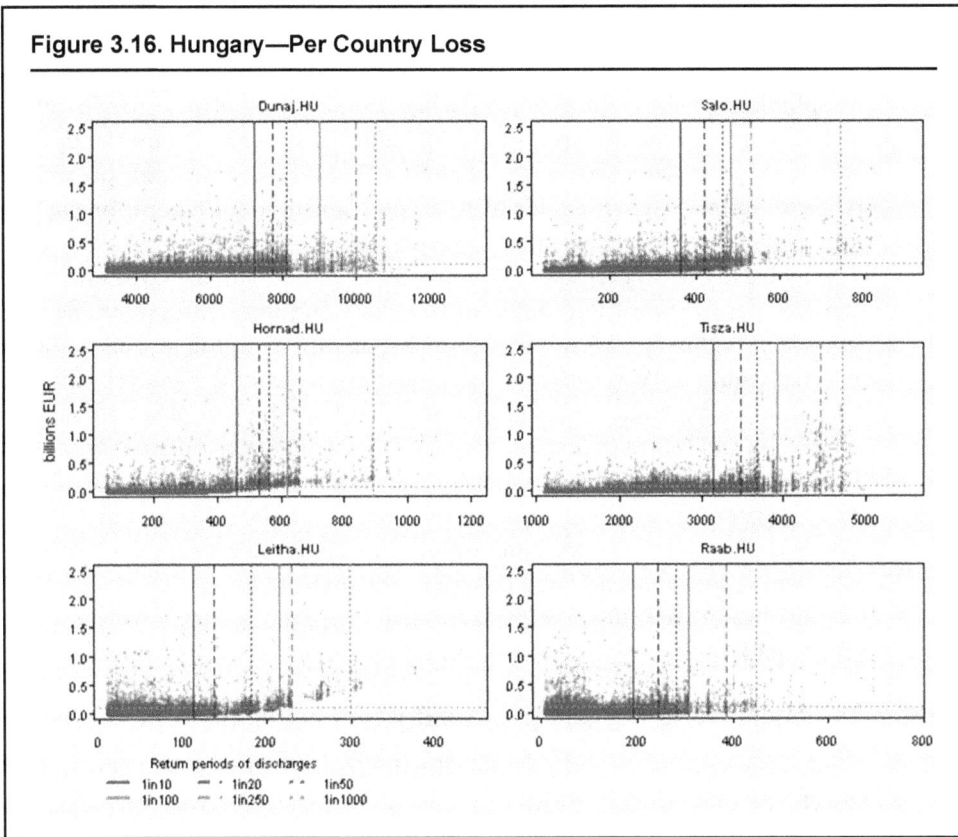

Source: Aon Benfield.
Note: Horizontal line corresponds to 1 in 10 RTP.

Figure 3.17. Poland—Per Country Loss

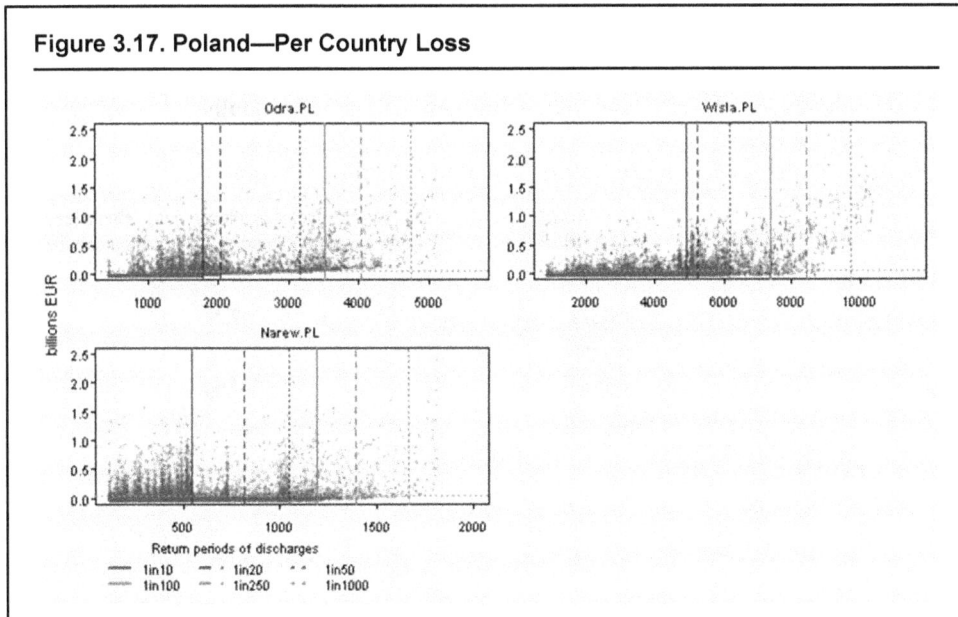

Source: Aon Benfield.
Note: Horizontal line corresponds to 1 in 10 RTP.

Performance of optimized criteria

Some important issues to be considered are the following:

- The optimization algorithm generated a high number of local maxima. Therefore, one had to rerun it with various starting values in order to obtain the optimal value. Even then, when manually changing the values, it was still possible to find better results. Therefore, this manual complement to the algorithm was performed, and the results are believed to be as close to optimal as possible.
- It is possible to find hyper-planes defining the event set with the same optimized criteria but with completely different triggers using linear programming. Unfortunately, highly specialized software able to cope with millions of variables would be required. With software equipment available for the analysis, the triggers had to be manually adjusted in a way that kept the best obtained value of the criterion and return periods of triggers. For example, two options for Morava (CZ) were available for CEE thresholds of 200 million, 500 million, 1,000 million, and the trigger was as a return period of either 100, 1,000, 350 years or 100, 650, 1,000 years. In such a case, the latter option was preferred because the return periods formed an increasing function of the CEE threshold.
- One can always reach 100 percent of correctly triggered events; however, this is at the cost of significantly increasing the number of incorrectly triggered events.

Setting Threshold Flood Triggers per Country for Parametric Contract Design

This section describes the result of the model with different conditions related to the valuation of assets and property. The previous model discussed earlier, was run on insured market data (and was based on existing insurance policies, thus allowing a more exact quantification of exposed values). Since Chapter 2 discussed the exposure model using all property and infrastructure, including insured plus uninsured private sector assets, this section applies those data values to the parametric trigger correlation analysis. Thus the property values in each region were modified accordingly to observe the behavior of losses and the flood triggering levels. The model was run witvh proportionally scaled value exposures and the adjusted losses thus changed proportionally.

Table 3.14. Model for Exposure Using Total Insured and Uninsured Assets

	Value exposed in EUR '000	Loss scale factor applied to every single loss, compared to the results in the earlier section
Czech Republic	241,245	60%
Slovak Republic	120,379	123%
Hungary	171,423	108%
Poland	533,789	132%
Total	1,066,835	—

Source: Aon Benfield.

Applying the above broader data, the model was run against the EUR 200 million and EUR 500 million levels of losses to determine the 'trigger' flood magnitudes (expressed as measured water flow in cubic meters per second). It should be qualified that the model yet needs better specification to include all public sector asset exposures including their locational and vulnerability functions, thus the figures below are, while useful, still illustrative. Additional flood trigger modeling would be required, depending on each government's preferences for assets and locations to be most protected.

As well, the figures below imply event probabilities which provide some bias toward quicker triggering of losses in the Czech Republic. This probably occurs because the model was initially based on insured data and it appears that under such data a larger proportion of Czech private assets in the sample were insured against catastrophic flood risks. This therefore, appears to give the Czech Republic smaller (more frequent) return periods or a higher probability of triggering. However, this can be corrected through the application of a broader public and private sector exposure asset model which would apply values that are not necessarily insured against catastrophes (for example, some public sector infrastructure and some private household or business uninsured properties). This would result in less of a bias toward loss triggering for those countries with the most private insurance against catastrophes specifically.

Table 3.15. List of Optimized Triggers as Return Period and Relevant Flow Discharge (in Cubic Meters per Second), for Loss Threshold of EUR 200 Million

Return Period/ *Discharge*	Czech Republic (200 mil)		Slovak Republic (200 mil)		Hungary (200 mil)		Poland (200 mil)
Odra-CZ	49	Dunaj-SK	833	Ipel-HU	—	Odra-PL	100
	1,571		13,834		—		3,510
Morava-CZ	14	Vah-SK	93	Dunaj-HU	—	Wisla-PL	53
	565		1,964		—		6,284
Dyje-CZ	40	Hornad-SK	125	Salo-HU	333	Narew-PL	1,000
	632		1,038		534		1,670
Vltava-CZ	16	Bodrog-SK	833	Hornad-HU	143		
	2,452		1,877		635		
Labe-CZ	19			Tisza-HU	233		
	3,258				4,440		
				Leitha-HU	91		
					212		
				Raab-HU	—		
					—		

Source: Aon Benfield.

Table 3.16. List of Optimized Triggers as Return Period and Relevant Discharge (in Cubic Meters per Second) for Loss Thresholds of EUR 500 Million

Return Period/ Discharge	Czech Republic (200 mil)		Slovak Republic (200 mil)		Hungary (200 mil)		Poland (200 mil)
Odra-CZ	500	Dunaj-SK	1,000	Ipel-HU	—	Odra-PL	476
	2,410		14,014		—		4,344
Morava-CZ	125	Vah-SK	127	Dunaj-HU	—	Wisla-PL	263
	785		2,037		—		8,486
Dyje-CZ	333	Hornad-SK	500	Salo-HU	1,429	Narew-PL	10,000
	918		1,278		758		1,805
Vltava-CZ	33	Bodrog-SK	2,000	Hornad-HU	—		
	2,997		2,032		—		
Labe-CZ	39			Tisza-HU	5,000		
	3,751				4,810		
				Leitha-HU	769		
					276		
				Raab-HU	—		
					—		

Source: Aon Benfield.

Conclusion

Losses on a country basis showed a much smaller correlation among each other, a positive sign for risk pooling prospects. Only the Slovak Republic and Hungary showed a moderate correlation of losses. This is likely a result that all the Slovak Republic rivers direct to Hungary. Cross correlation for other countries were small (below a 0.35 correlation coefficient).

Even though the rank correlation between countries is small, it may be worth considering having a pooled setting (where the sum of various country losses together, trigger the payment threshold, where compensation is then shared proportionately) versus individual countries triggers that would make individual country payments solely in terms of individual thresholds. A pooled setting decreases the overall average and standard deviation of retained losses and countries with small losses still benefit.

In terms of relative efficiency (correctly triggered vs. incorrectly triggered events) the model varies across countries and catchments. For the purposes of designing parametric contracts with pooled settings, additional work would be required to arrive at a high ratio of correctly triggered events as well as consistency in such ratios across the countries. The percentage of correctly triggered events (out of all which exceed the threshold) is around 75 percent for the EUR 200 and 500 million thresholds. As the thresholds increase, the efficiency decreases to less than 50 percent for example, for EUR 4 billion.

The reliability of the presented results, when applied to a decision making process on whether to buy alternative reinsurance covering uninsured public properties, depends on the similarity in behavior between such public properties and the private property data used in this chapter. Such behavior includes similarity in terms of the vulnerability factors and size of the aggregate values at risk of loss. As the data in chapter 2 covered public properties, additional correlation tests (for the purposes of setting triggers) would need to be tested to validate these triggers.

Annex: Monthly Correlations between Catchments

This annex illustrates matrices of rank correlation between discharges at a particular river catchment station, versus the rest of the stations. These are shown in figures 3A.1–3A.4. The Y axis represents the coefficient of correlation. The figure M within the charts means median of the monthly values, and the figure A is the simple average of the monthly correlation values.

The subject station always has correlation one with itself. The numerical figures within the graphs represent each month of the year. A smaller spread shows the same seasonality patterns, for example, Vltava will have almost the same behaviour as Labe since Vltava contributes with a bigger inflow than Labe at the confluence at Melnik (in the Czech Republic).

Figure 3A.1. Czech Republic

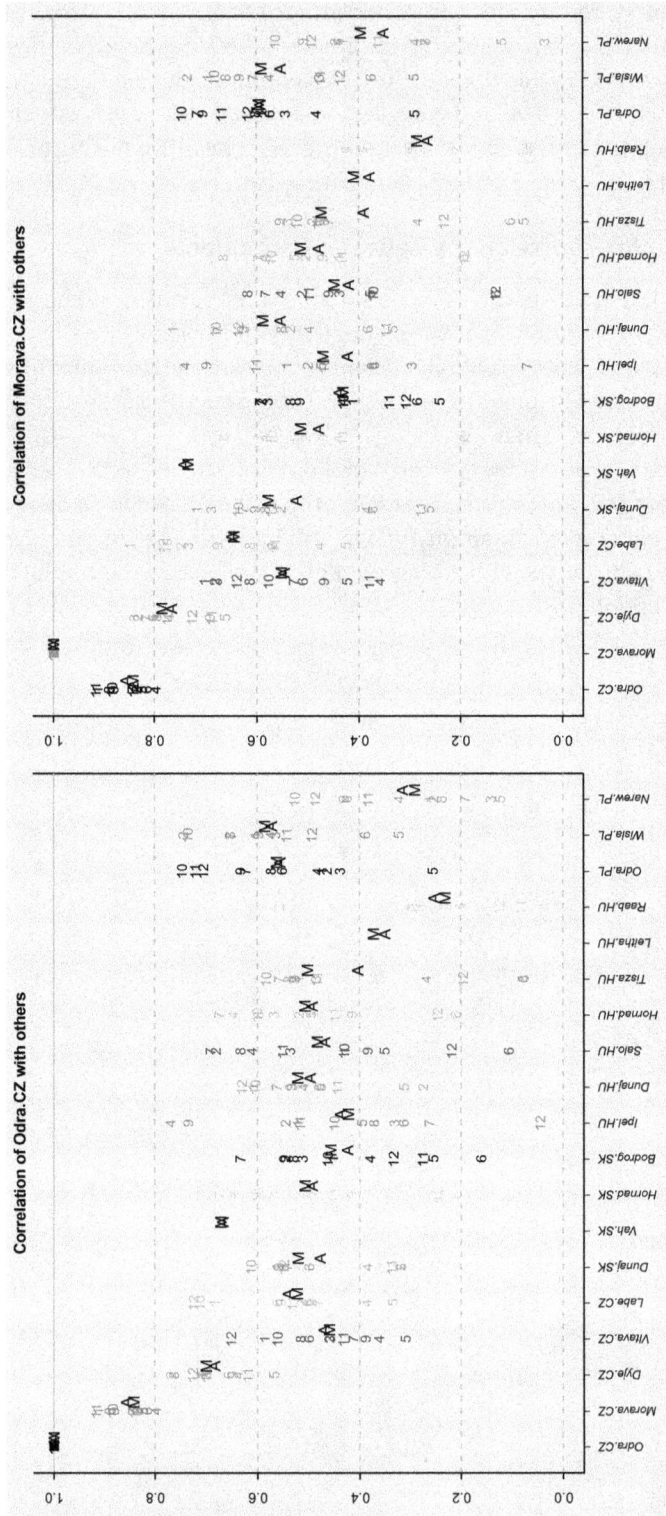

(Figure continues on next page)

Figure 3A.1 (continued)

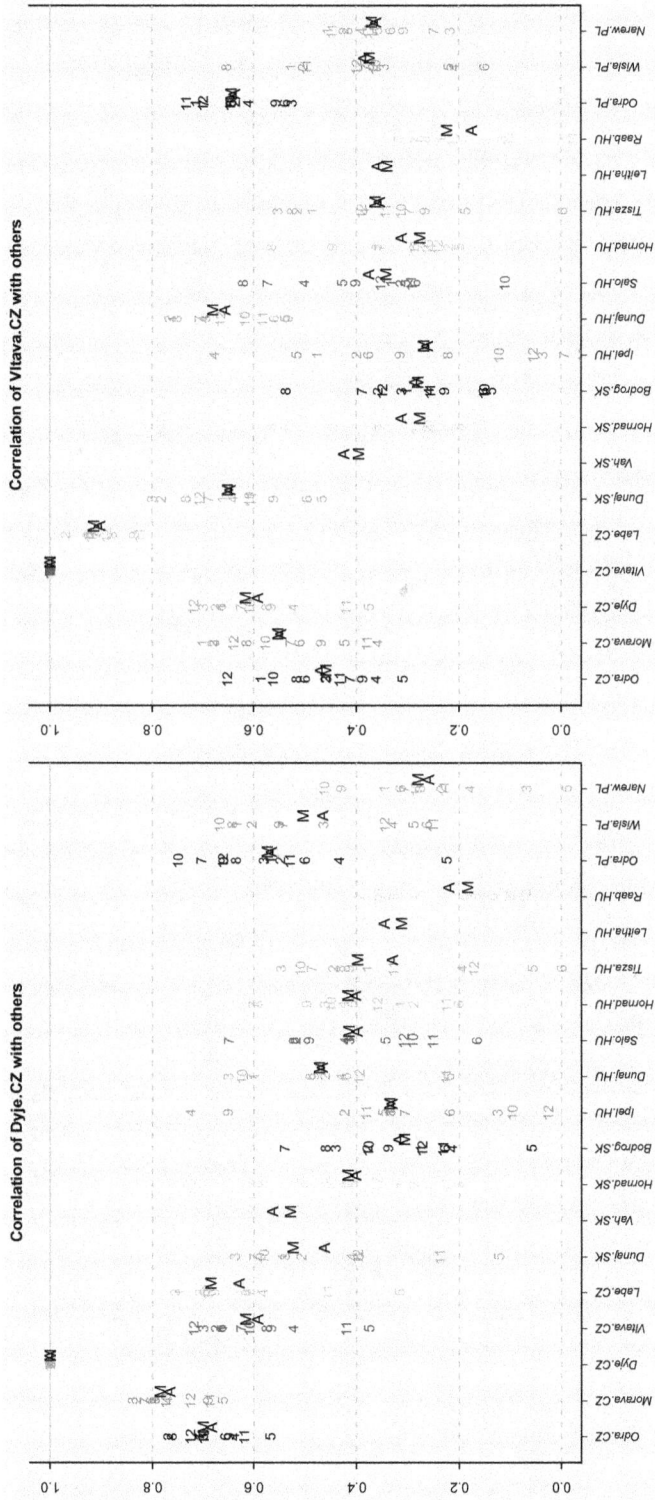

(Figure continues on next page)

Figure 3A.1 (continued)

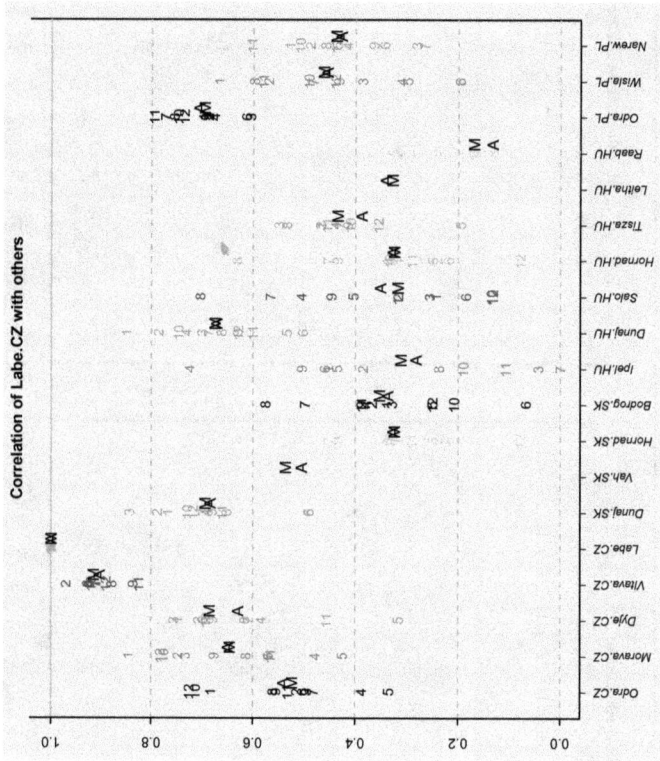

Figure 3A.2. The Slovak Republic

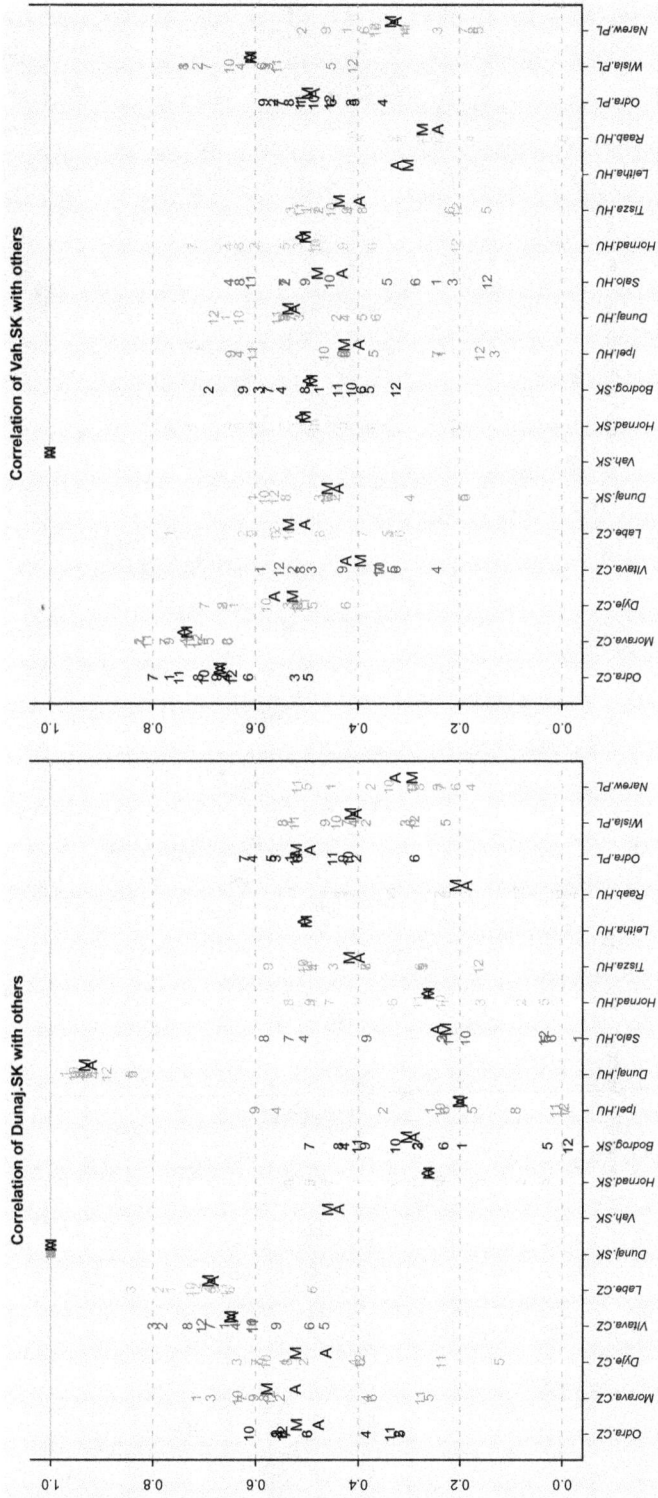

(Figure continues on next page)

Figure 3A.2 (continued)

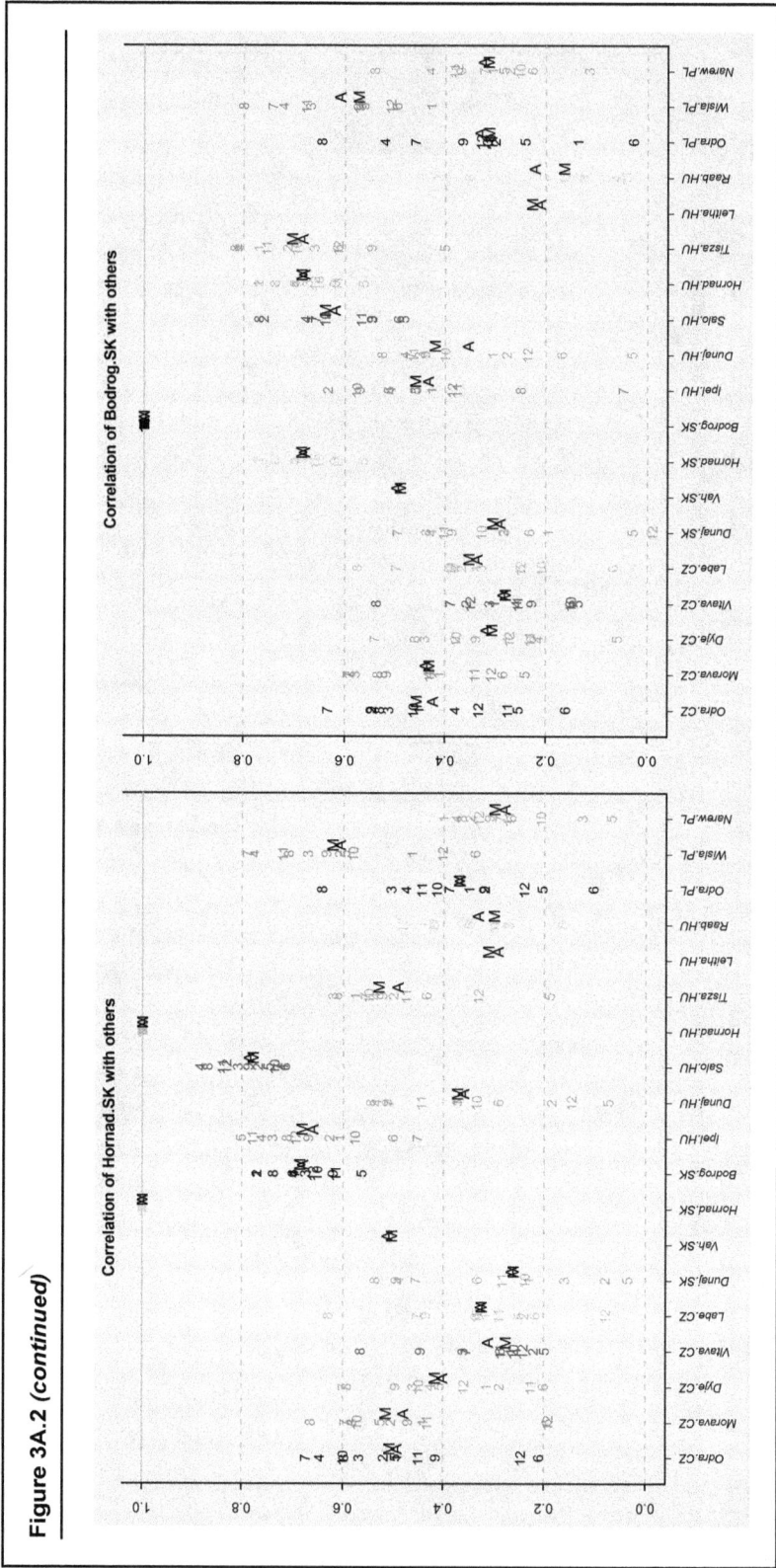

Source: Aon Benfield.

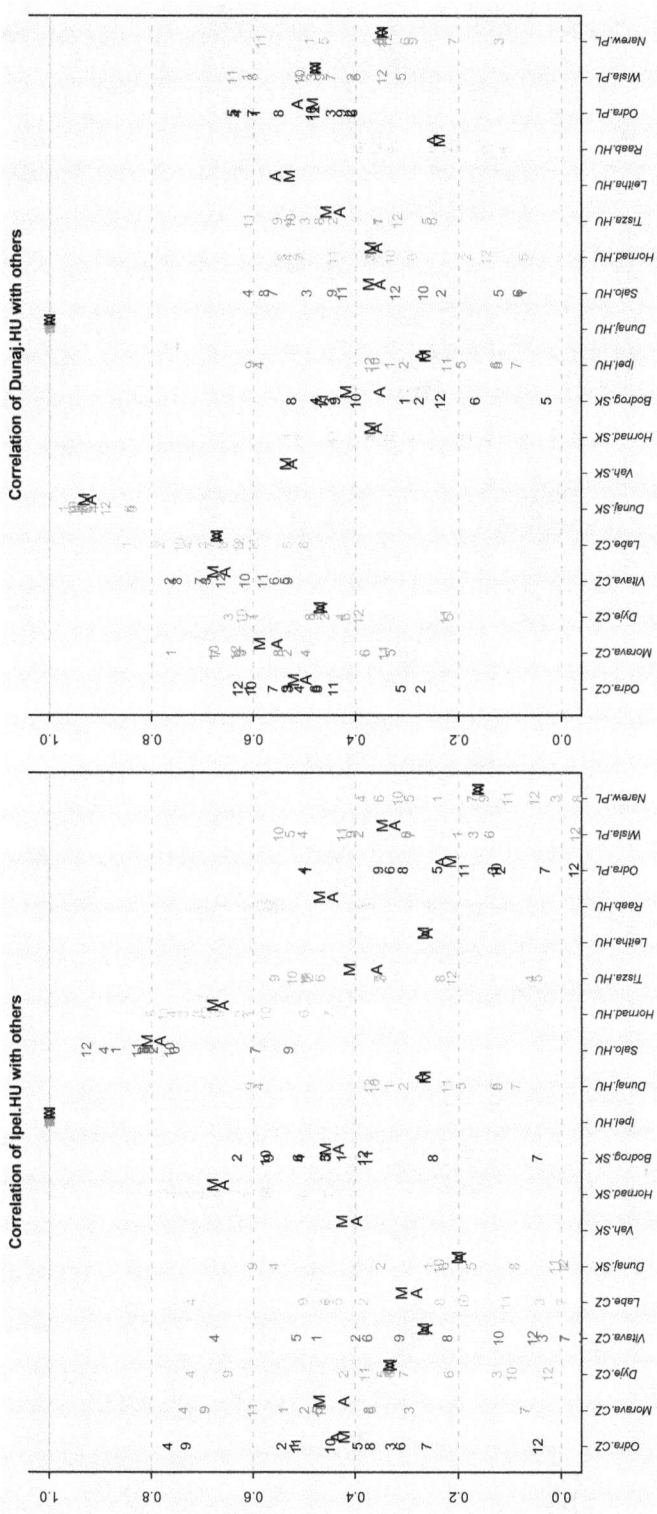

Figure 3A.3. Hungary

(Figure continues on next page)

Figure 3A.3 *(continued)*

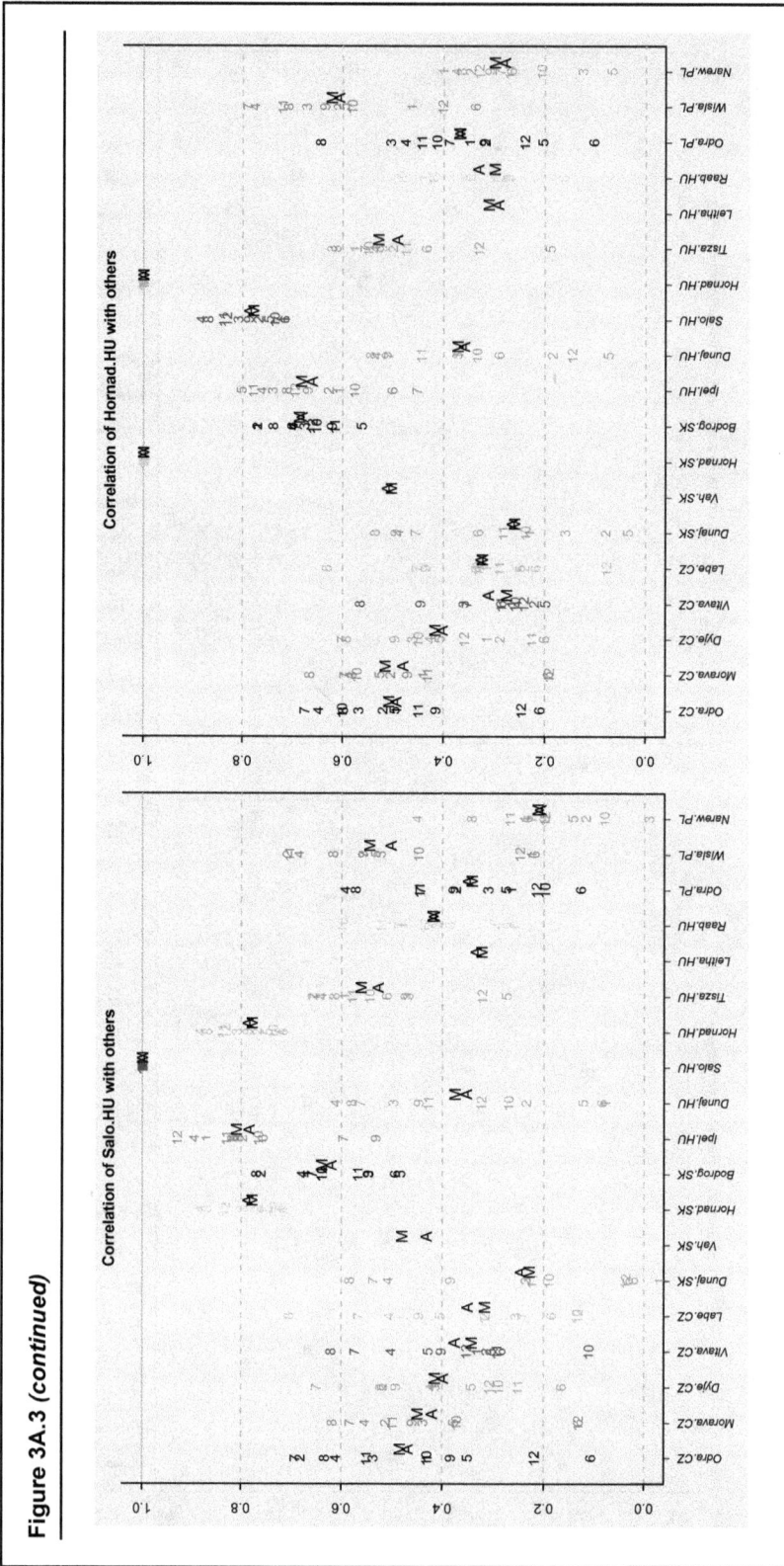

(Figure continues on next page)

Figure 3A.3 (continued)

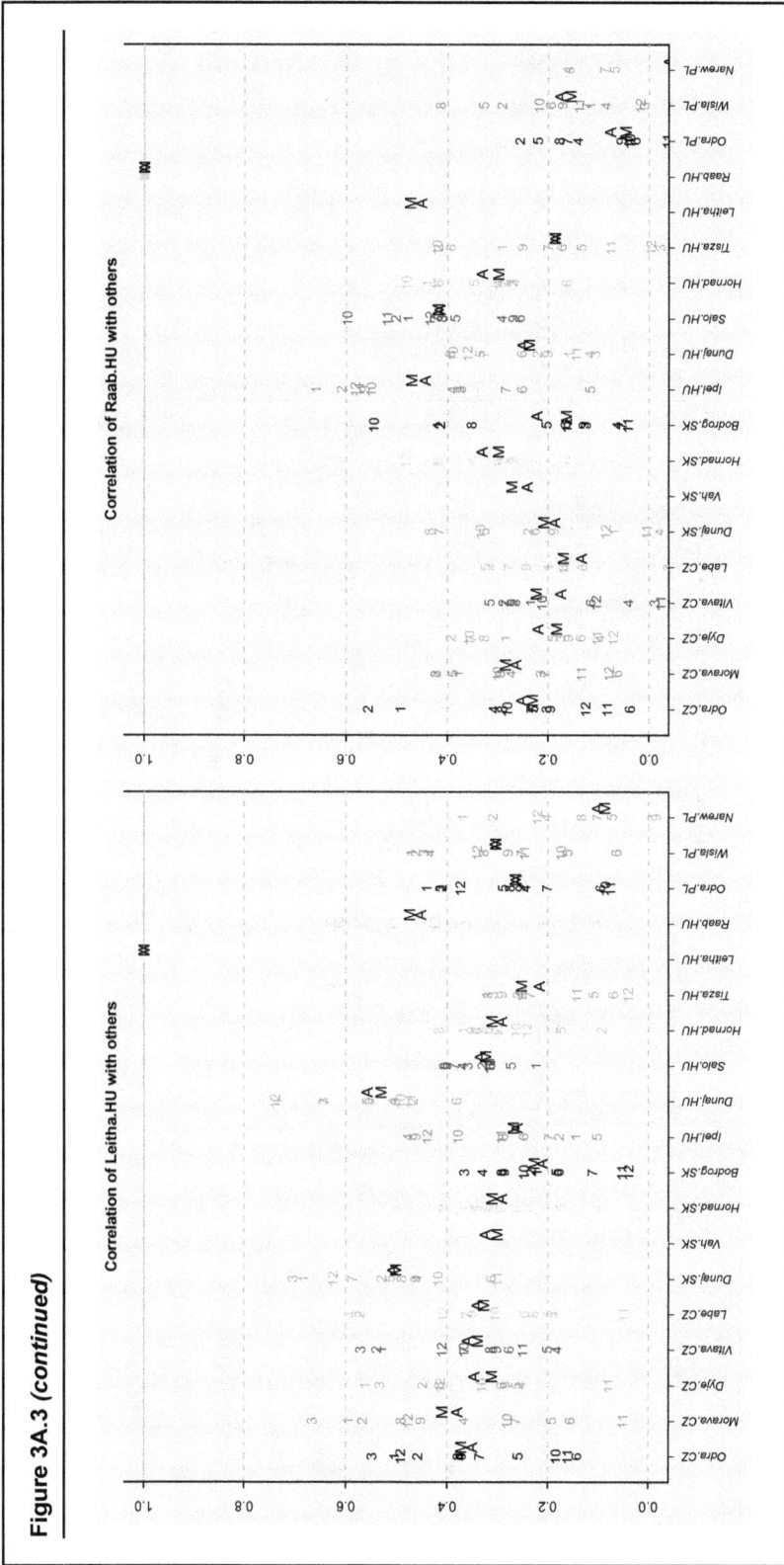

(Figure continues on next page)

Figure 3A.3 (continued)

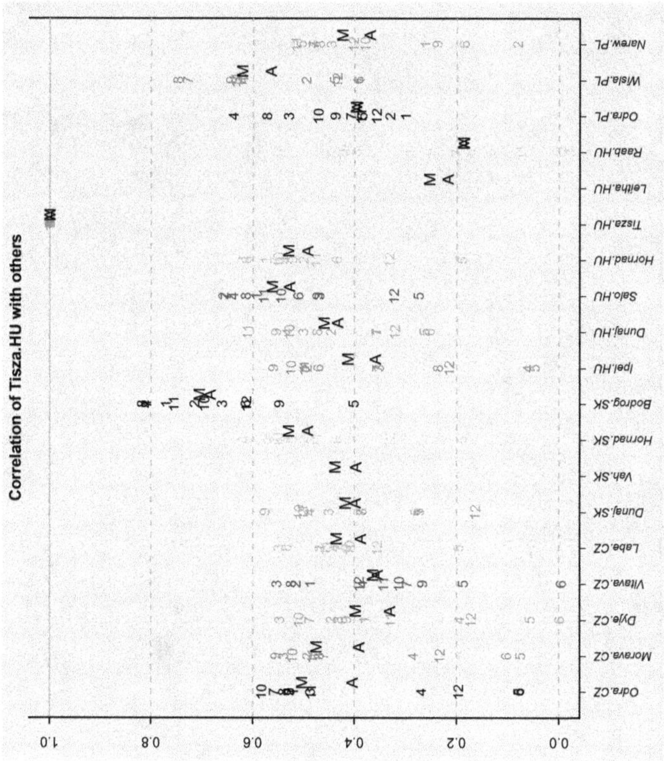

Source: Aon Benfield.

Figure 3A.4. Poland

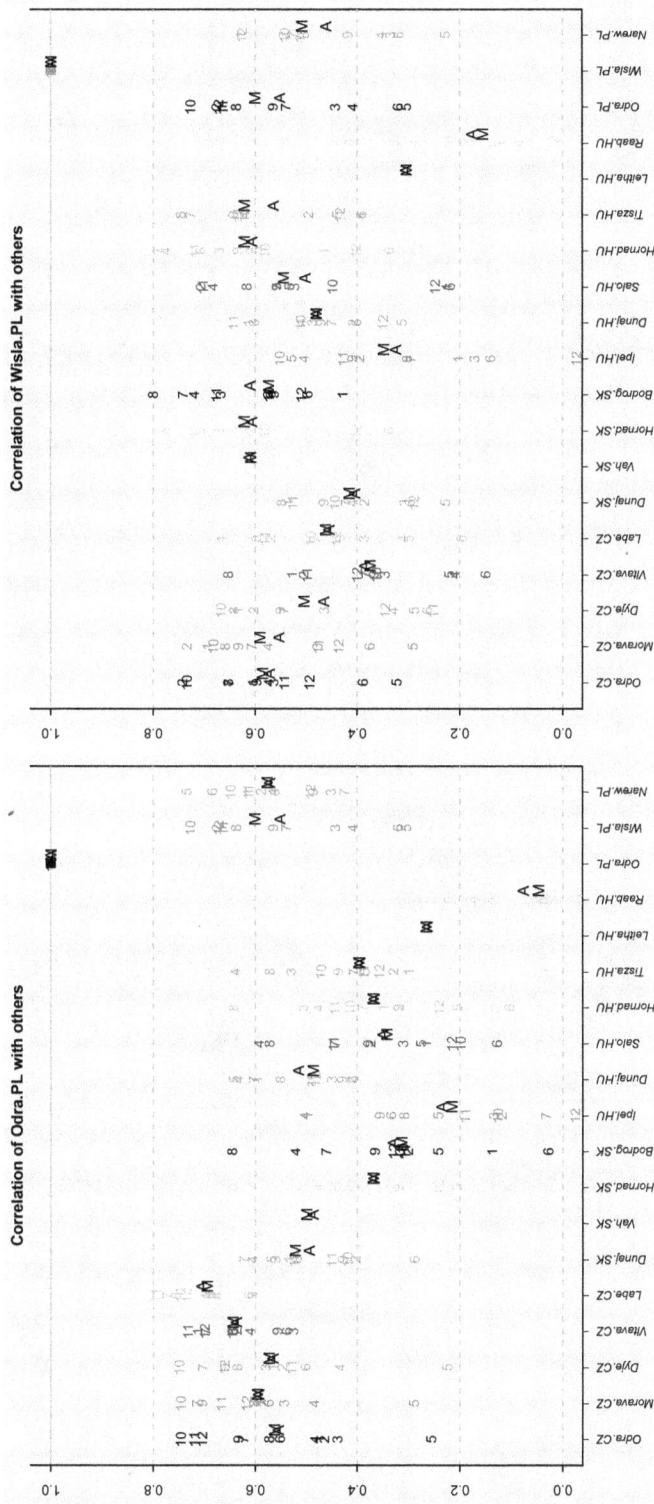

(Figure continues on next page)

Figure 3A.4 (continued)

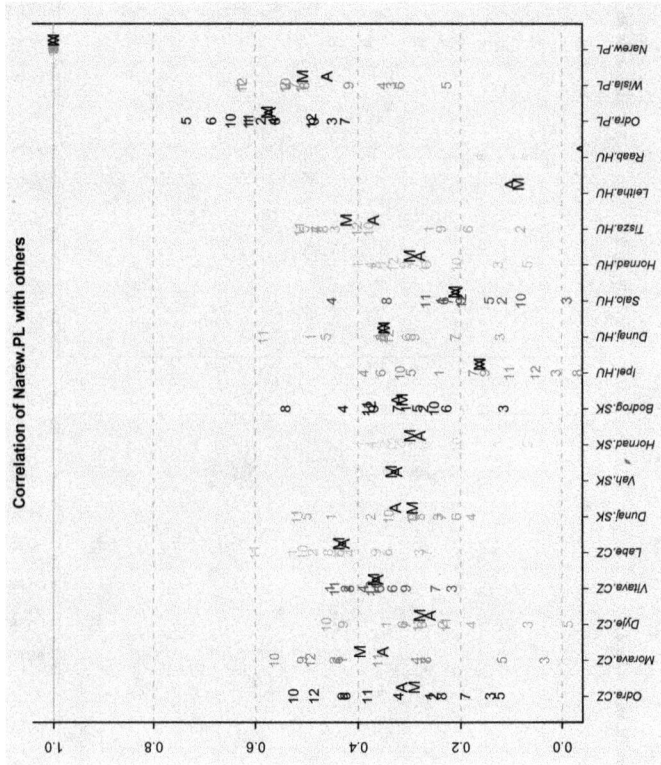

Source: Aon Benfield.

CHAPTER 4

Private Insurance Markets and Public Disaster Financing Mechanisms

Overview

Central Europe's Risk Exposure to Natural Hazards

This chapter comprises a review of government post-disaster safety nets as well as those provided by the private insurance market in the Czech Republic, Hungary, Poland, and the Slovak Republic.

As frequency and severity of major natural hazards and economic and insured losses caused by them have considerably increased world-wide, the countries of Central Europe have been no exception. Central Europe is vulnerable to a number of natural hazards, such as flood, landslide/mudslide/debris-flow, avalanche, windstorm, weight of snow, and fluctuations of extreme temperature.

Between 1980 and 2006, Europe witnessed a major growth in the scale and frequency of extreme weather events, which represented 89 per cent (238 billion of euro) out of the 366 billion of euro overall losses from disasters caused by the impact of natural hazards in this region. The European Environmental Agency's current projections suggest that South Eastern, Mediterranean and Central Europe regions are among the most vulnerable to climate change. Considerable adverse impacts are expected to occur to natural and human systems that are already under pressure from changes in land use and settlement.

The 1997, 2005, and 2006 floods in Central Europe demonstrated that large disasters caused by the impact of natural hazards can be very costly and can have major negative impacts on national budgets. For instance, the 1997 floods caused over EUR 5.6 billion in economic damages mainly to Poland (2.9 billion - 3.5 billion), the Czech Republic (1.8 billion) and the Slovak Republic (0.06 billion).

The 1997 floods were followed by another devastating flood across the Central European region in 2002. In that year, total economic losses from floods in Central Europe exceeded EUR 3 billion During this event, the Vltava river exceeded the water level of the major 1890 floods in Prague. Some 200,000 Czech residents were evacuated during the flooding, which caused the total economic loss of EUR 2.3 billion in the Czech Republic alone. Later, the 2006 floods affected Hungary, Bulgaria and Romania with economic damages estimated in excess of EUR 0.5 billion

Despite considerable economic loss potential from floods in the region, Central Europe appears to fare much better than most disaster prone areas in the world in terms of its financial preparedness for natural disasters. On average, over 50 percent of homeowners across the region are insured against natural disasters and governments, cognizant of devastating floods at the turn of the last century, have been allocating significant budgetary resources annually for emergency preparedness and post-disaster reconstruction and aid.

Fiscal Disaster Risk Financing Mechanisms at the Country Level

In all surveyed CEE V-4 countries, national annual budgetary allocations for emergencies are significant. All national emergency funds are annual non-accruing funds, meaning that they maintain the same statutory size in budget percentage terms and cannot be accumulated or carried forward from one year to another.

In all surveyed CEE V-4 countries, the emergency assistance aid can be made available to households, businesses, and local governments. None of the surveyed countries have a means testing requirement as a precondition for emergency assistance, although in Poland local officials have a considerable discretion in determining the eligibility for post-disaster aid. Overall, there is no clear delineation of government and private sector liabilities when it comes to funding economic damages in the aftermath of a disaster.

In all four countries the government stands ready to provide post-disaster financial assistance to the victims of natural disasters both for emergency relief and reconstruction purposes. While the former comes in the form of grants, the latter form of assistance in provided in the form of low interest reconstruction loans and reconstruction grants.

The administrative process involved in mobilizing additional resources in cases of major disasters caused by the impact of natural hazards appears to rely by and large on the administrative capabilities of local governments, which are deeply involved in the whole process of post-disaster loss assessment and eventual distribution of the funds to beneficiaries. The emergency relief assistance appears to be delivered to victims of disasters within days.

The Role of Private Catastrophe Insurance in Disaster
Risk Financing in the CEE V-4 Countries

Due to the very large floods at the turn of century the insurance industry in the CEE V-4 is well prepared to handle large catastrophic events. The big floods have also helped to increase the public awareness of risk which translated into a rather high level of property insurance penetration among households and SMEs. The unique feature of the the CEE V-4 markets is that traditionally catastrophe insurance perils have been included in the overall scope of coverage under the homeowners' policy rather than being an optional policy endorsement, which is the case in most other markets. As a result, almost all households with a fire policy are also automatically covered against flood, windstorm, landslides, hails and avalanches. Table 4.1 summarizes our estimates of catastrophe insurance penetration in the CEE V-4 region by country.

Table 4.1. Catastrophe Insurance Penetration in Central European Countries (Estimates)

Country	Homeowners with catastrophe insurance (%)
Czech Republic	49–65
Poland	56–40
Slovak Republic	51–60
Hungary	60–73

Source: AXCO, Swiss Re, World Bank.

The cost of catastrophe insurance coverage varies considerably across the region, not only because of different levels of disaster risk exposure in different countries but also because of varying levels of market discipline over risk pricing. For instance, if in the Czech Republic, most insurers charge adequate risk premium for the catastrophe portion of the risk, in Poland the situation is markedly different as the risk premium is driven more by the market competition than by the technical fundamentals.

On the supply side, as the market is dominated predominantly by large international insurance groups, except for Poland where the state-owned insurer PZU still holds the lion's share of the market. Reinsurance for individual country subsidiaries is typically placed in a centralized fashion through reinsurance departments of mother companies, which in turn place the cover for the whole group. This approach allows realizing considerable savings which translates into lower premiums for homeowners. In the case of PZU, the sheer size of the company allows it to pool the risk country-wide which results in a well-diversified risk exposure and highly affordable pricing.

Insurance regulators in CEE V-4 countries seem to be well aware of the importance of adequate catastrophe risk management in insurance companies. In the Czech Republic, for instance, the Insurance Regulator requires companies to supply estimates of their overall Probable Maximum Loss from a 200-year event as well as the details of their reinsurance programs. In Poland, catastrophe risk scenarios have been incorporated into a planned stress testing for the whole market.

Policy Recommendations

Despite considerable risk exposure to natural disasters the existing risk financing mechanisms in the countries of Central Europe are relatively well developed to address the consequences of large catastrophic events. The financial preparedness of the CEE V-4 countries to natural disasters manifests itself in rather high levels of catastrophe insurance coverage (well over 50 percent) as well as in the commitment of government resources in national budgets for emergency situations.

Several recommendations emerge from this analysis. They are intended to guide government policy makers in developing and applying national and regional disaster risk financing strategies, suggest ways in which the Bank can better address catastrophe risk financing in their dialogue with clients, and provide information and ideas that may be of value to other stakeholders, such as international donor organizations, NGOs, academics, and the general public.

Lessening the impact of natural disasters on government budgets. Despite a relatively high level of insurance penetration in the CEE V-4 countries, governments still carry a considerable budgetary exposure to catastrophic floods. The current regulatory frameworks in the Czech Republic and Poland, for instance, make it a government obligation to assist homeowners in post-disaster recovery and reconstruction efforts. Moreover, in the case of 1997 flood, the Czech government paid an equal compensation to both insured and uninsured homeowners for equity reasons. The post-disaster compensation was funded by additional government borrowing.

This approach to disaster compensation does not seem to optimal. In the case of disaster compensation, governments should clearly find a way to separate between public and private liabilities. While the provision of disaster relief, reconstruction of national life-lines (for example, utilities, roads, schools and hospitals) is clearly the government responsibility, recovery of private assets should be funded by individual savings and insurance. This is particularly the case when such insurance is widely available and quite affordable.

To this end, the governments of the CEE V-4 countries may consider changing the existing post-disaster compensation policies for housing reconstruction by introducing a strong element of private responsibility for losses inflicted by natural disasters. Such a policy change is likely not only to considerably increase insurance penetration among homeowners but also will help significantly reducing government fiscal exposures to natural disasters.

Reducing the financial vulnerability of homeowners and SMEs to natural hazards. While the analysis documented rather high levels of catastrophe insurance penetration among homeowners and SMEs in Central Europe, large portions of population still remains uninsured. In this context, the governments should consider investing in increasing public risk awareness as well as changing the existing post-disaster compensation policy (see above). In addition, those countries of the region, which have a lower level of property insurance coverage among homeowners, should consider introducing a stand-alone catastrophe insurance coverage for homeowners and small business owners, which can be backed by a dedicated reinsurance capacity at the regional level. As has been demonstrated by international experience, such programs can provide highly affordable coverage by realizing the benefits of region-wide risk diversification, economies of scale and the ability to obtain better pricing terms from the global reinsurance market.

Enhancing the ability of local regulators to assess the solvency implications of insurers' catastrophe risk exposures. Although the analysis documented a considerable level of technical sophistication on the part of CEE V-4 insurance supervisors in monitoring and regulating insurers' risk exposures to natural disasters, the capacity of CEE V-4 insurance regulatory bodies in catastrophe risk management would benefit from further investments in regulatory (risk assessment and monitoring) tools and specialized staff training.

The Impact of Natural Catastrophes on Central Europe

This section includes a review of government post-disaster safety nets as well as those provided by the private insurance market in the CEE V-4 countries. Although several natural hazards affect the regions, most of disaster related losses in can be attributed to the risk of flood.

Objectives, Scope, and Methodology

The analysis attempts to establish the extent of financial vulnerability of governments and households to natural hazards in four countries of the CEE V-4 by examining:

- The fiscal policy of the four Central European countries in the areas of post-disaster relief and reconstruction.
- The extent of catastrophe insurance coverage provided by the private insurance industry in the region as well as the technical capacity of national insurance markets to manage catastrophe insurance risk.

Besides documenting the current state of government and market-based safety nets for homeowners and SMEs affected by natural disasters, the analysis also suggests a range of practical solutions and policy recommendations with the view of reducing the financial vulnerability of the region to natural disasters. The analysis was prepared based on a series of written surveys followed by interviews with key government officials, government experts and insurers in the four countries.

Survey of Catastrophe Insurance Markets in Central Europe

Central Europe's Risk Exposure to Natural Hazards

The CEE V-4 countries are highly vulnerable to natural disasters such as flood, landslide, mudslide, debris-flow, windstorm, weight of snow, and extreme temperature fluctuations, with the risk of flood being the most significant. As shown in table 4.2, economic and insured losses in four countries of the region from the 1997 flood alone- which is considered to be the most catastrophic event in the region over the last 200 years—were in excess of US$5 billion.

Table 4.2. Economic and Insured Losses from 1997 Flood in Central Europe

Country	Poland	Czech Republic	The Slovak Republic
Economic loss (US$ million)	2,900	1,800	60
Insured loss (US$ million)	450	305	10

Source: Swiss Re and Munich Re (1997).

Catastrophe Risk Policy Coverage

Over the last 10 years, the non-life insurance industry in Central European countries has been transformed by the rapid consolidation, privatization and entrance in the market of large multinational insurance groups (such as Generali, Allianz, ERGO (Munich Re Group), and VIG), which currently control the lion's share of the market in all countries of the region, except Poland where the state-owned PZU still remains the biggest player. As a result, the insurance terms and conditions offered by most companies to homeowners and SMEs in the market under the FLEXA[1] cover are rather standard, with only slight variations across different companies.

Natural Hazards Covered

In all the CEE V-4 countries, insurers offer "all-risks" homeowners coverage which insurers property damage to private dwellings from FLEXA and all major natural perils such as flood, land-slide, windstorm, avalanche, hail, earthquake. Most FLEXA policies offered by the market in Central Europe do not allow the insured to decline natural hazards cover, which is an integral part of individual property insurance policy. Small businesses, industrial and commercial customers however can choose perils to be covered by their insurance policy, which to a large extent explains why a considerably larger percent of homeowners is covered against natural disasters. Specifically, while in the case of homeowners, almost 100 percent of those insured against the risk of fire are also insured against natural perils, only 40-50 percent of SMEs with a FLEXA cover have coverage against natural perils.

Catastrophe Insurance Penetration

In general, the CEE V-4 countries have a rather high level of insurance coverage for natural perils—well over 50 percent, which is considerably higher than in most OECD countries without a mandatory catastrophe insurance scheme. In comparison, catastrophe insurance penetration in Germany during the 2001 floods stood at a meager 7 percent.

The main drivers of such a high level of catastrophe insurance coverage have been a heightened level of risk awareness by the public after the 1997 and 2001 major floods, the expansion of the mortgage lending industry (as lenders typically require a proof of property insurance), considerably improved distribution and marketing capabilities of local insurance companies and, finally, rapid economic growth, which translated into stronger demand for insurance.

Insured limits. Insured policy limits for natural perils are typically the same as the sum insured under the underlying FLEXA policy. The limits of coverage however vary significantly from one country to another. It is worth mentioning that in some Central European countries the insured limits remain artificially low due to the fact that they are linked to the historic book property values, which have not updated since the early 1990s.

Deductibles. As deductibles are not very popular with individuals and corporations in Central European countries, they rarely exceed two percent of sum insured or a few hundred euros. Many companies do not have any deductibles at all under their all-risk property policies.

Premium rates. The pricing of 'all-risk' property coverage varies significantly throughout the region based on the local market conditions and the pricing sophistication of insurers. The premiums for all-inclusive property coverage range from 1 to 4 per mille, for example, (0.01 percent to 0.04 percent). The variation in the rates can be mainly attributed to the level of competition in each market rather than to risk characteristics of insured dwellings. In some countries however insurers refuse coverage to dwellings located in the most flood prone areas, for example, in Zone IV.

Terms of coverage. The terms of coverage for catastrophic perils offered by the local market appear rather generous as insurance policies cover all risks (for example, FLEXA and natural hazards) with low deductibles. In most cases, FLEXA policies include provide coverage for damage to the building structure alone, with contents of the building insured under a separate policy.

Indemnification basis. In covering catastrophic perils, insurers are often faced with the problem of underinsurance arising of policyholders buying less coverage than the replacement cost of their property. To deal with this problem, insurers include underinsurance penalties into the terms and conditions of the policy which have the effect of reducing the amount of indemnity paid in the aftermath of a disaster proportionately to the rate of underinsurance.[2] However, as many insurance policies are sold in conjunction with mortgage loans, the insured limits are typically set to cover the replacement cost of mortgaged property to protect mortgage lenders against the loss or damage to their collateral that may be caused by fires or natural perils.

Claims settlement. In the CEE V-4 countries, loss adjustment is typically carried out by loss adjusters from insurance companies, although for complex and large commercial/industrial losses external professional loss adjusters may be engaged as well. Reinsurers may also be involved if losses exceed a pre-agreed value.

In most countries of the region, claims settlement is typically done either on the new replacement cost or residual value basis. The residual value approach enables the insured to reduce the insured limit (initially set at a historic book value) by the amount of accrued depreciation and hence pay less for coverage which consequently, in the case of a loss, results in a corresponding reduction of the indemnity payment. Under the new replacement cost approach the insured limit is set based on the estimated current replacement cost of the dwelling, which is updated annually, which naturally results in higher insurance premiums as well as indemnity payments.

Risk management. In all Central European markets, large insurance companies have the necessary risk management skills and expertise to adequately manage their catastrophic risk. As catastrophe risk accumulations of local insurers can be quite significant relative to their capital base, large companies actively monitor their risk accumulations and buy considerable amounts of catastrophe excess-of-loss (XL) reinsurance to reduce their overall risk exposures to major floods. In the case of large insurance groups, reinsurance is typically placed at a group level for all country subsidiaries, which results in a considerably improved quality and amount of available reinsurance protection.

Typically, reinsurance treaties are concluded with large reputable international reinsurance companies. The amount of reinsurance bought by large groups is sufficient to cover catastrophic events with a 250-year return period. Most of surveyed large insurers had quantitative estimates of their probable maximum loss (PML) potentials for different return periods, as probabilistic commercial flood risk models have been made available by several European risk modeling companies (Prague-based Intermap, that conducted the analysis in chapter 2, is one example) as well as large reinsurers (Swiss Re and Munich Re) and commercial reinsurance brokers. As a result, several companies reported that they use at least 2-3 risk models before committing to a given estimate of PML for a chosen return period (typically 200-250 return periods are used).

The above described level of sophistication in risk management is rarely the case for smaller companies, which do not have the necessary capital and human resources to afford sophisticated risk management systems. Those however, account for 10-15 percent of market share and hence are unlikely to pose a systemic threat to the market in case of a major flood event.

Insurance laws and regulations. None of the countries of the region, except for Czech Republic have any specific requirements for pricing, reserving, reinsuring or reporting catastrophe risk underwritten by local insurers. The Czech Insurance Regulator requires companies to regularly report their estimates of 250 year PMLs (based on their own risk models) as well as the details of their reinsurance treaties. In Poland, the monitoring of companies' catastrophe risk exposures is viewed by the local regulator as an integral part of preparatory work for Solvency II. Hence, plans have been made to incorporate catastrophe risk scenarios into the stress testing of insurers scheduled for the next year.

Poland is in the process of developing a mandatory catastrophe insurance law which would make catastrophe insurance obligatory for all homeowners. The law however is at the very early stages of development.

Product distribution channels. In the CEE V-4 region, to distribute their products, insurers use mainly their own sales forces, and often tied agents. Bank-assurance is also becoming more common.

Czech Republic—Catastrophe Insurance Market Overview

Country Disaster Risk Profile

Flood is by far the main natural hazard in the Czech Republic, causing insured losses of CZK 9.8 billion (US$305.8 billion) in 1997 and CZK 36.79 billion (US$1.13 billion) in 2002. Floods result from the limited drainage capacity and the lack of regulation of some of the country's major rivers. Flooding normally occurs in the summer months when annual rainfall is at its highest but can also be caused by snow melt. The most hazardous areas are the river valleys of Moravia and East Bohemia, some of which form narrow, steep-sided channels that deeply cut through the surrounding plateau lands. As the July 1997 floods demonstrated, however, almost every part of the country is potentially exposed.

Flooding is an annual occurrence in the Czech Republic, but was regarded as little more than a nuisance until the catastrophic floods of July 1997, which inundated 35 percent of the country. This led to a huge increase in the penetration of industrial and residential flood insurance, with the result that further floods in August 2002 caused insured losses of CZK 36.79 billion (US$1.13 billion), up from CZK 9.78 billion (US$305.8 billion) in 1997. Events of this magnitude are reckoned to have a return period of 500 years on the Vltava and Labe rivers and 250 years on the Berounka, though the fact that two catastrophes occurred only five years apart must throw all such calculations into doubt. A list of major recent flood events in the Czech Republic is presented in table 4.3.

Table 4.3. Historical Disaster Losses in the Czech Republic

Date	Area	Losses
December 1993	South and west Bohemia	Insured losses CZK 750 mln to CZK 1 bln (US$26 mln to US$34 mln)
June 1995	Central Bohemia	Estimated loss CZK 200 mln (US$7.5 mln)
May 1996	Central and south Bohemia, north and south Moravia	Estimated loss CZK 500 mln (US$18 mln)
September 1996	North Moravia	Estimated loss CZK 220 mln (US$8 mln)
July 1997	East Bohemia, north and south Moravia	Worst floods since 1903 caused by rainfall of up to 300 litres per square metre of ground. One-third of the country under water. 60 fatalities. Total material damage estimated at CZK 63 bln (US$1.99 bln), of which insured losses were CZK 9.78 bln (US$305.8 mln)
July 1998	East Bohemia	Total economic losses CZK 1.8 bln (US$55.8 mln). 10 dead. Estimated insured losses CZK 569.5 mln (US$17.6 mln) including two commercial claims at CZK 100 mln each (US$3.1 mln)
March 2000	North and east Bohemia	Estimated losses CZK 2 bln (US$49.0 mln), including CZK 200 mln (US$4.9 mln) in respect of VW Skoda car plant
April 2000	Flash flooding hit the Juta textile mill	Insured loss CZK 400 mln (US$10.4 mln)
August 2002	Catastrophic flooding affecting 15% of the land area, including the capital, Prague	Estimated economic losses CZK 73 bln (US$2.23 bln). Estimated insured losses CZK 36.79 bln (US$1.13 bln)
April 2006		Flooding caused by snow melt and rain. Estimated insured losses in excess of CZK 2.0 bln (US$88.5 mln)

Source: AXCO Country Report, 2008.
Note: mln = million; bln = billion.

The country is also exposed to a greater or lesser extent to windstorm, hail, weight of snow, snow melt, and earthquake, although the latter is very insignificant. The risks of windstorm and weight of snow, however, appear to be quite real. For instance, there have been two unexpected windstorm catastrophes in the last two years caused by "Kyrill" and "Emma" causing over EUR 100 million in damages. An atmospheric hazard which caused unexpectedly high losses in 2006 was weight of snow, followed by flooding caused by snow-melt.

Contrary to initial indications, most of the damage was caused by flooding rather than weight of snow, which mainly affected disused buildings in the residential and small business sectors. There is no published estimate for the total market loss, though Ceska Pojistovna alone paid weather-related claims of CZK 1.5 billion (US$66.37 billion) in the first half of 2006, which would be an equivalent of about US$180 million for the whole market.

Natural Hazards Insurance

Currently, the local insurance market offers an all-risk inclusive property insurance policy, which besides traditional FLEXA perils also provides coverage against almost all known types of natural disasters. While in theory, homeowners can exclude natural perils from their coverage, in practice very few are doing so as the design of homeowners policies by most companies does not provide consumers with an option to opt out of natural perils coverage. There are no stand-alone catastrophe insurance policies in the market today.

The scope of coverage under the homeowners' policies includes damage to structures and internal fixtures. House contents must be insured under a separate policy. A standard contents coverage includes a small insurance sublimit on the value of insured contents in house basements, which are the most vulnerable to floods. The sublimit can be increased for an additional premium.

Due to the floods of 1997 and 2002 and the rapid growth the market has experienced ever since, the number of individual property policies at the end of 2007 stood at 1,875,523.[3] This corresponds to about 49 percent of all residential dwellings in the Czech Republic, which is a rather high level of catastrophe insurance penetration by OECD standards. This high number however conceals the problem of obtaining coverage for people living in flood prone areas as most insurers do not provide the coverage.

In contrast to Hungary, however, non-availability of flood cover has not become a political issue and there is no pressure for the establishment of a national flood insurance pool. The problem with insurability of houses located in close proximity to rivers is also being gradually addressed by the government investments in flood protection barriers as well as the government decision to prohibit housing reconstruction in the most flood prone areas.

The main drivers behind such a high level of catastrophe insurance coverage among homeowners have been the tremendously increased risk awareness among the population after the two major consecutive floods, exponential growth in mortgage lending (as banks require proof of property insurance) and the overall economic expansion experienced by the Czech Republic over the last 10 years. The level of catastrophe insurance penetration among SMEs is considerably lower as enterprises can opt out of natural perils coverage and those located in relatively low flood exposure zones do so.

Most property insurance policies are typically with a small deductible of about 2 percent. The sum insured for natural hazards is the same as for FLEXA perils and is typically established at the time of policy issuance. However, the insured limits are typically small for most of the existing policies (around US$18,405–US$30,675)[4] due to several factors. First, non-life policies in the Czech Republic are commonly issued for an indefinite term or for an annual period with an automatic renewal. This means that the terms and conditions of coverage remain the same until the policy is cancelled, or a policy-holder requests a new insured limit, or agrees to switch from the currently prevalent book-value claims settlement to a replacement cost approach which will considerably increase the insured limit.

The main reason behind homeowners' reluctance to switch to a replacement cost approach is a considerable increase in annual insurance premiums entailed by such a change. Also, as a result of the August 2002 floods, some insurers limit flood coverage to 20-50 percent of the total sum insured, which limits the market average for overall individual coverage limits. While floods are unlikely to cause complete property loss for most homeowners, such low limits of coverage are likely to trigger considerable under-insurance penalties in case of a major claim, and in the case of loss, claims are settled by insurance companies' own loss adjusters.

As 75 percent of the residential property insurance market is controlled by only two companies—Generali and Kooperativa (VIG), competition on residential property rates for the existing business is rather weak, which enables insurers to charge actuarially sound rates for the coverage and remain profitable. The situation with the rates was however dramatically different before the major floods of 1997 and 2002, which served as a major catalyst for re-pricing the flood risk by the market. After the 2002 floods, the premium rates have been increased by 400 percent and currently remain at around 250 percent level of the pre-2002 flood rates. A summary of flood premium rates charged by the market is presented in table 4.4.

Despite the fact that at least 20–25 percent of risk premium is paid back to insurance agents in the form of sales commissions, these rates still compare rather well with other flood prone countries in Europe, such as Poland, where the premium rates are driven predominantly by competition rather than by actuarial risk models. Virtually, all homeowners policies are sold through companies' own sale force, agents, or bank-assurance channels.

Since the 2002 floods the risk management capabilities of the local market have been transformed and are now on par with best international practice. Most companies adopt-

Table 4.4. Flood Premium Rates in Different Flood Risk Zones

Flood zones (return periods in years)	HHs and SMEs premium rates (per mille)	Commercial and industrial premium rates[a] (per mille)
Zone I (risk of flood is highly remote)	0.4	0.7
Zone II (50 or above)	0.8	1.4
Zone III (20–50)	2.0	3.0
Zone IV (<20)	—	—

Source: Country regulators and industry; V-4 countries.
Note: — = not applicable.
a. Commercial and industrial are defined as policies with insured limit in excess of Kcz 100 million.

ed highly sophisticated risk accumulation control systems that enable them to link each insured property to a geo-code and hence trace their risk accumulations in real time. In addition, due to the efforts of large international reinsurance brokers (Aon Benfield) and reinsurers (Swiss Re and Munich Re), the local insurance market now has rather accurate flood risk modeling tools which are used to determine companies' probable maximum loss (PML) potentials by risk accumulation and at the portfolio level.

Model generated estimates of risk are used by companies to determine the amount of reinsurance they need to protect themselves against severe catastrophic events. Currently, most companies buy reinsurance protection with the view of surviving a 1-in-200 or 250 loss scenario. This roughly comes to about a EUR 1.5 billion insured loss for the whole Czech market. In comparison, the 1997 and 2002 floods caused insured losses of US$305 billion and US$1.13 billion, respectively. To reduce the uncertainty of risk modeling estimates large companies use at least 2 external models, as well as their own. One company recently hired the Prague University to review major risk models currently in use by the market to validate the assumptions and methodology employed by the external modelers.

However, the above description of risk management capabilities of the Czech market applies only to large international insurance groups as the remaining few small domestically owned companies still do business the old-fashioned way. The problem of inadequate risk management capabilities in small insurance companies is further exacerbated by the fact that they must aggressively compete on price with large players, which leaves them with insufficient premium for placing adequate reinsurance protection (for example, with reputable reinsurers and of sufficient quantity).

The insurance market is regulated by the Czech National Bank (CNB). Despite the fact that the insurance supervision of catastrophe risk management in the market began only in 2006 it is currently rather advanced by international standards. In brief, companies are required to submit their reinsurance programs along with estimates of net catastrophe risk exposure derived from internal risk models. The regulator requires at least a 200-300 year PML estimate for the whole risk portfolio along with the calculation of aggregate company's risk retentions under all reinsurance treaties. A ratio of net retentions arising from a 200-250 year flood event to solvency capital should not exceed 2-5 percent. From this year onwards, besides the aggregate retentions, the CNB will also be requesting all sums insured by flood risk zones that were covered by reinsurance treaties.

The CNB appears to be cognizant of the possibility of larger size catastrophe events that may threaten insurers' solvency but deems it impractical to require the level of claims paying capacity in excess of those required by 1-in-250 year events. The government appears to be clearly committed to provide necessary financial assistance to the insurance industry in the case of such an unlikely catastrophic scenario. During the 1997 floods, for instance, the government paid claims for an insolvent locally owned insurer, whose claims paying capacity was clearly insufficient to survive such a catastrophic event.

The CNB also plans in the very near future to have the technical capacity to validate internal companies' catastrophe risk models. To this effect, the CNB is in the process of establishing a special risk-based solvency group with advanced quantitative capabilities.

Government Post-disaster Safety Nets

According to the Czech Ministry of Finance, the existing regulatory framework provides for two types of budgetary emergency allocations in the aftermath of natural disasters. These are as follows:

- *Budgetary allocations for emergency and immediate measures aimed at rescue and health protection of affected population.* To this effect, according to Regulatory Acts No. 239/2000 Sb. and No.240/2000 Sb, the government makes an annual CZK 100 million allocation in the state budget under the chapter of Public Treasury Administration. Mentioned financial aid can reach ultimate beneficiaries within hours if necessary, as was demonstrated during the 2002 flood. A similar structure of emergency financial aid exists at the level of local administrations.
- *Budgetary allocations for property reconstruction and revitalization.* There are several short to medium time programs managed by the Ministry of Industry and Trade and the Ministry for Regional Development which allocate government post-disaster financial aid for the purposes of reconstruction of destroyed property in the form of interest-free loans to municipalities, firms and households. This type of assistance is based on Acts No. 12/200 Sb and No.186/2002 Sb.—titled "State Aid for Territorial Restoration." This assistance is funded by a 0.3 percent annual state budget allocation. In 2009, this amount was CZK 3.5 billion. The speed with which assistance is delivered to ultimate beneficiaries depends on individual case by case evaluations of the needs of aid applicants.[5]

Disaster reconstruction can also be funded from the following additional sources:

- Insurance indemnities (Act No.: 218/2000 *on Budget Rules* explicitly provides for the possibility of insuring state property);
- Local and regional budgets;
- State budget chapters (that is, government departments) by the savings or inhibition of some governmental expenditure of the current year;
- State budget by the global or selective reduction of the expenditures of state budget chapters of the current year based on the government decision and Parliament approval in certain cases (so called government packages);
- Proceeds from the privatization of state property (for example, in 2005, the privatization of ČEZ and OSINEK generated CZK 5 billion for the state treasury);
- Issuance of state bonds as stipulated by Act No.: 163/1997. For instance, in the aftermath of the 1997 flood, in 1997–98, the Ministry of Finance issued CZK 5 billion of bonds to finance reconstruction and rehabilitation efforts;
- Issuance of bonds and other debt obligations by the regions and local authorities;
- Commercial loans.

Poland—Catastrophe Insurance Market Overview

Country Disaster Risk Profile

Although the country is exposed to a variety of natural perils, flood is by far the most common and significant. Of all historical events, the 1997 Odra river flood was the most devastating to the country and the insurance industry. The overall economic losses caused by the event were US$3.7 billion, with most of them uninsured. Although large floods in the Odra River and its tributaries are rather frequent—in the nineteenth century, four major floods were recorded in 1813, 1829, 1854 and 1880, while in the twentieth century 12 large floods were recorded—the 1997 event was the biggest on record. The July 1997 flood was caused by extremely heavy rain, with some meteorological stations recording as much as 400 millimeters over a four-day period, which was four times of the long-term average. A brief summary of the most recent floods is presented in table 4.5.

Table 4.5. Most Significant Floods in Poland (1997–2008)

Year	Date	Description of event	Economic impact
1997	July/August	Devastating floods in July and August 1997 affected large areas of central Europe. In Poland, a total area of 31,000 square kilometers, about 10 percent of the country, was affected, with the loss of 2,000 km of railway line, 3,000 km of roads, 900 bridges and 100,000 houses. More than 50 people died. The flooded areas extended along the rivers Odra, Nysa and Wisla together with their catchment areas.	The economic loss was estimated at US$3.7 bln in Poland, and the insurance industry bore losses of over US$225 mln.
2001	July/August	Beginning 9 July, torrential rainfall and consequent flooding affected southern Poland. The hardest hit areas were the cities and towns along the Vistula river, where 300 hectares of land were flooded. Bridges, sewage systems, water and gas supplies, houses and livelihoods were destroyed. Some 25 people died.	The economic loss was estimated at US$700 mln.
2005	March	Flooding caused by melting snow and heavy rainfall. Tributaries of the Odra river burst their banks near the south-western city of Wroclaw, and sections of the main road from Warsaw to Gdansk were cut.	No significant damage was reported.
2006	March	The central European floods of March 2006 mainly affected agricultural land.	No information.
2006	August	Rain caused severe flooding in the south-west.	Insurance market losses were estimated to be below PLN 40 mln (US$12.8 mln).

Source: AXCO Country Report, 2008.
Note: bln = billion; mln = million; km = kilometers.

The existing hazard risk models offered by major reinsurance brokers imply an insured market loss of about US$2 billion from a 1-in-200-year event—an event of severity of the 1997 flood. Poland is also exposed to wind storms, although the risk is relatively low compared to that of floods. In comparison, a 1-in-200 wind storm is likely to cause only 1/10 of economic damage expected from a similar frequency flood.

Hazard Insurance

All natural perils, including flood, are automatically covered by a homeowners' policy offered by most local insurers. The most common design of the insurance policy simply does not provide for an option to opt out of natural hazards coverage. For agricultural buildings, property insurance cover (including that for flood cover and other acts of god) is obligatory,[6] but the legislation is not well enforced and many risks remain uninsured. As a result of increased flood risk awareness and a growing number of mortgage-financed properties among newly constructed dwellings, 56 percent of homes in Poland are insured today against natural perils. This can be considered quite an achievement for a country where insurance coverage was quite low even 15 years ago.

Figure 4.1. Catastrophe Insurance Coverage Penetration among Homeowners

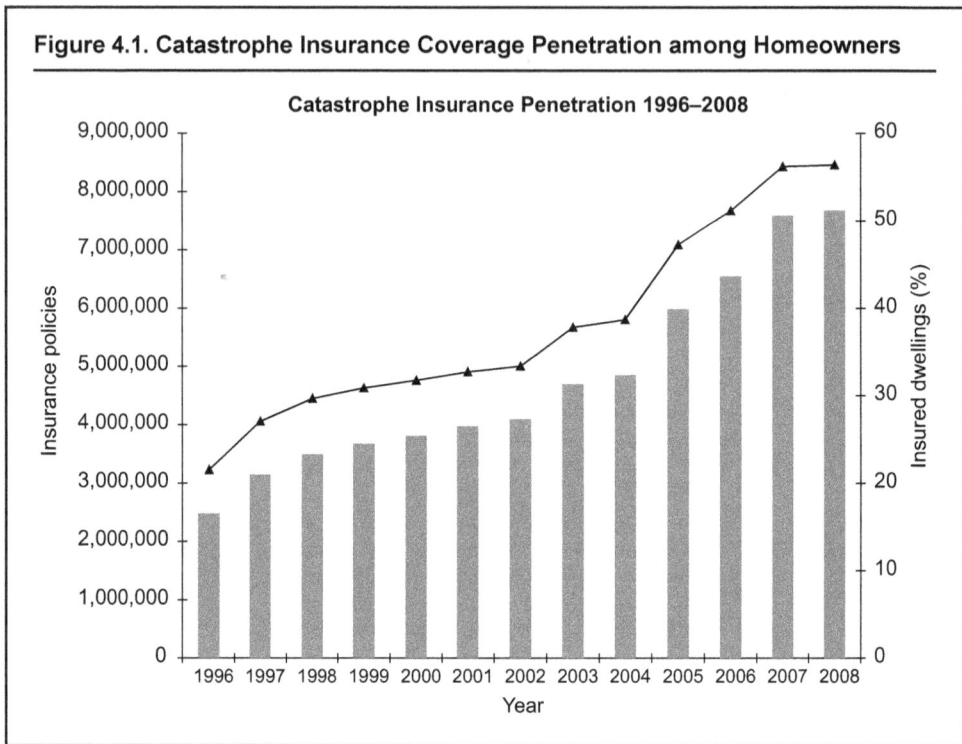

Catastrophe Insurance Penetration 1996–2008

Source: Authors, based on the data provided by the Polish Insurance Regulator, 2009

The potential for expansion is noteworthy due to the growing segment of mortgage-financed construction, which is 100 percent insured due to the banks' requirements. In 2007 alone, Poland's central bank (NBP) reported that mortgage lending increased by 50.4 percent to PLN 116.84 billion (US$41.1 billion), which mirrors the significant growth experienced in prior years. As can be seen from figure 4.1, today 7.7 million Polish households (or 56 percent of homeowners) have property flood coverage. This compares to less than 2.5 million policies in 1996.

Typically, companies do not limit sums insured for flood coverage under the offered policies. As a result, most of homeowners' policies do not have flood sublimits, except for the areas that are highly exposed to floods. Due to the increasing competition for the residential property business, which still remains highly profitable despite a considerable increase in the number of market players, premium rates are rather low by international or even Central European standards. The basic additional premium rate for flood cover historically has been 20 percent of the basic fire rate, but in the current extreme competitive climate coverage is often included in a global rate. Nevertheless, with an average loss ratio of 40 percent, the residential property business remains highly profitable.

For instance, PZU, the biggest player in the market has been offering all-perils property covers (for example, FLEXA and NATCAT) for less than 0.1 percent of insured value, as compared to 0.25 percent in the neighboring Czech Republic. The average premium generated per risk is around PLN 99 (US$44) each for buildings and contents. Despite the low pricing, the company remains highly profitable and appears to have sufficient claims paying capacity (comprising reinsurance, own reserves and surplus) to survive a 1-in-200 year flood. PZU's ability to maintain such low pricing without losing its profitability can be mainly explained by its country-wide diversification of the risk and a very large share of the market it commands.

Also, for reasons of competition, most policies in Poland have very low deductibles. In the case of PZU, for instance, deductibles on a residential property insurance policy are EUR 100, but even then, they are applied only if the loss is below that amount. Deductibles for flood and other natural perils are usually the same as for the main FLEXA policy.

Perhaps, one of the key limitations of the current insurance practice is the low insured limits that rarely approximate the true value of insured dwellings and contents. The average amount of cover for contents is PLN 15,000 (US$6,700) and for buildings PLN 130,000 (US$57,800). Insured limits under most existing policies are set based on the depreciated book value. However, newly issued policies use the current market value rather than the historic replacement cost as a basis for claims settlement. These terms of coverage cannot be changed unless a policy-holder requests it, which most policy-holders are reluctant to do because of a potential increase in premium. Hence, in the case of complete loss of a dwelling, most homeowners will face severe underinsurance penalties—as the rule of "averaging" is quite common.

As opposed to the residential property segment, most Polish owned SMEs do not buy any insurance, though awareness is increasing. Companies with foreign capital are generally better insured and protected. Government property risks in many cases are insured on written-down book values, and not on current or replacement values.

Although the Polish insurance market does not have a commonly shared flood risk model or high resolution flood risk maps, most companies use their own proprietary accumulation control systems, which enables them to underwrite, price and monitor residential risk accumulations in flood-prone areas by postal code. For corporations, address based monitoring is used. The PZU, for instance, uses a customized version of MapInfo program for monitoring its own risk aggregates. For instance, according to S&P's 2006 credit report, the PZU estimates its probable maximum loss to be between PLN 860 billion (US$382 billion) and PLN 920 billion (US$408 billion) based on a one-in-200-year event.

There are several commercial flood risk models in the market which are offered by large reinsurance brokers (Aon Benfield, Guy Carpenter), reinsurers (Swiss Re), and risk modeling companies (RMS). All these models allow monitoring flood risk aggregates at least by postcode and making estimates of probable maximum loss from events with different return periods. It is not uncommon for large companies to use several models at the same time to reduce the level of uncertainty in their estimates of the required claims paying capacity, and ultimately, the amount of reinsurance protection needed. Local companies' risk management efforts are further stimulated by the local regulatory requirements to report the 10 biggest risks as well as by the accumulation control requirements from the international rating agencies, which are concerned about companies' excessive risk exposure to catastrophic risks.

Due to the growing risk retention capabilities of the local market—mainly due to the market consolidation and buy-outs of locally owned companies by large foreign insurers—the amount of reinsurance placed with foreign reinsurers has been declining in relative terms (for example, as a percent of gross premium written). Nevertheless, for smaller size insurers, reinsurance provides most of claims paying capacity in catastrophic events as their retentions remain rather insignificant—5-10 percent, vs. 98.5 percent in the case of the PZU. The growing risk retentions by larger local companies are partially driven by the regulatory allowance for claims equalization reserves. The reserves must be set up by all companies in operation for five years and over. Retentions on any one risk must not exceed 25 percent of total technical reserves and own capital, although the regulator can approve a higher figure in justifiable cases.

While there are no specific catastrophe risk related regulatory requirements; as part of Solvency II calibration tests (QIS IV), the Insurance Regulator asked companies to include in their solvency calculations catastrophe risk scenarios for flood and hurricanes with a 200-year return period. Further market stress tests are planned by the Regulator this year, which inter-alia will include major catastrophe risk scenarios and validation of the modeling methodology used by insurers.

Since the 1997 floods, the government has been trying to limit land development in flood prone areas and has been investing heavily into flood protection infrastructure. For instance, in March 2007, the country borrowed US$189 million from the World Bank for the Odra River Basin Flood Protection Project. The main development objective of the project was to protect the population in the Odra basin against loss of life and damage to property caused by severe flooding. This will be achieved by reducing the extreme flood peaks through storage in a dry polder on the Odra river, just upstream of Raciborz town, enabling a reduction of the flood peak downstream of the reservoir, and by increasing the flood carrying capacity of the Odra river channels through and around Wroclaw. The project would protect more than 2.5 million people in towns such as Raciborz, Kedzierzyn, Kozle, Krapkowice, Opole, Brzeg, Olawa and Wroclaw, and settlements in the three vovoidships of Slaskie, Opolskie and Dolnoslaskie.

Government Post-disaster Safety Nets

Since 1997, the government has allocated PZN 753 million (EUR 171 million) in its annual budget for emergencies. The funds can be used for (a) disaster risk prevention activities, such as flood protection works, (b) liquidation of property damages caused by natural disasters through financial assistance to local governments for housing or infrastructure reconstruction, and (c) post-disaster assistance to individuals. The latter can be eligible for small grants (up to EUR 1,500) to pay for living expenses incurred due to natural disasters or housing reconstruction grants.

Although there is no official limit to the size of individual reconstruction grants, the ultimate decision on the individual eligibility and the amount of reconstruction assistance rests with local government officials. There appears to be a considerable room for government discretion in making such decisions as the eligibility for government assistance is linked to the demonstrable deterioration of living conditions as a consequence of a natural disaster. On average it takes up to 1 month for the funds to reach the beneficiaries, which is relatively quick by international standards.

Currently, the Ministry of Interior, which is in charge of allocating post-disaster aid in Poland, is working on the first draft of a compulsory catastrophe insurance law, which will make flood insurance compulsory for all homeowners in the country. At the moment, only rural dwellings are subject to this requirement. Under the proposed plan, the two state-owned companies—PZU and Warta- will offer a stand-alone flood insurance policy to homeowners, which will be made compulsory by the proposed catastrophe insurance law. The risk will be then partially retained by the companies and partially reinsured in the international reinsurance market. No special risk pooling mechanism is envisaged under the plan.

The Slovak Republic—Catastrophe Insurance Market Overview

Country Disaster Risk Profile

The Slovak Republic is subject to flood risk. It has minimal exposure to earthquake risk, and is not considered to be an area for that particular hazard. The four seismic stations in the Slovak Republic associated with the Geophysics Institute occasionally record weak tremors below Richter level 4. The latest recorded earthquake occurrence was registered in the eastern Slovak Republic on 21 May 2003. The tremor measured 4.2 Richter and damaged more than 120 of the 135 houses in one village. The insured damage is not known, but Allianz Slovenska stated that some policies only pay when the tremor exceeds Richter level 5 or 6.

Traditionally the Slovak Republic was considered a greater flood risk than the Czech Republic. Floods occurred when rivers overflowed due to water from melting snow or exceptional rainfall and endangered areas along the river valleys in the lowlands. However, after the disastrous floods in 1964, a system of dams and dykes was built on the Danube in the Slovak Republic and Hungary in order to prevent the recurrence of a similar event. The small losses in the Slovak Republic in the summer of 2002 seem to indicate that the flood control system is now quite effective and that the country's hazard risk profile has been reduced considerably.

Floods following heavy rain have occurred in recent years, but damage has been significantly lower than in Austria or the Czech Republic. In July 1998, flooding rivers devastated villages and Romany camps in both the Czech and the Slovak Republics. In the Slovak Republic, this resulted in the loss of at least 44 lives. Around 2,500 insurance claims were filed and approximately SKK 54 million (US$2.81 million) claims were paid.

In 1999 and 2000, there were more occurrences of floods and severe rain damage. These events were less severe than the 1998 floods. Areas in the eastern Slovak Republic with low concentration of domestic or commercial risks were the most affected. The disastrous floods of the summer of 2002 caused greater devastation in the Czech Republic and other countries than in the Slovak Republic. Bratislava was in a state of emergency for eight days in August, however. Preventive measures including sandbags and evacuation were effective, and there was only one fatality. It was the highest water level in Bratislava for 65 years.

The Slovak government estimate of total economic damage from that event and earlier floods in March and July was SKK 1.8 billion (US$93.654 billion). Insured damage was relatively light as many affected dwellings were not insured: the insurance association estimated a market loss of SKK 140 billion (US$7.28 billion). In 2004, the National Contact Centre for Civilian Security registered nine flood events, the biggest ones in July in the Kosice and Presov areas. The insured loss was insignificant.

Aon Benfield (a reinsurance broker) has the only fully probabilistic model in the country, which has been available since 2003. They also help clients to calculate their probable maximum losses for insured portfolios for the purpose of placing reinsurance coverage. Despite the increasing competition, so far the average market loss ratio for property has been rather low as the Slovak Republic typically remains unaffected by windstorms such as Emma which frequently cause considerable property damages in Austria and the Czech Republic. A full probabilistic flood model has existed.

Hazard Insurance

In contrast to Poland and the Czech Republic, where property owners cannot opt out of natural perils coverage, in the Slovak Republic coverage for all major natural perils, including flood, earthquake, hail, wind, burden of slow and landslide is optional and can be obtained for an additional premium in addition to the standard insurance package of FLEXA perils. As a result of this consumer discretion over the scope of coverage, over 30 percent of insured homeowners opt out of the catastrophe insurance coverage. A similar percentage of SMEs—30 percent—with general property insurance coverage do not have optional flood and earthquake endorsements.

Yet, the estimated level of catastrophe insurance penetration in the Slovak Republic is still relatively high—about 51 percent of all homes (for example, 0.952 million dwellings) are covered against catastrophic perils. This can be considered quite an achievement for a country where insurance coverage was quite low even 20 years ago. There is potential for further expansion due to the growing segment of mortgage-financed construction, which is 100 percent insured due to lenders' requirements.

Deductibles for natural perils are virtually non-existent or very small. Instead, since the floods of August 2002, insurers typically use sublimits of about of 20-30 percent of sums insured under the FLEXA policy. Some insurers check the loss history for new risks and exclude flood altogether if a risk had a flood loss within the last 10 years. Replacement is the basis for indemnity of property damage most of the time; though very occasionally cover is placed on a "book value" basis. No indications of premium rates are available, since they can vary widely depending on the area where flood coverage is requested.

Insurers track the flood risk mainly for insured properties in low-lying areas close to rivers and for the earthquake risk by Catastrophe Risk Evaluating and Standardizing Target (CRESTA) zone. Following the 2002 floods, many companies are now looking into acquiring more sophisticated flood risk accumulation control tools. In response to the growing interest from the market in flood modeling tools, Aon Benfield has produced a flood reinsurance model mainly to calculate aggregate risk exposures and probable maximum losses from events with different return periods. Swiss Re has been working with the Slovak Insurance Association and a software company to develop a rating model for floods in the Slovak Republic, which can also allow monitoring aggregate risk exposures and estimating probable maximum portfolio losses. The model is very similar to that developed by the company for the Czech Republic.

Large companies appear to track their aggregate accumulations and use modeling tools to determine their PMLs. A return period of 250-years is used for internal risk management purposes in calculating insurers' own risk exposures. The existing *Aquarius* model now allows calculating probable maximum portfolio losses in each of four flood zones for different return periods. It has been almost 50 years since there was a major flooding incident when the Danube burst its banks. Since then a dam has been built to contain any future loss exposure. In response to the flood management regulations, a national program has been set up to reinforce flood prone areas and build dykes and dams where necessary.

Government Risk Financing

The Ministry of Environment of the Slovak Republic is the main government body responsible for flood control. The budgetary appropriations for flood management and post-flood recovery are made under the budgetary chapter Všeobecná pokladničná správa (General Treasury Administration) which is administered by the Ministry of Finance. The Law of the National Council of the Slovak Republic Nr. 42/1994 Z.z. (and in the wording of subsequent directives) regarding the civil protection of the population defines an extraordinary event as natural disaster, accident, catastrophe or terrorist attack. Since the time the law has been adopted, flood is always classified as a natural disaster.

The Ministry of Environment is responsible for preparing an annual flood damage report. The report serves as a basis for budgetary allocations for rescue and relief work as well as for post-disaster reconstruction and prevention. The government disaster risk financing mechanism typically involves a budgetary transfer from the Ministry of Finance to the Ministry of Environment (or other government agencies involved in disaster relief or rehabilitation work), which in turn make the funds available to the final beneficiaries: municipalities, regional environment administration offices, and state-owned hydropower stations. The regional offices of the Ministry of Environment further allocate the funds to villages and private citizens.

The existing national legislative framework for disaster risk management and financing is described in the following legislation:

- Law Nr. 666/2004 on flood prevention;
- Decree Nr. 386/2005 issued by the Ministry of Environment on monitoring flood related damages and undertaken response measures;
- Decree Nr. 387/2005 by the Ministry of Environment evaluation of damages and compensation of flood-related damages.

Typically, it takes at least half a year to get the aid to the flood victims. The Ministry of Environment does not provide any additional resources besides those envisaged under the above described budgetary allocation from the Ministry of Finance. The provision of post-disaster subsidies is not contingent upon availability of private insurance. Also, there is no maximum pre-set in advance amount of financial assistance to victims of disasters and no means testing requirements.

Hungary—Catastrophe Insurance Market Overview

Country Disaster Risk Profile

Hungary's risk exposure to natural perils is by-and-large limited to flood and earthquake. However, the country's overall economic exposure to these perils is rather moderate. Hungary's exposure to earthquake results from the compressive motions of the Eurasian and African plates, which elevated the Carpathian Mountains to the north and east of the great Hungarian Plain (see table 4.6 and figure 4.2).

A relic of past crustal movements can also be seen in the long-extinct volcanoes on the northern shores of Lake Balaton. Earthquake is regarded as a minor hazard by most of the local companies, though the risk appears to be under-estimated and therefore under-rated. The local market works on the assumption of a moderate earthquake every 30 to 35 years and a severe earthquake every 90 years.

Table 4.6. History of Sizeable Earthquakes in Hungary

Date	Area	Magnitude	Intensity
1978	Bekes	—	6.5
1956	Dunaharaszti	5.1	8.0
1956	Pakscz	4.2	6.0
1953	Ukkturje	4.0	6.5
1951	Tereske	4.4	7.0
1942	Bekonybel	3.6	6.0
1942	Tapiosuly	4.1	6.0
1939	Almoso	4.5	5.5
1939	Eger	3.0	6.0
1937	Tarcal	4.2	6.0
1934	Bucsuszentlaszlg	4.5	6.5
1931	Beregdaroc	4.0	6.0
1930	Cserharsurame	3.9	6.0
1927	Varpalcta	3.4	7.0
1927	Varpalcta	3.7	7.0
1925	Eser	5.2	8.5
1925	Naskanizsa	4.3	6.5
1922	Pecs	3.8	5.5
1917	Gasztcny	4.0	6.0

Source: AXCO, 2009.
Note: — = not applicable.

There is an earthquake construction code which applies to concrete slab and steel frame and concrete buildings. Most buildings in Hungary either pre-date the code, however, or are not covered by it. There is said to be a Richter 5 event every year, but damage is usually negligible. The last significant event was in 1985 in the area north of Lake Balaton. The estimated loss was HUF 200 billion (approximately US$2.4 billion) falling mainly on the household account. Recorded events in excess of intensity 5 from 1917 onwards are listed below:

Hungary's risk exposure to floods arises from the presence of two main rivers on its territory—Tisza flowing through Szeged, and the Danube that flows through Budapest. The country's flood plain areas are estimated at 5,450 square kilometers, out of which 900 square kilometers were flooded in 2006 (table 4.7).

In the more distant past Hungary suffered a number of catastrophic floods, two of the most notable being the Danube flood of 1838 which destroyed Pest and the Tisza flood of 1879 which destroyed Szeged. Such major events have been largely eradicated, however, by river improvement schemes and the building of dikes to create flood basins along the courses of the major rivers. The success of these measures was dramatically proven in April 2006 when the Danube rose to its highest level for nearly 150 years but caused almost no insured flood losses. The river Tisza in the east of the country produced severe floods in March 1999, 2000, and 2001 but insured losses were low.

Figure 4.2. Earthquake Map of South Eastern Europe

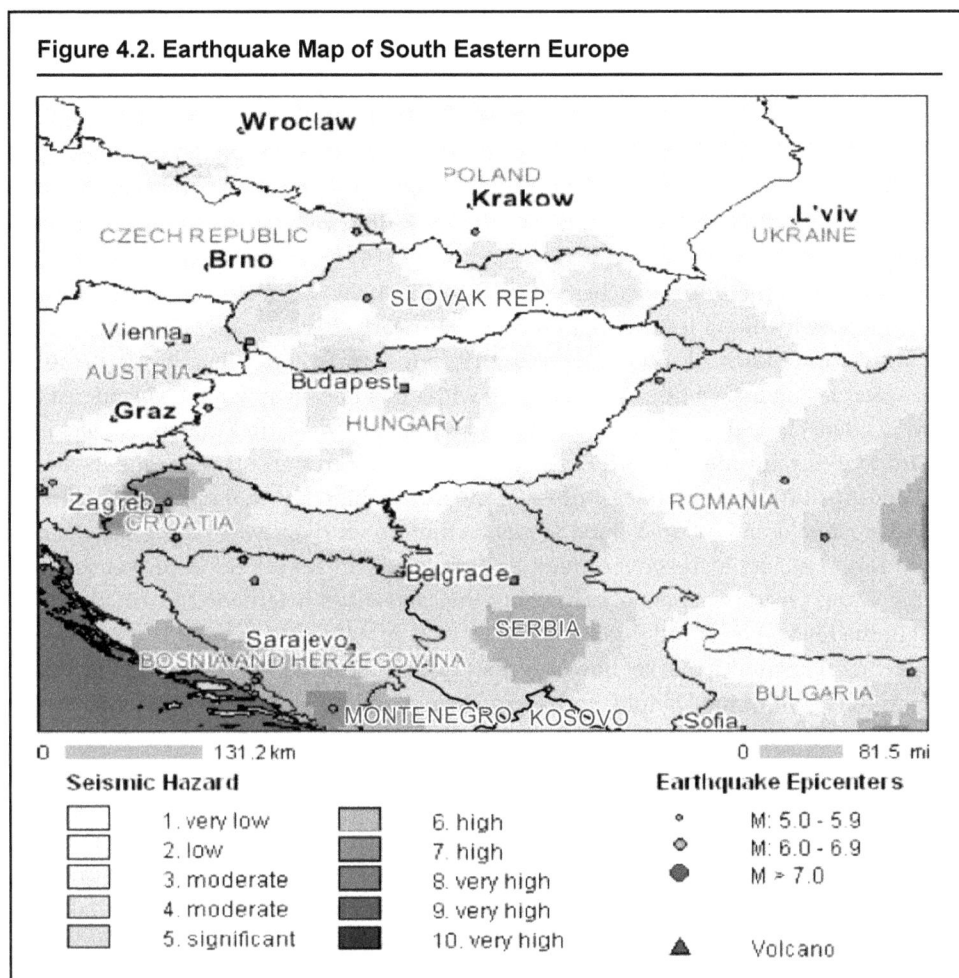

Source: Swiss Re.

Table 4.7. Hungary's Flood Exposure

	Hungary (km²)
Size of morphological plain[a]	5,450
Size of recent floodplain (loss in %)	900 (85%)
Flooded in 2006	882
Artificial polder opening	0
Potential restoration area	700[b]; 80[c]
Flooded potential restoration area (% of total potential restoration area flooded)	60[d] (80%)

Source: AXCO Country Report, 2009.

Note: km² = square kilometers.

a. Floodplain only, without groundwater influenced areas. b. Vasarhelyi Plan. c. Bodrog mouth. d. Novi Becej, and Bodrog mouth identified in GEF study.

Hungary's floods are normally caused by rainfall and snow-melt in the Carpathian and Tatra mountains, outside Hungary itself. The most exposed areas are the northern reaches of the Tisza where it enters Hungary from the Ukraine, the Koros where it enters Hungary from Romania, and the southern reaches of the Tisza after its confluence with the Koros. There is also a risk of flooding from the Danube south of Budapest. Altogether, an estimated two million hectares of land are exposed to 1:100 year flooding. Between 1999 and 2001 there was a marked increase in severe flood incidents in the east of the country.

Flooding on the upper reaches of the Tisza in 1999 was regarded as a 1:100 year event, and yet the flood level in March 2000 was nearly 20 centimeters higher. In a further incident in March 2001 the level of the Tisza rose by 8 meters in a day as a result of melt-water from the Carpathians coinciding with unusually heavy rains. This increase in flood incidents is said to be the result of deforestation in the Tatra Mountains increasing the amount of rainwater run-off. Flood waters draining from central Europe in August 2002 and April 2006 raised the Danube to dangerously high levels, but the embankments in Budapest held and insured flood losses further down-river were negligible. As a result of recent incidents the government has initiated a 10-year flood improvement plan for the Tisza. Overflow channels are being dug and dikes heightened to 1m above the level of the highest recorded flood.

The local insurance market however does not see the flood PML as being significant, even in the event of the Danube and Tisza rivers flooding simultaneously. One reason for a low PML is the fact that the most flood-prone rivers, the Tisza and the Koros, flow through agricultural areas where insurance penetration is low and there is relatively little industrial development. Insurers have also taken comfort from the fact that recent floods have been relatively localized and have affected different stretches of the Tisza valley each year. In 2001, for example, only four villages were inundated. Insurers are also protected by restrictive policy wordings, which exclude non-flood-protected properties, and by specific underwriting measures, such as the exclusion of properties of mud brick construction. The overall insured loss statistics for the last decade are summarized in table 4.8 below.

Table 4.8. Insured Flood Losses

Flood date	Total losses	Insured losses
March 1999	HUF 82 bln/US$345.8 mln	Not known
March 2000	Not known	HUF 500 mln/US$1.8 mln
March 2001	HUF 23 bln/US$80.3 mln	HUF 3.2 bln/US$11.2 mln

Source: AXCO Report, 2009.
Note: bln = billion; mln = million; km = kilometers.

Most damage was caused to roads, bridges and village houses. A surprising feature of the floods was the number of total loss buildings claims. These arose because many rural homes are built of mud brick which can become saturated and unstable after prolonged exposure to standing water.

Hazard Insurance

At the time this analysis was being prepared there were 30 insurance companies supervised in Hungary, of which 10 were non-life, 10 life and 10 composite. A total of 11 branches have been established by EU insurers on a freedom of establishment basis, though most of these are inactive. Non-life insurance is also written by 34 insurance associations which are mainly active in agriculture and motor. Every insurance company except the state export credit insurer is foreign-owned. The market is dominated by Allianz Hungaria, which retains a market share of around 35 percent.

An unusual feature of the Hungarian property insurance market is the high level of penetration of household business. According to our estimates, in 2009 the local insurers held around 2.9 million residential property policies in their portfolios, which represents a penetration rate of over 70 percent of households. OTP Garancia, Generali-Providencia, Aegon and Allianz Hungaria have all in excess of 500,000 household policies on their books, which accounts for a high proportion of their catastrophe accumulations.

As catastrophe insurance coverage is typically offered by the local market as part of the all-risk property policy at a very competitive rate, very few homeowners (around 5 percent) opt out of it. In fact, it appears that such opting out of the natural hazards coverage is only possible in the case of smaller insurance companies which use this feature to remain competitive. Such a high level of property insurance coverage among households can at least be partially explained by the mandatory insurance coverage requirement introduced by local banks for all new mortgage borrowers. In response to the government interest rate subsidies for new mortgage borrowers, the mortgage lending market grew rapidly between 2002 and 2006, hence driving up the level of property insurance penetration among the Hungarian homeowners. The recent phasing out of mortgage subsidies has reduced the amount of household new business, and insurers are now trying to increase their premiums per policy by selling assistance, legal protection, life and personal accident riders.

A typical comprehensive policy includes the perils of fire, lightning, explosion, aircraft, storm, hail, weight of snow, landslide, collapse of underground cavities, impact by vehicles, cloudburst, flood, earthquake, burst pipes, burglary and glass breakage. Flood wordings generally exclude damage to houses built of mud brick and houses situated between river banks and flood protection dikes. Policies are normally issued on a reinstatement basis and sums insured are index-linked. Many policies specify the level of security protections required for varying sums insured. "Condominium" policies are available to provide collective insurance on the buildings of apartment blocks.

The earthquake peril includes earthquake fire, landslip and collapse following subsidence. Most companies define earthquake as "shaking reaching the fifth degree on the MSK-64 scale," and thus avoid liability for damage to buildings with inadequate earthquake resistance. Although there are virtually no deductibles, earthquake is insured either on a replacement or cash value basis and with a sublimit above the sum insured specified in the contract—typically up to US$25,000, for example, if aggregate losses from flood or earthquake exceed that amount, individual property damage claims are scaled down proportionately, based on sum insured.

While earthquake insurance is almost universal for foreign-invested enterprises and householders, penetration is lower for Hungarian enterprises, but it is still estimated that 80 percent of industrial risks are covered against earthquake. The survey of the market for this analysis indicates that there are about 300,000 all-risk property insurance covers for SMEs in Hungary. Household earthquake rates are the same across Hungary, whereas industrial rates can vary by region. Because of intense competition, most insurers charge inclusive fire and perils rates with only a minimal allocation of premium for earthquake.

In addition to earthquake, all-risk residential property policies cover two types of flood, namely cloudburst and flood. Cloudburst is defined as damage caused by standing water resulting from excessive rainfall, excluding the effects of rising ground water. Flood is defined as the "overflow of any permanent or seasonal, natural or artificial waterways, lakes, ponds or reservoirs which inundates flood-protected areas." The limitation to flood-protected areas effectively excludes properties located in the flood basins between riverbanks and dikes, as well as properties which are not protected by dikes or embankments.

Insurers generally survey flood-exposed properties within 15 km of a river and exclude those for which the risk is unacceptably high. Some companies automatically decline risks in areas around the upper reaches of the Tisza which were affected by flooding in 1999 to 2001. Others take the view that since the floods occurred in different places in different years, the average incidence of risk along the Tisza remains acceptable. Some insurers decline mud-brick houses in flood-prone areas because prolonged exposure to standing water can lead to structural failure. Similarly to earthquake, flood is insured on a replacement value basis, with losses subject to a sublimit above the maximum loss threshold specified in the insurance policy. It is estimated that approximately 95 percent of household policies and 80 percent of commercial policies are extended to include flood. Flood is included in the overall special perils rate, which is the same across the country.

A *Law on Social Flood Insurance* (popularly known as the *Miklos Wesselenyi Law* after a nineteenth century Hungarian river regulator) was passed in August 2003. The law authorized the establishment of a state-backed flood insurance fund for the benefit of homeowners who are unable to obtain commercial flood insurance because their properties are situated in unprotected flood plains. The fund provides maximum cover of HUF 15 billion (US$87,057) per property and compensation is available to any eligible homeowner who elects to pay premiums. The fund is administered by the state and there is no involvement by the commercial insurance sector.

The main purpose of the Miklos Wesselenyi Flood Protection Fund is to save the government from having to make *ex gratia* payments to uninsured flood victims. Because many of those who live on unprotected flood plains are poor farmers with low insurance consciousness and below-average incomes, the number of people buying protection from the fund is virtually zero. It therefore seems that the main beneficiaries of the scheme are the insurance companies, which will no longer be under political pressure to underwrite flood risks in exposed areas.

Rating levels are low, largely because of the need to remain competitive. A typical buildings rate for an all-perils-policy, which would be applied throughout Hungary, is 1.06 percent. Some companies however make an effort to charge more. Contents rates are 1.5 percent in the country but up to 3.6 percent in Budapest because of the higher burglary risk. Policies are normally issued with nil deductibles. The average household premium in 2006 was HUF 25,000 (US$125) and of earthquake cover HUF 2,000 (about US$10). Average limits reach US$100,000 for residential and US$400,000 for commercial properties.

Risk accumulations are monitored on a postcode basis. All companies are said to base their catastrophe PMLs on a severe earthquake affecting Budapest, though there is no generally accepted earthquake model for Hungary and therefore no consensus about the appropriate level of catastrophe protection. Some models produce PMLs which seem unrealistically high, while others produce PMLs which are unaccountably lower. Companies which have either produced or are working on Budapest earthquake models include Munich Re, Equecat, Benfield Group and Aon Re. The companies are also required to report their risk aggregates for earthquake and flood to the local insurance regulator. Since most of the local companies are foreign owned, most of reinsurance is placed with the parent companies.

Government Risk Financing

According to the Ministry of Local Governments and the National Directorate General for Disaster Management, the government annually allocates HUF 3-4 billion (US$15–20 million equivalent) to the national Force Majeure Fund. The fund proceeds are used for the purposes of reconstructing government owned assets destroyed by natural disasters. The size of the fund can be increased by a government decree. In addition to the central FMF, all local and regional governments must be allocated at least 2-3 percent of their annual budgets for emergency situations. There are 19 counties and 3200 Local Government offices. Interestingly, government financial assistance to homeowners that have been adversely affected by natural disasters is not predicated upon proof of insurance.

Typically, it takes 2–3 weeks from the declaration of a national disaster by the government for the aid from the Calamity fund to reach disaster victims. Local government offices perform the role of a payment agent. The County Disaster management Office and insurance companies are involved in evaluating the extent of loss. There is no statutory maximum amount of financial aid to be paid per household and amount of assistance may vary significantly from one catastrophe event to another based on the government assessment of overall economic damages from a disaster. Unused funds in the National Calamity Fund can be carried forward in addition to the new budget.

Conclusion

Despite considerable risk exposure to natural disasters, the existing private risk financing mechanisms in the countries of Central Europe are relatively well advanced to mitigate the consequences of large catastrophic events. Several recommendations emerge from this analysis. They are intended to guide government policymakers in developing and applying national and regional disaster risk financing strategies, suggest ways in which specialists can better address catastrophe risk financing in their dialogue with clients, and provide information and ideas that may be of value to other stakeholders, such as international donor organizations, NGOs, academics, and the general public.

Lessening the impact of natural disasters on government budgets. Despite a relatively high level of insurance penetration in the CEE V-4 countries, governments still carry a considerable budgetary exposure to catastrophic floods. The current regulatory frameworks in the Czech Republic and Poland, for instance, make it a government obligation to assist homeowners in post-disaster recovery and reconstruction efforts. Moreover, in the case of 1997 flood, the Czech government paid an equal compensation to both insured and uninsured homeowners for equity reasons. The post-disaster compensation was funded by additional government borrowing.

This approach to disaster compensation does not seem optimal. In the case of disaster compensation, governments should clearly find a way to separate between public and private liabilities. While the reconstruction of the former is clearly the government responsibility, the latter should be covered by private insurance. This is particularly the case when such insurance is widely available and quite affordable. To this end, the governments of the CEE V-4 countries may consider changing the existing post-disaster compensation policies for housing reconstruction by introducing a strong element of private responsibility for losses inflicted by natural disasters. Such a policy change is likely to not only considerably increase insurance penetration among homeowners but also will help significantly reducing government fiscal exposures to natural disasters. As well, for purely public sector losses, governments should consider risk transfer mechanisms to provide additional budgetary support for mega disasters.

Reducing the financial vulnerability of homeowners and SMEs to natural hazards. While this analysis documented rather high levels of catastrophe insurance penetration among homeowners and SMEs in the CEE V-4 countries, up to possibly 50 percent of the population still remains uninsured. In this context, the governments of CEE V-4 should consider investing in increasing public risk awareness as well as changing the post-disaster compensation policy. In addition, those CEE V-4 countries which have a lower level of property insurance coverage among homeowners should consider introducing a stand-alone catastrophe insurance to homeowners and small business owners, backed by a dedicated reinsurance capacity at the country or in the case of smaller economies (such as the Slovak Republic) at the regional level.

As has been demonstrated by the international experience, programs can provide highly affordable coverage by realizing the benefits of country-wide risk diversification, economies of scale and the ability to obtain better pricing terms from the global reinsurance market. The first country wide catastrophe risk pool in an emerging market known as the Turkish Catastrophe Insurance Pool (TCIP) was pioneered and successfully launched with Bank assistance in Turkey in 2000. As well, a Caribbean Catastrophe Risk Financing Facility (CCRIF) was established in 2007 to provide government fiscal budgetary support in the event of hurricanes or earthquakes for 16 country governments and territories in the Caribbean region. Work on a similar program for the countries of South Eastern Europe and the Caucauses has reached a fairly advanced stage, and this initiative, the SECE CRIF, may enable insurers selling a stand-alone catastrophe insurance cover to receive access to a dedicated reinsurance capacity on highly attractive terms.

Enhancing the ability of local regulators to assess the solvency implications of insurers' catastrophe risk exposures. Although this analysis documented a considerable level of technical sophistication on the part of CEE V-4 insurance supervisors in monitoring and regulating insurers' risk exposures to natural disasters, the capacity of CEE V-4 insurance regulatory bodies in catastrophe risk management would benefit from further investments in regulatory risk assessment and monitoring tools and specialized staff training.

Notes

1. FLEXA is an abbreviation for the following five insured perils, which are typically covered under one insurance policy: fire, lightning, explosion, and aviation.
2. In the insurance industry, this approach is known as a rule of averaging or the average clause.
3. See Annual Report of the Czech Insurance Association, 2007, p. 62.
4. See AXCO Country Report for the Czech Republic, 2008.
5. For more detailed information there is a link on MRD web pages: *http://www.mmr.cz/Regionalni-politika/Programy-Dotace/Poskytovani-statni-pomoci-po-zivelni-nebo-jine-poh*.
6. Act of 22 May 2003 on Compulsory Insurance, the Insurance Guarantee Fund and the Motor Insurers' Bureau

CHAPTER 5

Fiscal Sustainability Effects of Natural Disaster Shocks

Natural disasters constitute a major shock to public finances and debt sustainability because of their impact on output and the need for reconstruction and relief expenses. The analysis in this chapter uses a Panel Vector Auto Regression (PVAR) model to systematically estimate the impact of geological, climatic, and other types of natural disasters on government expenditures and revenues using annual data for high- and middle-income countries over 1975–2008.

The analysis finds that all disasters cause declines in real GDP. For the average country, budget deficits increase after climatic disasters—for lower-middle-income countries the increase in deficits is widespread. Disasters do not lead to larger output declines in countries with higher initial government debt possibly because their access to capital markets allow them to smooth their long-term funding programs. Countries with high financial development suffer smaller real consequences from disasters, but deficits expand further in these countries likely due to increases in debt given their easier access to capital markets. Disasters in countries with high insurance penetration also have smaller real consequences and do not result in deficit expansions. From an ex post perspective, the availability of insurance seems to offer the best combination of real and fiscal consequences from catastrophic natural disasters.

Background and Context

Recent observations suggest that natural catastrophes, especially climatic ones, are increasing both in intensity and frequency. UNEP (2005) stresses that the world is facing an increasing frequency and intensity of disasters that have had devastating impacts based on figures reported by the secretariat of the International Strategy for Disaster Reduction where the 10 years prior to 2005 have seen 478,100 people killed, more than 2.5 billion people affected, and about US$690 billion in economic losses. Hoppe and Grimm (2008), form the Geo Risks Research Department of Munich Re, document that there have been increasing signs that the steady advance of global warming is progressively affecting the frequency and intensity of natural catastrophes.

In addition to their direct costs, usually measured in terms of damages, casualties, and output losses (Raddatz, 2009; Rasmussen, 2004), natural disasters have the potential to constitute a major issue for public finances, and debt sustainability in particular (Borensztein et al., 2008; Rasmussen, 2004; International Monetary Fund, 2009; Inter American Development Bank, 2009; World Bank, 2003; World Bank, 2001). The reconstruction of public infrastructure destroyed by a disaster requires increases in government expenditures at the same time that the contraction in economic activity may reduce the government's ability to gather resources from standard tax collections. Furthermore, governments facing large disasters may need to mobilize resources to provide emergency relief, aid, and social safety nets to those individuals directly affected by these catastrophes. While international aid may help mitigate some of the immediate consequences of disasters, the amounts involved are usually smaller than the tens of billions that a large disaster may cost, and are not promptly available.

The consequences of disasters for public finance and debt sustainability will depend on the nature of the government's reaction to the disasters. Whether governments respond to disasters by increasing expenditures to provide reconstruction and relief after a natural disaster will depend on their capacity to gather resources by increasing fiscal revenues or borrow resources from domestic or international sources, or benefit from previously contracted fiscal policy insurance or other hedges. In absence of these financing options, the governments' only option would be to maintain or even decrease the level of expenditures, limiting its ability to provide reconstruction and relief and potentially increasing the economic consequences of the disaster.

The route followed by different governments concerning the combination of expenditures, revenues, and borrowing will likely depend to the access to lending, its cost, and on the demand for government services. For instance, countries that can borrow at low cost and face the burden of reconstruction and relief may prefer that route to increasing revenues through taxation or restraining expenditures. And countries where private insurance markets share a large fraction of the reconstruction costs (for example, by financing the reconstruction of private and public capital) may focus on emergency relief, face smaller funding requirements, and expanding expenditures moderately.

This chapter estimates the impact of natural disasters on fiscal sustainability by characterizing how government expenditures and revenues typically respond to different types of disasters, and how these responses relate to a government's ability to borrow and to the availability of private sources of financing for private and public reconstruction. Following Raddatz (2009), the analysis does this by estimating the parameters of a PVAR model that includes real output, government expenditures, government revenues, measures of the occurrence of geological, climatic, and other disasters, as well as other external shocks and standard macroeconomic variables like inflation and interest rates.[1] The three categories of natural disasters considered follow Skidmore and Toya (2002) and are defined as follows: geological disasters including earthquakes, landslides, volcano eruptions, and tidal waves; climatic disasters including floods, droughts, extreme temperatures, and windstorms; and other disasters including famines, epidemics, insect plagues, wild fires, miscellaneous accidents, industrial accidents, and transport accidents.

Using the parameters of the model one can predict the dynamic response of each of the variables of interest to the occurrence of any type of disaster the same year the disaster occurs and in the years following the disaster. The model is estimated using annual data for high and middle-income countries during the period 1975-2008. While low income countries are also of interest, data availability and the importance of aid flows for government financing makes them hard to compare to countries that participate more actively in international financial markets.

The response of all variables in the model are identified against the occurrence of each type of natural disaster by assuming that these disasters are acts of God whose occurrence is exogenous to a country's economic condition. After estimating the average fiscal responses to disasters of all countries in the sample, the responses of different country groups are contrasted based on income levels, financial development, and insurance penetration. The contrasts allow to test whether differences in these country characteristics that proxy for a country's ability to borrow, and the availability of non-governmental sources of funds for reconstruction, are associated with different fiscal behaviors and macroeconomic costs of disasters. Crucially, when comparing the responses of countries across groups, differences in income levels across these groups are controlled for.[2]

For middle- and high-income countries, it is found that all three types of disasters cause unambiguous declines in GDP of about 1 percent for a climatic disaster, 7 percent for a geological disaster, and 5 percent for other disasters. However, clear budget consequences are observed more prominently after climatic disasters. While not confirmed, this could possibly be due to the wider area scope of such disasters, for example, when rains, windstorms, or hurricanes cover large swathes of territory thus causing multi-jurisdictional damages. The financial consequences thus occur due to expanding expenditure (by 15 percent) and declining revenue (by 10 percent) after these episodes.

While governments try to proactively attenuate the impact of climatic disasters, they incur significant budget deficits (increases by 25 percent from initial levels). The GDP impact of climatic shocks, however, is the smallest as a result of theses government fiscal injections. For geological disasters, governments appear to respond less with deficit financing to achieve a fiscal impulse, and this seems to result in higher real consequences for these disasters. This lack of an offsetting fiscal impulse could be driven by government preferences or simply a constrained fiscal space,[3] and the analysis tries to shed some light on the merit of these two interpretations by further controlling for initial debt levels and financial market development.

It appears that initial debt levels do not constrain a government's fiscal space available for disaster response in the sample, for which it is conjectured that in this sample high initial debt levels proxy for a better access to capital markets. Furthermore, financially developed countries are found to always strongly increase government expenditures after disasters (by 55 percent). While deficits increase relatively more in financially developed countries (by 75 percent as opposed to 10 percent in less financially developed countries), the resources that an efficient financial system can mobilize may help dealing with the economic consequences of disasters more effectively. The output loss for financially less developed countries appear to be 2 to 10 percent of GDP versus on average, no significant loss for financially more developed countries. In contrast, countries with high levels of insurance penetration can deal with the economic consequences of disasters without engaging in deficit financing of expenditures.

In addition to quantifying the impact of natural disasters on output and fiscal variables for different groups of countries, this analysis leaves three main messages concerning the use of fiscal-policy financial instruments. First, one needs to be careful when associating high debt levels with a government's limited ability to borrow. A country's stock of debt is the equilibrium outcome of supply and demand factors. Countries with high debt levels may be those that face a larger supply of loans. For those countries, debt levels proxy for a good access to credit rather than a tighter credit constraint. In the sample of high- and middle-income countries, this seems to be the case. Second, countries with more developed credit and bond markets or more developed insurance markets suffer less from disasters (smaller output declines). However, the way they achieve it differs in both cases.

In financially developed credit and bond markets, governments are able to raise funds and increase deficits. Presumably, this response helps alleviate the impact of the disasters. Thus, it seems that governments in such financially developed countries have better access to debt markets to attenuate shocks. In contrast, in countries with high insurance penetration, the smaller impact of disasters occurs without an important fiscal expansion. Countries with smaller insurance markets expand deficits more, yet still suffer more from disasters in terms of the effect on GDP. The availability of insurance seems to reduce the real consequences without requiring an increase in fiscal burdens. It seems, therefore, that while overall financial development helps deal with disasters, the prevalence of insurance does it in a more efficient ex post manner. Of course, properly weighting these two options requires an explicit consideration of the costs of both strategies: the net present value of interest costs associated with further borrowing from the financial system versus insurance premium costs.

Given the recent emphasis on the use of insurance related strategies to deal with disasters (catastrophe insurance); it is useful to discuss the implications of the results of this strategy. Although the results here relate to insurance penetration in the private sector, fiscal insurance policies could have a similar positive hedging effect and help enhance the disaster relief response and reconstruction, and further diminish the real consequences of disasters in a fiscally sustainable manner. The reason is that, based on the analysis results, the availability of insurance seems to dampen the impact of disasters by taking some of the losses and helping the government to focus fiscal expenses on the remaining un-hedged risks. This mechanism should also apply to fiscal insurance.

If this is the case, governments could avoid jeopardizing fiscal sustainability after natural disasters by purchasing financial products that transfer and disperse some of the financial risks from the natural disasters into financial markets. However, challenges in pricing and cost-benefit analysis concerning these products often leave countries hesitant to use them, assuming they will be able to meet the financial costs of disasters with their current expenditures and the help of official aid. Nevertheless, recent experience suggests that, despite these challenges, countries would like to arrange for some risk transfer mechanism as part of their climate-change risk mitigation strategies (Borensztein et al., 2008). The remainder of the chapter is structured as follows: section 2 describes the data and section 3 explains the estimation methodology. Section 4 presents and discusses the estimation results including for subgroups of countries based on income levels, regional location, and financial deepening. Section 5 concludes.

Methodological Approach

The analysis estimates the impact of natural disasters on output and fiscal variables across countries using a PVAR model that relates the variables of interest to its lagged values, and to contemporaneous and lagged indicators of the occurrence of various types of natural disasters. For a given country, the baseline specification of the model corresponds to

$$A_0 x_{i,t} = \sum_{j=1}^{q} A_j x_{i,t-j} + \sum_{j=1}^{q} B_j D_{i,t-j} + \theta_i + \theta_t + \gamma_i t + \varepsilon_{it} \tag{1}$$

where

$$x_{i,t} = (TT_{i,t}, \; y_{i,t})', \; TT_{i,t}$$

is the (growth of) a terms-of-trade index, and

$$y_{i,t} = (EXP_{i,t}, \; GDP_{i,t}, \; INF_{i,t}, \; R_{i,t}, \; REV_{i,t})'$$

is a vector of endogenous variables that includes the (log of) real government expenditures (*EXP*), GDP per capita (in constant 2000 US dollars) (*GDP*), the inflation rate (*INF*), nominal interest rate (*R*), and government revenues (*REV*).

The main focus of the analysis is on *EXP*, *GDP*, and *REV*, but inflation and interest rates are included in the y vector as controls for other macroeconomic conditions. This set includes all the conventional macroeconomic variables typically included in macro models (see Monacelli (2005), Linde et al (2008), and Adolfson (2001), among others). The vector

$$D_{i,t} = (GEO_{i,t}, \; CLIM_{i,t}, \; OTH_{i,t})'$$

includes variables capturing the occurrence of geological, climatic, or other disasters, as described in the next section. The parameters θ_i and θ_t are country and year fixed-effects that capture long run differences in all the variables across countries, and the impact of global factors that are common to all countries in the sample and can be understood as the world business cycle. The coefficient g_i captures a country-specific trend and is included when the model is estimated in levels only (see below). The residual term ∂_{it} corresponds to an error term that is assumed i.i.d. The number of lags, q, is assumed to be equal in both summatories. Relaxing this assumption does not importantly change the results. The parameters of the model are matrices, denoted by Aj, and the structural interpretation of the results depends on the identification of the parameters of the contemporaneous matrix A_0.

Data

To conduct the analysis, data was collected on the incidence of disasters and several measures of macroeconomic and fiscal performance for middle- and high-income countries (see table 5A.1). Low-income countries are not included because their fiscal expenditures, revenues, and overall debt are typically related to official and multilateral aid support. Therefore, the fiscal responses to shocks are likely to differ qualitatively from those of other countries and depend on exogenous aid allocation.

Data for natural disasters were obtained from the Emergency Disasters Database (EM-DAT) maintained by the Center for Research on the Epidemiology of Disasters (CRED, 2008). This is a comprehensive database that includes data on the occurrence and effects of over 12,800 mass-disasters in the world since 1900, and is compiled from a diversity of sources. As a general principle, to enter into the database an event has to meet any of the following conditions: there are ten or more people reported killed; there are 100 or more people reported affected; a state of emergency is declared; or there is a call for international assistance.

The data contain information on various types of disasters that, following Skidmore and Toya (2002) are classified in three broad categories. Geological disasters include earthquakes, landslides, volcano eruptions, and tidal waves. An important characteristic of this type of events is their unpredictability and relatively fast onset. The second category is climatic disasters. This category includes floods, droughts, extreme temperatures, and windstorms (for example, hurricanes). Compared to the previous category, some of these disasters can be forecasted well in advance (so precautions can be undertaken) and some have a relatively long onset. The final category is a residual group that includes famines, epidemics, insect plagues, wild fires, miscellaneous accidents, industrial accidents, and transport accidents.

In each category, the incidence of disasters is measured by counting the annual number of events that classify as large disasters according to the following criteria established by the International Monetary Fund (see Fund (2003)); that is, the event either affects at least half a percent of a country's population, or causes damages to the capital stock, housing, human lives, other, of at least half a percent of national GDP; or results in more than one fatality for every 10,000 people.

Starting from this variable, a different measure is constructed that not only counts the number of disasters, but also takes into account the month of the year when the disaster occurs, in a manner similar to Noy (2009). This allows disasters occurring early in the year to have a different contemporaneous impact that those that happen near the end of the year. Taking into account the date of occurrence, produces an estimate of the output cost of a disaster occurring January 1st.

Data on macroeconomic performance, fiscal stance, and other types of external shocks (used as controls in part of the analysis) come from various sources. Real GDP per-capita is measured in constant 2000 US dollars and obtained from the World Bank's (2008) World Development Indicators (WDI). The terms-of-trade index is the ratio of export prices to import prices computed using the current and constant price values of exports and imports from the national accounts component of the Penn World Tables (version 6.1) and updated using the terms-of-trade data from WDI.

Data on government expenditures and revenues came from WDI, IFS, and EIU. Data on total government debt came mainly from Panizza et al. (2008), complemented with data from WDI, IFS, and EIU. Government expenses are cash payments for goods and services incurred by the government, including wages compensation and interest payments. Revenues include receipts from taxes, social contributions, and fees, excluding grants. Data on a country's CPI and inflation rate came from WDI.

Finally, data on money market, discount, and deposit interest rates came from the International Monetary Fund's (2010) International Financial Statistics. To increase the cross-country coverage of the sample the three definitions above the interest rate series with the longest spell during the sample period were selected, with preference for the money market rates when two or more series had the same coverage. Summary statistics for these variables for the sample of countries during the period of analysis are presented in table 5A.2. To improve coverage on all macroeconomic and disaster variables, the final sample used in the econometric analysis below was restricted to the post Bretton Woods, 1975–2006 period.

Table 5A.3 takes a first look at the data by comparing within the sample, the average macroeconomic performance for years with and without disasters. The results show that expenditures grow slightly faster in years with Geological and Climatic disasters, but not significantly so. In the year of a geological disaster, expenditures grow 5.6 percent on average, compared to only 2.6 percent for the remaining years. However, both averages have wide dispersion and a two-sided test rejects the hypothesis that those two averages are identical, only at the 12 percent level. The differences are much smaller and also insignificant for climatic disasters, which result in expenditure growth of 2.7 percent, compared to 2.6 percent for the average year without a climatic disaster.

On the revenue side, revenue growth is also higher in the year of a geological disaster than in other years (4.4 versus 3.1 percent, respectively), but is lower in the year of a climatic disaster than in a normal year (2.4 versus 3.3 percent). These unconditional comparisons show only a small increase in the fiscal deficit during a disaster. However, a proper estimation of the impact of a disaster on any macroeconomic variable requires conditioning on the behavior of other variables, as well as global fluctuations in economic activity. The methodological approach outlined in section 2 takes care of that.

The Impact of Disasters on Expenditures and Output

The impulse responses that are presented in the next section summarize the response of the key variables included in the VAR (output, government expenses, and revenues) against the occurrence of a large natural disaster. As such, each one of them conveys information on the evolution of the whole system of variables after a shock, and on the full set of relations among variables. These interactions may lead to some apparently unintuitive results that are useful to discuss at this stage.

For instance, the response to a disaster of a simple system that includes only output, fiscal expenditure, and fiscal revenue, is considered. One can assume that initially the disaster leads to a decline in output, an increase in expenditure, and that revenue passively follows output. After the initial impact, the evolution of each of these variables will depend on their contemporaneous and lagged relations. In particular, in this example the sign and magnitude of the expenditure multiplier will play a crucial role. If an increase in expenditures leads to an increase in output, this multiplier effect will dampen the initial output decline resulting from the disaster. If the multiplier is large enough, output may actually end up increasing shortly after the disaster instead of declining.

Thus, in the above example, it is possible to obtain small and even positive responses of output to disasters depending on the impact of the disaster on expenditures and the relation between expenditures and output. It is also possible that a disaster will not lead to an increase in government expenditures if a government does not have the fiscal space for deficit financing. In such a case, expenditures will not react immediately to the shock but follow the declining revenues. Depending on the sign and magnitude of the fiscal multiplier, this may reinforce or dampen the response of output. Of course, if revenues do not follow output passively, the final behavior of all variables will also depend on the impact of a disaster on revenues and the relation between revenues and output and expenditures. Also, if other variables are added to the PVAR their behavior should be considered when tracing down the impact of a shock.

These simple examples highlight that one must be careful when interpreting the results of the impulse-response functions because they do not only convey isolated relations among pairs of variables. One could in principle trace down the transmission mechanism looking at the full set of IRF for each of the structural shocks. For instance, in the example above one could look at the IRF of output to an expenditure shock, to gauge the sign and significance of the multiplier and decompose the direct and indirect transmission of a disaster to output. However, as discussed above, while the assumptions for the identification of the impact of disasters and other exogenous variables are relatively uncontroversial, identifying fiscal shocks from causal ordering using annual data has many pitfalls. Thus, the impulse responses to structural shocks to endogenous variables must be taken with caution.

Results

This section presents and discusses in detail the estimated impact of natural disasters on output, fiscal expenditures, fiscal revenues, and the deficit. Other macroeconomic variables, like inflation and interest rates, are included in the estimation to control for their behavior around disasters but their response to disasters is not discussed, for reasons of space. For the baseline estimation, the annex to this chapter reports on the full set of impulse-response functions. First discussed are the baseline results for the full sample of countries included in the analysis. Then the differential responses across income levels are documented, as well as proxies for the fiscal space, and the development of the financial and insurance markets. The annex presents a detailed discussion of the impact of disasters for different regions.

Baseline Results

Figure 5A.1 shows the cumulative impulse response functions of real per capita GDP, government deficits, government expenditures, and government revenues. Since the variables are expressed in logarithms, the non-cumulative IRFs show the percentage deviation of the variable with respect to its trend level at each point in time, and the cumulative IRFs displayed show the cumulative percentage deviation of a variable at each moment. In the long-run, the cumulative IRFs show the total percentage deviation of the variable from its trend resulting from a shock.

In this and most of the analysis, government expenditures and revenues are expressed as a fraction of government deficit using the sample average shares of each deficit component. This means that the evolution of the deficit can be directly obtained by subtracting the evolution of expenditures and revenues.[4] This evolution is the one shown in the second column of graphs, because the deficit is not directly part of the model specified in equation (1). Obtaining the evolution of deficit as a fraction of GDP only requires subtracting the evolution of real GDP from the evolution of the deficit.

For the average middle- and high-income country, all three types of disasters have a significantly negative impact on GDP (figure 5A.1, first column). The cumulative output decline is about 1 percent for a climatic disaster, 7 percent for a geological disaster, and 5 percent for other disasters (the residual category). As mentioned above, the residual disaster category is qualitatively different from the other two, so the impact of these disasters must be taken with caution. Henceforth, more emphasis will be placed in the discussion, of the better-defined geological and climatic disasters.

Fiscal variables respond to disasters. The impulse responses reported in figure 5A.1 show the evolution of government expenditures and revenues as a share of the government deficit, so that the difference between these two series measures the impact of the shock on the deficit. The evolution of the deficit computed in this way is also reported in the second column of the figure. Government expenditures increase in response to climatic and geological disasters, although only the latter cumulative response reaches significance two years after the shock. On the contrary, expenditures contract strongly after a residual disaster. Revenues decline strongly after a climatic disaster (a decline corresponding to 20 percent of the deficit), but experience an insignificant increase after a geological disaster. After other types of disasters, revenues decline but not significantly.

The combination of the increase in expenditures and the decline in revenues after a climatic shock leads to an important increase in the government deficit (20 percent increase in real terms). After a geological disaster, the increases in expenditures and revenues cancel out, resulting in an insignificant movement in the level of the deficit. However, the large simultaneous decline in output implies that even in this case the deficit is increasing as a share of GDP. Somewhat surprisingly, deficits decline in real per capita terms after other types of disasters. This decline is larger than the decline in GDP, so that the deficit declines relative to GDP as well. As mentioned above, this may just reflect the heterogeneity and sparsity of the disasters included in this category.

Several of these results are similar to those obtained using a specification in differences (figure 5A.2). In this case, the responses of expenditures to climatic and geological disasters are smaller and less significant. The conclusions regarding the deficit, however, are largely unaffected: the deficit increases after a climatic disaster, fluctuates very little after a geological disaster (sometimes with the opposite sign, showing a contraction of the deficit), and is insignificant but changes sign after other disasters.

Overall, the baseline results show unambiguous GDP declines after each type of disaster, but clearer budget consequences following climatic disasters. These consequences come from an expansion of the expenditure and a decline of the revenue after these episodes. It seems that governments actively try to attenuate the impact of these disasters (possibly due to their broad geographical impact) by incurring deficit financing. Coincidentally, the output impact of climatic shocks is the smallest. Following a geological disaster, expenditures and revenues move in similar directions, resulting in a small budget adjustment.

After a typical geological disaster, fluctuations in expenses are highly correlated with fiscal revenues. Governments do not massively resort to deficit financing after a geological disaster and this seems to end in higher real consequences for these disasters. This lack of deficit financing may be due to demand factors (government choice) or because of a small fiscal space. Results below controlling for the level of initial debt and financial market development will shed more light on the merit of these two interpretations.

Robustness

There were several modeling choices made in the estimation of the baseline results. This section briefly explores the robustness of the results to these choices. The discussion above already showed that the use of a model in levels or differences does not importantly affect the results. In what follows the role of the number of lags, the measure of disasters, the measure of output, and the order of the variables in the VAR, are explored.

The results of each of these exercises, reported in figures 5A.3 to 5A.7, show that the findings discussed above are not crucially driven by these modeling choices. Adding a third lag turns positive the point estimate for the GDP impact of climatic disasters, but as in the previous case, the impact is not statistically significant (figure 5A.3). The conclusions regarding deficits, expenditures, and revenues are largely unaffected.

Two different indicators of the occurrence of disasters are used. First, a simple index that takes the value of 1 if at least one disaster of each category took place in a given year (figure 5A.4, panel A). Second, a more complex index takes into account the month when the disaster occurs, thus reporting the impact of a disaster occurring January 1st (figure 5A.4, panel B). In both cases, the output and fiscal impacts of disasters are similar to those reported in the baseline results. Similar results are also obtained when using the PWT measure of real per capita GDP that adjusts for purchasing power parity instead of the measure in constant dollars (figure 5A.5).

As explained in section 3, the baseline estimation in levels, included the changes in the (log) interest rate instead of the level of this variable because in some cases its impulse responses suggested non-stationary behavior. While this choice makes a difference for the estimated responses of this variable, it does not importantly affect the estimated responses of output and the fiscal variables to disasters, as shown in figure 5A.6.

Finally, changing the order of variables in the VAR, so that expenditures are located after output inflation, and interest rates, and just before revenues, does not change the main results either (figure 5A.7). Overall, these exercises indicate that the broad patterns documented above are robust features of the data and do not depend crucially on specific modeling choices. In what follows, the focus is only on the baseline model estimated in levels, because of its precision relative to the model in differences.

The Impact of Disasters across Income Levels

The baseline results group all middle and high-income countries together. As discussed in section 3, this increases the number of disasters included in the sample, raising the statistical power of the procedure. The cost is that assuming homogeneity in the parameters may significantly bias the estimates. A possible way of advancing, in allowing heterogeneity while retaining statistical power, is to estimate separately the model for groups of relatively homogeneous countries. One straightforward manner of grouping countries is according to their per-capita income level, which proxies for their overall level of development. The results of this exercise are reported below.

Climatic and geological disasters have a smaller output impact among high-income countries than in the whole sample (figure 5A.8, first column). Climatic disasters induce a small contemporaneous decline of a few basis points that quickly reverses and become close to zero (and insignificant) from a statistical perspective. Geological disasters have a cumulative output effect of about 3 percent (half that of the baseline) that is not significant either. The only large significant impact is that of other disasters. However, as shown in table 5A.1, there are very few and concentrated episodes of Geological and Other disasters among high-income countries. The only country in this group that has experienced large geological disasters is Greece, on three occasions, and the only country affected by other disasters is Barbados. Only for climatic disasters is there enough statistical variation for identification (27 disasters spread across several countries).

Thus, the results for Geological and Other disasters in this group of countries are unlikely to be reliable and therefore what follows, focuses on Climatic disasters. On the fiscal side, both expenditures and revenues increase after a climatic disaster (annex table 5A.1, columns (3) and (4)). This comovement results in insignificant impacts on the budget deficit. This suggests that high-income countries increase their expenditures and revenues in response to such disasters. They can mitigate the impact of these shocks without going into deficit financing, presumably due to a positive multiplier effect of public expenditures.

The situation is different for middle-income countries (figure 5A.9). The output impact of disasters is much larger in this group, with a cumulative output decline of about

1.5 percent for climatic disasters and about 7 percent for Geological disasters. Contrary to high-income countries, in this (larger) group of countries there are many episodes of disasters across several countries, so the results are not driven by a single country or a cluster of episodes.

On the fiscal side, disasters are typically associated with increases in expenditures. These increases reach about 10 and 50 percent of the average budget deficit after a climatic and geological disaster, respectively. On the revenue side, there are important differences between climatic and geological disasters. While revenues decline by about 30 percent of the deficit after a climatic disaster, they increase by a similar magnitude after a geological disaster. As a result, the cumulative budget deficit increases by about 20 percent following a climatic or geological disaster, but only after a climatic disaster is this increase statistically significant. Of course, given the decline in output, the cumulative deficit increase as a fraction of GDP would be higher.

Overall, governments in middle-income countries react to disasters by increasing expenditures and relying on deficit financing, thus increasing their overall debt levels. However, despite these attempts, the disasters still result in important output costs that further reduce their ability to service debt, presumably due to a small fiscal multiplier and a larger direct impact of disasters on economic activity.

In the sample used, the group of middle-income countries encompasses 73 countries. It is thus possible that the group is still too heterogeneous and that the responses discussed above may be contaminated by this heterogeneity. To further check for this possibility, this group was separated into two sub-groups of lower- and higher-middle-income countries, again following the World Bank's classification. The results are reported in figures 5A.10 and 5A.11.

Lower-middle-income countries are shown to be much more heavily affected by disasters than higher-middle-income ones. In the former group, a climatic disaster results in a 4 percent cumulative output decline, while in the latter it leads to a similar output increase. Similarly, geological disasters lead to an 11 percent cumulative output decline among lower-middle-income countries and to a negligible decline among higher middle-income countries. The small decline in higher-middle-income countries following a geological disaster is not very robust and when looking at the specification in differences there is a similar decline to that for lower-middle-income countries. However, the increase following a climatic disaster in higher-middle-income countries persists across specifications and is unlikely to be driven by specific episodes because there are 77 episodes of climatic disasters among the 28 countries in this group.

Although it may initially look contradictory, it is worth reminding that from a theoretical point of view, the impact of a disaster on economic activity is ambiguous. A disaster may destroy capital and other factors of production reducing the amount of output that can be produced with a given amount of labor. However, it also makes people intertemporally poorer, increasing the incentives to work through a standard wealth effect. The final response of output depends on which of these effects dominate. Thus, one possible interpretation of these findings is that, among higher-middle-income countries the wealth effect associated with a disaster dominates the factor destruction effect, leading to a slowly accumulating increase in output.

On the fiscal side, there are completely opposite responses to disasters between these two groups of middle-income countries. Lower-middle-income countries reduce (increase) expenditure and revenue after a climatic (geological) disaster. Higher-middle-income countries follow the exactly opposite pattern for climatic disasters. However, these different patterns yield more similar results for the behavior of the budget deficit. In both groups of countries, the deficit increases after a climatic disaster, although the increase is larger and more significant among lower-middle income ones (30 percent versus 20 percent). The increase in the deficit after a geological disaster is not significant in both cases, although the point estimate is also considerably higher among lower-middle-income countries (50 percent increase versus 10 percent decline).

Overall, these results suggest that most of the previous conclusions regarding middle-income countries are driven by the behavior of lower-middle income ones. Among these countries, governments react to disasters by engaging in deficit financing and increasing debt, but are still more affected by the disasters on the real side, further reducing their ability to repay. This coincides with the common observation that relatively poorer countries have lower capacity to efficiently and effectively execute government expenditures.

Of course, another possibility is that the direct output impact of disasters could be higher among these countries. For instance, a smaller stock of capital in lower-middle-income countries could be associated with a higher marginal product of capital, so the output losses associated with a decline in the capital stock would be higher. Another possibility is that the wealth effects that push for an increase in output after a disaster are smaller among these countries.

Indebtedness and the Effect of a Country's Response to Disasters

The previous results suggest that middle-income countries, especially the poorer ones engage in deficit financing after a disaster without being able to mitigate the impact of these events on the real side of the economy. However, even the ability to engage in deficit financing of expenditure will likely depend on a country's debt level, its access to domestic or international debt markets, and the ability to raise revenues through taxation. In this section some insights are shed on the role of initial debt on a country's ability to engage in deficit financing, by comparing the output and fiscal response to disasters of countries with different initial levels of total government debt.

Despite government debt being an important macroeconomic variable, data on total debt levels is relatively scarce and available for few countries in recent years. Thus, looking at the role of debt severely reduces the sample of countries under consideration. With this caveat in mind, the results of this exercise are reported in figure 5A.12.

Contrary to expectations, countries with high levels of initial debt (panel B) do not suffer more from disasters than those with low levels of debt (panel A). Climatic shocks induce similar output declines in the two groups, and Geological disasters have larger impact on countries with lower initial debt levels (panel A). Also, despite similar declines in revenue after a climatic disaster, countries with higher initial levels of debt expand government expenditures relatively more and run higher increases in the deficit. Only for Geological Disasters there is a larger deficit increase among countries with lower debt levels, but this larger increase is associated with a larger decline in revenue relative to countries with higher debt levels. At least in this sample, it seems that initial debt levels do not constrain a government's fiscal space. This apparent paradox is partly explained by the composition of countries in the sample with high and low debt levels.

There are many more high-income countries among those with high initial debt levels than among those with low initial debt levels. Also, among upper middle-income countries, those with higher initial debt levels have higher income per capita than those with lower debt. The average GDP per capita (PPP adjusted) among countries with high debt is about US$9,900 but only US$8,600 dollars for countries with lower initial debt. In this sample, governments of relatively richer countries have enjoyed better access to debt. This access seems to be serially correlated, so that good access in the past, signals good access in the future rather than a reduced fiscal space.

To check to what extent these differences are driven by income levels an estimation was made of a variation of the model described in equation (1), that, instead of splitting the sample in two groups, allows the impact of external shocks to vary parametrically with the initial level of debt and a country's level of income. This means that the B_j matrices in equation (1), and the block of the A_j matrices associated with the terms-of-trade fluctuations will vary with the levels of debt and income.

After estimating this model, it is possible to construct the IRFs for countries with high and low levels of debt controlling for differences in income. Figure 5A.13 reports these IRFs. Each of the panels in the figure reports the impact of a type of disaster on output and fiscal variables for hypothetical countries with low and high debt levels (25th and 75th percentile of the debt to GDP ratios across sample countries), along their one standard deviation confidence bands. These figures show that the patterns documented above survive controlling for differences in average income levels.

Countries with higher initial debt levels experience a smaller decline in GDP after a geological disaster, a larger expansion of government expenditures and a smaller contraction of revenues after all types of disasters. In sum, the hypothesis that high initial debt levels are proxying for better access to funds in this sample, is not rejected by controlling for differences in average GDP per capita.

Financial Development and Insurance Penetration

A disaster typically affects a country's productive capacity by destroying physical and human capital. Replacing that capital is costly and may take time (especially in the case of damages to infrastructure). While there is no way around the time required to rebuild capital and infrastructure; and human capital lost may never be replaced; having quick access to financial resources will certainly reduce the time it takes to reconstruct a country's productive capacity.

Even though governments may try to provide relief and resources for this reconstruction, a large part of it will likely come from market sources. Therefore, having a well-developed financial system that can finance the reconstruction ex post or that can gather and price the risks ex-ante through insurance schemes, may substantially reduce the need for government financing in the aftermath of a disaster, and make government spending more productive.[5]

Next, the relation between financial and insurance market development is observed, as well as the consequences of disasters in relation to government financing and output (GDP), by grouping countries according to the development of these markets and comparing the impact of disasters across these groups. To maintain as many observations and disasters as possible in each group, the sample between countries is first divided among those with measures of financial development and insurance penetration above and below the sample median respectively.

The analysis shows that climatic and geological shocks have a large negative output impact on countries with low levels of financial development, as measured by the average ratio of private credit to GDP from 1975 to 2008 (figure 5A.14). Among these countries, a climatic shock results in a cumulative output decline of almost 2 percent, and a geological disaster results in a decline of about 9 percent. In contrast, among more financially developed countries a climatic disaster has rather positive impact on output while a geological disaster has no impact on output.[6]

Government expenditure does not increase after climatic disasters in financially underdeveloped countries, but a large significant increase of 60 percent of the average budget deficit occurs among more financially developed ones (figure 5A.14, panel B, column 3). The latter occurs despite an important contraction of revenue of about 30 percent of the average deficit. As a result, the budget deficit increases importantly in financially developed countries, and only modestly and not significantly among financially underdeveloped ones.

Controlling for income does not change the conclusions. The comparison of the responses to disasters of GDP and fiscal variables in countries with high and low levels of financial development (figure 5A.15) (25th and 75th sample percentiles, respectively) confirms that more financially developed countries suffer smaller output contractions after disasters, although the differences are not significant. The figure also confirms that expenditures always expand in financially developed countries, and revenues expand after geological disasters and contracts after climatic disasters. As before, deficits always increase relatively more in financially developed countries.

These results indicate that governments can borrow more easily in financially developed countries, and that the real consequences of shocks, at least for the more frequent climatic ones, are smaller. This is consistent with the financial system facilitating resources both for government financing (for example, by allowing the issuance of domestic debt) and for private reconstruction. Having access to the resources, which can be mobilized by an efficient financial system, helps dealing with disasters. This is confirmed by unreported results that interest rates also decline in financially developed countries following a climatic shock (while they remain unaltered among financially underdeveloped countries), and suggests that the larger deficit expansion in these countries does not necessarily lead to a larger increase in government debt burdens or concerns about an excessive debt burden that would significantly increase the interest rate risk premium for the governments.

The results are different when countries are compared according to the degree of insurance penetration, as measured by the total value of premiums to GDP (figure 5A.16). It is important to keep in mind that data on insurance penetration is not widely available, so the subset of countries with data is biased toward higher income countries. Thus, the important aspect of this exercise is the comparison between the two groups rather than the estimated responses for each individual group. Comparing the real consequences of shocks, countries with relatively low insurance penetration (panel A) suffer larger output declines in response to climatic and geological disasters than countries with high insurance penetration (panel B). At the same time, deficits increase considerably more in countries with low insurance penetration. In countries with high insurance penetration, expenditures and revenues move together resulting in a small change in the fiscal deficit.

Most of these patterns survive controlling for differences in income (figure 5A.17). Countries with low insurance penetration suffer significantly more after disasters (first column) and expand expenses relatively more (although this difference is not significant). The only difference is that while revenues decline relatively more for countries with low insurance penetration, they move similarly in both groups after a geological disaster. As a result, deficits increase relatively more after a climatic disaster for countries with low insurance penetration, but increase relatively less after a geological disaster. Nonetheless, when computed as a fraction of GDP, deficits always increase relatively more for countries with low insurance penetration.

Overall, countries with low insurance penetration expand their government deficits after disasters but do not manage to reduce the negative consequences of disasters as much as in those countries with high insurance penetration. One likely interpretation of these findings is that countries with high insurance penetration quickly allocate the resources from existing insurance coverage to recover productive capacity, and little fiscal effort is required to dampen the macro consequences of these events. Fiscal resources can then be devoted to relief, and the simultaneous increase in expenditures and revenues suggests that the fiscal effort is mainly redistributive (for example, providing relief to those affected by increasing revenues from those not affected by the disaster).

Finally, a comparison of these results with those obtained when comparing countries with different levels of financial development show that these two dimensions play different roles in the transmission of disasters to the fiscal purse. While countries with high financial development or high insurance penetration suffer relatively less from disasters in terms of output decline, a developed financial system allows governments to borrow and finance a deficit possibly at low interest rates to reduce the real consequences of disasters.

In contrast, countries with high levels of insurance penetration can deal with these real macro consequences without engaging in deficit financing of the expenditures. It seems, therefore, that while overall financial development helps deal with disasters, the prevalence of insurance does it in a more efficient ex post manner. Of course, insurance has an ex-ante cost that must be considered for welfare comparisons, another dimension to consider and as discussed earlier in chapter 1.

Conclusion

This chapter estimated the implications of natural disasters for public finances by analyzing the cumulative responses of government expenditures, revenues, and fiscal deficit to disaster shocks. The analysis found that climatic, geological, and other disasters have an important negative impact on the fiscal stance by decreasing output and increasing deficits, especially in lower middle-income countries.

When controlling for income, there is no clear relation between initial debt and the fiscal impact of disasters. In the sample used, countries that were more indebted seem to be those with better access to debt, so that debt levels proxy for better access to capital markets rather than constrained fiscal space. Furthermore, countries with more developed financial or insurance markets suffered less from disasters in terms of output declines. The way this was achieved differed in each case, however. In financially developed markets, governments are able to raise funds and increase deficits. And presumably this response helps alleviate the impact of the disasters. In contrast, in countries with high insurance penetration, the smaller impact of disasters on GDP occurs without an important fiscal expansion.

Countries with smaller insurance markets expand deficits more, and still suffer more from disasters. Thus, it seems that the availability of insurance reduces the real consequences without requiring an increase in fiscal burdens. By extending the implication of this finding, financial markets and development institutions could help in the development and more in depth use of fiscal insurance policies or hedging instruments to further diminish disaster consequences. The future research could focus on better identification of the fiscal responses to disasters and the implied consequences for fiscal stances, by employing higher frequency (quarterly) data and increasing the homogeneity of countries in the analyzed sample. This could exploit the potential efficiency gains through the use of appropriate estimation methods.

Notes

1. These types of models use the cross-country dimension of the data to increase the power of the estimation of time series models, and have been routinely used when short time series data is available, as it is the case in this paper.

2. This analysis also characterizes the different responses across regions in additional results.

3. Perotti (2007) puts forth two essential features of fiscal space that are used in the discussions henceforth. First, fiscal pace is determined by the inter-temporal government budget constraint and some notion of fiscal sustainability. This means that in order to increase some type of government expenditures at present one needs to either reduce other expenditures now or in the future, or increase current or future revenues or inflate away existing nominal debt. The ability to increase debt levels in a sustainable manner is thus consistent with having fiscal space available. Second, if one type of expenditure has a higher social marginal return than another and the same cost, resources should be moved from the second to the first type of expenditure.

4. By definition, the deficit is the difference between expenditures and revenues: . Log-linearizing this expression, the log deviations of deficit correspond to , where and are the shares of expenditures and revenues on deficit: and the lowercase letters with hats represent the log deviation of a variable with respect to its trend.

5. For instance, this may happen by allowing the government to focus on relief and public good provision instead of providing subsidized credits for the private sector.

6. This result is not robust to changes in the variable used for interest rates. When using only the money market rates (with the corresponding reduction in the sample), there is a decline in output as a result of a geological disaster, and only a small impact for climatic disasters.

Annex: Impact of Disasters for Different Regions

Table 5A.1. Summary Statistics

Country	Mean				Number of Events			Number of Observations
	GDP per capita	Expenditures/ GDP	Revenues/ GDP	Deficit/ GDP	Geological	Climatic	Other	
East Asia Pacific and South Asia								
China	901	0.156	0.144	-0.011	2	65	0	22
Fiji	1,803	0.285	0.244	-0.042	0	17	0	24
Indonesia	640	0.192	0.185	-0.007	2	1	3	30
Korea, Rep. of	5,704	0.162	0.175	0.013	0	1	0	23
Malaysia	2,545	0.291	0.243	-0.048	0	0	0	25
Philippines	942	0.166	0.153	-0.014	2	58	0	29
Sri Lanka	568	0.297	0.197	-0.100	0	29	0	26
Thailand	1,404	0.168	0.161	-0.007	0	20	0	27
Total	**1,734**	**0.214**	**0.187**	**-0.027**	**6**	**191**	**3**	**206**
Europe and Central Asia								
Albania	1,303	0.303	0.232	-0.071	0	3	0	14
Azerbaijan	933	0.261	0.217	-0.044	1	4	0	15
Belarus	1,462	0.293	0.322	0.028	0	1	0	16
Bulgaria	1,754	0.351	0.349	-0.002	0	2	0	17
Croatia	5,171	0.363	0.361	-0.001	0	3	0	13
Czech Republic	5,827	0.341	0.317	-0.024	0	2	0	14
Georgia	842	0.250	0.208	-0.042	1	3	0	12
Hungary	4,399	0.499	0.456	-0.043	0	3	0	26
Kazakhstan	1,402	0.238	0.222	-0.016	0	1	0	13
Latvia	3,741	0.373	0.359	-0.014	0	1	0	14

(Table continues on next page)

Table 5A.1 (continued)

Country	Mean				Number of Events			Number of Observations
	GDP per capita	Expenditures/ GDP	Revenues/ GDP	Deficit/ GDP	Geological	Climatic	Other	
Lithuania	3,814	0.346	0.317	-0.030	0	1	0	13
Macedonia, FYR	1,775	0.372	0.360	-0.012	0	2	1	15
Moldova	410	0.318	0.307	-0.011	0	3	0	12
Poland	4,034	0.334	0.301	-0.034	0	1	0	17
Romania	1,705	0.324	0.286	-0.038	0	2	0	7
Russian Federation	2,101	0.169	0.183	0.014	0	1	0	13
Slovak Republic	4,222	0.438	0.380	-0.058	0	2	0	12
Slovenia	10,388	0.471	0.462	-0.009	0	2	0	13
Turkey	3,559	0.237	0.175	-0.062	3	2	0	15
Ukraine	795	0.334	0.309	-0.025	0	3	0	15
Total	**3,039**	**0.338**	**0.313**	**-0.025**	**5**	**42**	**1**	**286**
Western Europe and North America								
Austria	17,636	0.372	0.333	-0.039	0	0	0	22
Belgium	17,256	0.493	0.429	-0.064	0	0	0	24
Denmark	23,307	0.381	0.368	-0.013	0	2	0	26
France	20,372	0.521	0.490	-0.032	0	2	0	25
Greece	9,497	0.289	0.201	-0.088	3	2	0	22
Luxembourg	29,981	0.407	0.431	0.024	0	4	0	17
Netherlands	20,934	0.513	0.487	-0.026	0	1	0	25
Portugal	7,939	0.406	0.301	-0.105	0	0	0	19
Sweden	23,397	0.371	0.355	-0.016	0	1	0	32
United States	29,635	0.205	0.180	-0.025	0	3	0	27
Total	**20,331**	**0.394**	**0.357**	**-0.037**	**3**	**15**	**0**	**239**

(Table continues on next page)

Table 5A.1 (continued)

Country	Mean				Number of Events			Number of Observations
	GDP per capita	Expenditures/ GDP	Revenues/ GDP	Deficit/ GDP	Geological	Climatic	Other	
Middle East, North Africa, and Sub-Saharan Africa								
Algeria	1,783	0.311	0.308	-0.003	0	1	0	17
Botswana	2,575	0.395	0.462	0.067	0	9	2	29
Cameroon	721	0.174	0.186	0.012	1	2	0	28
Cape Verde	1,280	0.365	0.301	-0.064	0	2	1	13
Egypt, Arab Rep.	1,099	0.376	0.342	-0.034	1	0	0	28
Iran, Islamic Rep.	2,025	0.455	0.410	-0.045	2	0	0	5
Israel	16,212	0.523	0.425	-0.097	0	1	0	19
Jordan	1,748	0.368	0.240	-0.128	0	4	0	27
Lebanon	3,707	0.294	0.116	-0.178	0	1	0	5
Lesotho	383	0.437	0.443	0.006	0	6	0	16
Mauritius	2,849	0.237	0.211	-0.025	0	6	1	26
Morocco	1,191	0.320	0.251	-0.069	1	3	0	22
Namibia	2,508	0.299	0.298	-0.002	0	5	0	6
Seychelles	6,106	0.538	0.473	-0.065	1	1	0	19
South Africa	3,218	0.267	0.237	-0.031	0	6	1	29
Swaziland	1,079	0.281	0.276	-0.005	0	12	0	27
Syrian Arab Republic	1,042	0.314	0.253	-0.061	0	1	0	21
Tunisia	1,595	0.340	0.309	-0.031	0	1	0	16
Total	**2,747**	**0.340**	**0.306**	**-0.034**	**6**	**61**	**5**	**354**

(Table continues on next page)

Table 5A.1 (continued)

Country	Mean				Number of Events			Number of Observations
	GDP per capita	Expenditures/ GDP	Revenues/ GDP	Deficit/ GDP	Geological	Climatic	Other	
Latin America and Caribbean								
Argentina	7,692	0.204	0.200	−0.004	0	3	0	15
Bahamas, The	15,611	0.188	0.174	−0.014	0	5	0	15
Barbados	8,304	0.320	0.285	−0.035	0	3	1	25
Belize	2,844	0.293	0.244	−0.049	0	7	0	25
Bolivia	1,039	0.255	0.165	−0.090	0	10	0	19
Brazil	3,408	0.276	0.264	−0.012	0	4	0	16
Chile	3,271	0.246	0.249	0.003	2	7	0	23
Colombia	2,393	0.277	0.263	−0.014	3	7	0	24
Costa Rica	3,281	0.163	0.134	−0.029	2	8	0	28
Dominican Republic	2,502	0.130	0.130	0.000	0	3	0	14
El Salvador	2,326	0.181	0.160	−0.021	2	4	1	10
Grenada	2,998	0.294	0.263	−0.031	0	0	0	5
Guatemala	1,607	0.120	0.100	−0.020	0	6	0	30
Guyana	882	0.412	0.346	−0.066	0	2	1	3
Honduras	1,121	0.210	0.164	−0.046	0	17	0	24
Jamaica	3,487	0.260	0.254	−0.006	0	1	0	11
Mexico	5,424	0.258	0.229	−0.029	1	8	1	29

(Table continues on next page)

Table 5A.1 (continued)

Country	Mean				Number of Events			Number of Observations
	GDP per capita	Expenditures/ GDP	Revenues/ GDP	Deficit/ GDP	Geological	Climatic	Other	
Nicaragua	805	0.227	0.164	−0.063	0	1	0	7
Panama	3,395	0.237	0.236	−0.001	1	2	0	14
Paraguay	1,415	0.159	0.157	−0.002	0	4	0	13
Peru	2,077	0.176	0.143	−0.033	1	11	2	32
St. Lucia	2,620	0.270	0.245	−0.025	0	2	0	10
St. Vincent and the Grenadines	2,264	0.330	0.286	−0.043	0	2	0	21
Uruguay	5,929	0.263	0.244	−0.019	0	3	0	29
Venezuela, RB	5,320	0.221	0.234	0.013	0	1	0	27
Total	**3,840**	**0.231**	**0.207**	**−0.024**	**12**	**121**	**6**	**469**

Note: The table provides descriptive statistics for each country, grouped by regions. Mean values are reported for real GDP per capita, and for government expenditures, government revenue and government deficit as a fraction of the GDP. The number of events by type of disaster, and the number of observations are also listed.

Table 5A.2. Unit Root and Cointegration Tests

Panel A. Unit root tests

Variable	Levels			Differences		
	LLC test (1)	IPS test (2)	Frac. Reject (ADF) (3)	LLC test (4)	IPS test (5)	Frac. Reject (ADF) (6)
GDP per capita	−19.3	−9.2	0.3	−37.0	−27.5	0.8
Government Expenditures	−3.7	−2.3	0.2	−31.7	−29.9	0.8
Government Revenues	−5.6	−3.9	0.2	−26.1	−27.6	0.8
Inflation	−52.2	−28.7	0.6	n.a.	n.a.	n.a.
Interest Rate	−4.6	−2.5	0.2	−50.8	−33.4	0.9
Terms of Trade	−6.9	−5.2	0.3	−39.4	−39.4	1.0

Panel B. Panel cointegration tests

VAR including TT, GEXP, GDP, GREV, INF, and R

Alt. hypothesis: common AR coefs.

	Statistic	Prob.
Panel v-Statistic	−0.72	0.76
Panel rho-Statistic	11.54	1.00
Panel PP-Statistic	−0.19	0.42
Panel ADF-Statistic	−1.50	0.07

Alt. hypothesis: individual AR coefs.

	Statistic	Prob.
Group rho-Statistic	14.97	1.00
Group PP-Statistic	-3.64	0.00
Group ADF-Statistic	-3.97	0.00

Note: Panel A shows the results of country-by-country and panel unit root tests performed for the main series used in the paper. Columns (1) to (3) show results for the variables in levels, and columns (4) to (6) for the variables in differences. The exception is inflation, which being the changes in the price level, is just included in levels. Columns (1) and (4) show the results of the Levin-Lin Chu panel unit root test, and Columns (2) and (5) the statistics for the Im, Pesaran, and Shin test. Columns (3) and (6) report the fraction of countries in the sample in which a standard, country-by-country augmented Dickey Fuller test could not reject the null hypothesis of a unit root. All the tests in level allow for a country-specific intercept and trend, and those in differences for the country-specific intercept only. Also, all tests use the Newey-West bandwidth selection with the Bartlett kernel for the estimation of the long run variance of the series. The table in Panel B reports the statistic and associated p-value of the different variants of Pedroni's (1999) panel cointegration test. The null hypothesis in each case is no cointegration. n.a. = not available.

Table 5A.3. Comparing Years With and Without Disasters: Two Sample Mean Tests

	GDP Growth		Expenditures Growth		Revenues Growth	
	Geological	Climatic	Geological	Climatic	Geological	Climatic
Mean						
No Disaster	0.026	0.026	0.026	0.025	0.033	0.034
Disaster	0.013	0.024	0.036	0.027	0.014	0.028
t-stat						
D = ND	0.141	0.569	0.638	0.779	0.636	0.670
ND > D	0.071	0.285	0.681	0.610	0.318	0.335
ND < D	0.929	0.715	0.319	0.390	0.682	0.665

Note: The table shows the t-test for the difference on the average growth of GDP, Expenditures and Revenues, in years when a disaster occurs (Disaster), and in years without disasters (No Disaster). D is the mean of the sample with at least one disaster, and ND is from the sample with zero disasters.

Figure 5A.1. Cumulative Impulse Response Functions of Levels

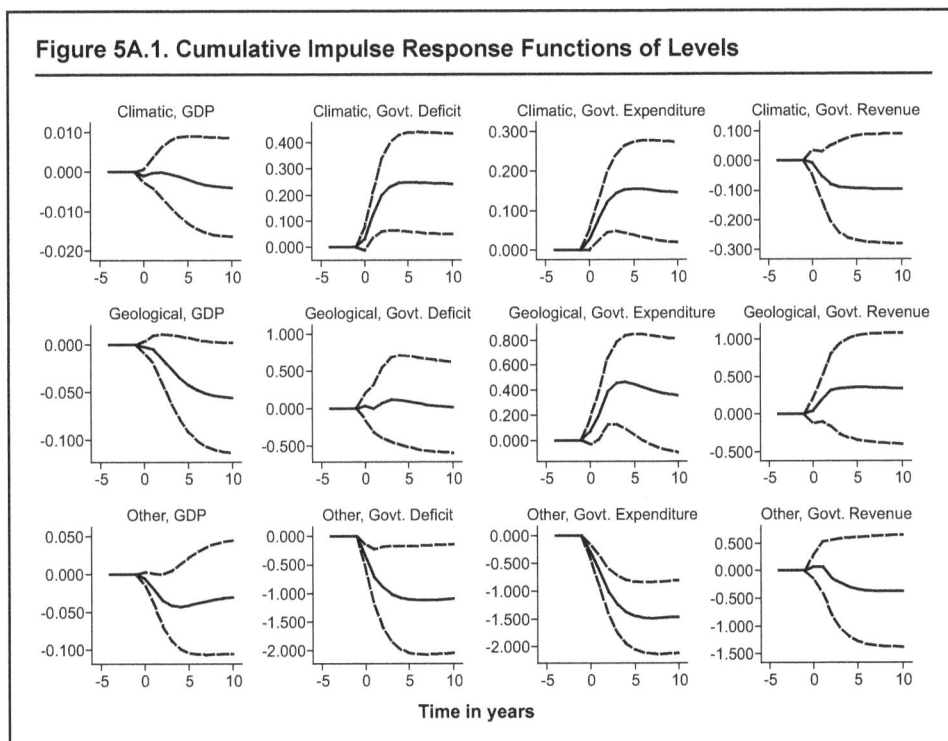

Note: The figure shows the cumulative impulse response functions (IRF) for GDP, government deficit, government expenditures, and government revenues. GDP and government deficit are expressed in real per capita terms; government expenditures and revenues are expressed as fractions of the long run government deficit. The parameters used to estimate the IRF come from the baseline specification with all variables expressed in levels (except the interest rate), and including two lags. The order of the endogenous variables entered in the VAR is the following: government expenditures, GDP, inflation, interest rate, and government revenues. The model also includes country specific means and trends, and with time fixed effects that capture global variables. The government deficit is obtained as the weighted difference of revenues and expenditures. The solid lines show the cumulative percentage deviation of each variable from its trend resulting from a climatic, geological or other natural disasters occurred at time 0 (time in years). The dotted lines show one standard deviation confidence bands.

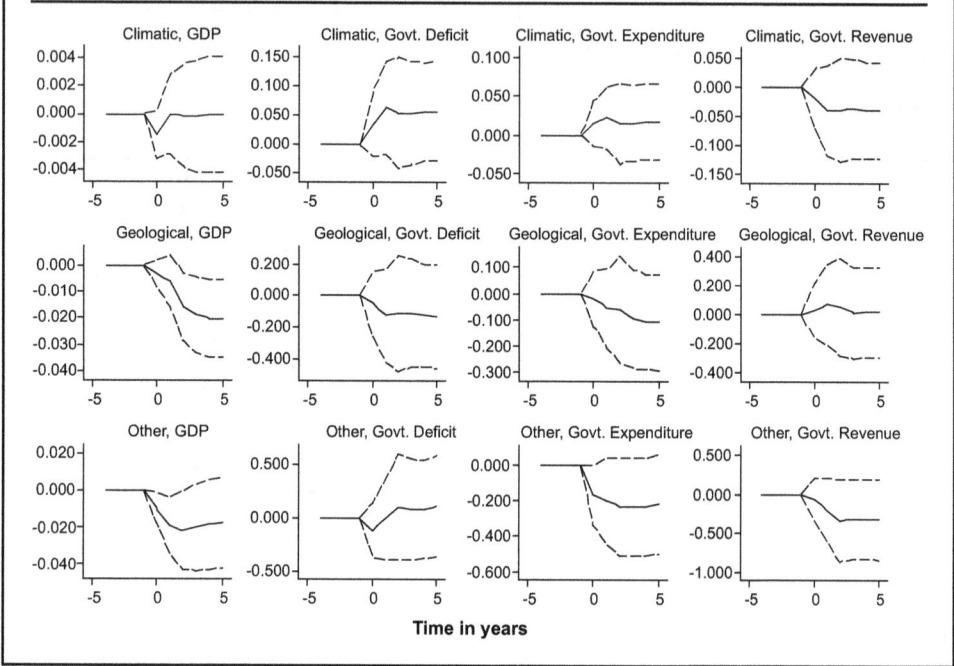

Figure 5A.2. Cumulative Impulse Response Functions of Differences

Note: The figure shows the cumulative impulse response functions (IRF) for GDP, government deficit, government expenditures, and government revenues. GDP and government deficit are expressed in real per capita terms; government expenditures and revenues are expressed as fractions of the long run government deficit. The parameters used to estimate the IRF come from a specification with all variables in differences, and including two lags. The order of the endogenous variables entered in the VAR is the following: government expenditures, GDP, inflation, interest rate, and government revenues. The model also includes time fixed effects that capture global variables. The government deficit is obtained as the weighted difference of revenues and expenditures. The solid lines show the cumulative percentage deviation of each variable from its trend resulting from a climatic, geological or other natural disasters occurred at time 0 (time in years). The dotted lines show one standard deviation confidence bands.

Figure 5A.3. Cumulative IRFs Adding Lags

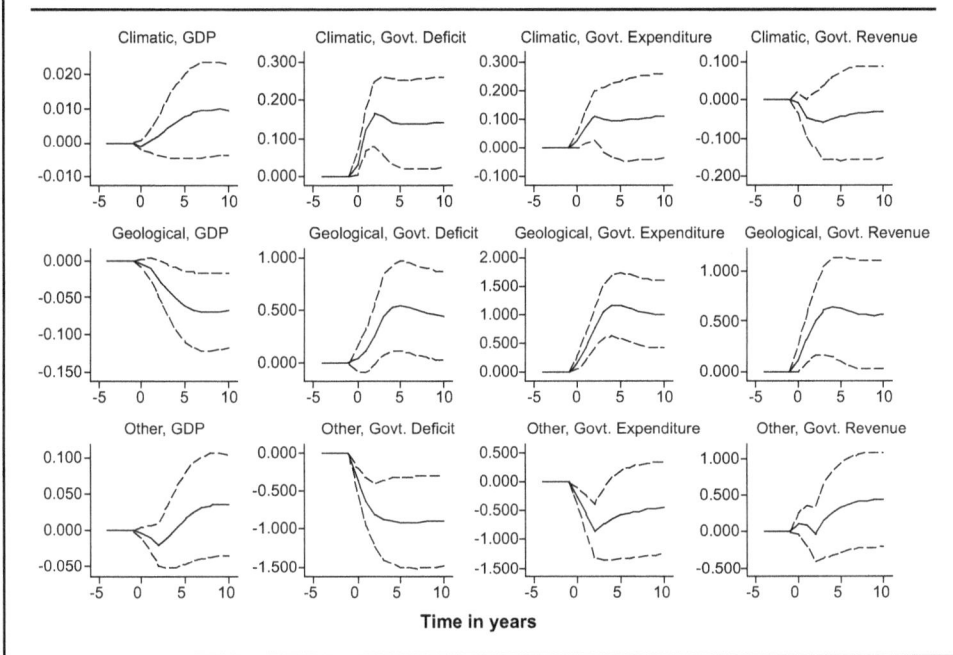

Note: The figure shows the cumulative impulse response functions (IRF) for GDP, government deficit, government expenditures, and government revenues. GDP and government deficit are expressed in real per capita terms; government expenditures and revenues are expressed as fractions of the long run government deficit. The parameters used to estimate the IRF come from the baseline specification with all variables expressed in levels (except the interest rate), and including three lags. The order of the endogenous variables entered in the VAR is the following: government expenditures, GDP, inflation, interest rate, and government revenues. The model also includes country specific means and trends, and with time fixed effects that capture global variables. The government deficit is obtained as the weighted difference of revenues and expenditures. The solid lines show the cumulative percentage deviation of each variable from its trend resulting from a climatic, geological or other natural disasters occurred at time 0 (time in years). The dotted lines show one standard deviation confidence bands.

Figure 5A.4. Cumulative IFRs Using Different Disaster Indicators

Panel A. Index by Category of Disaster

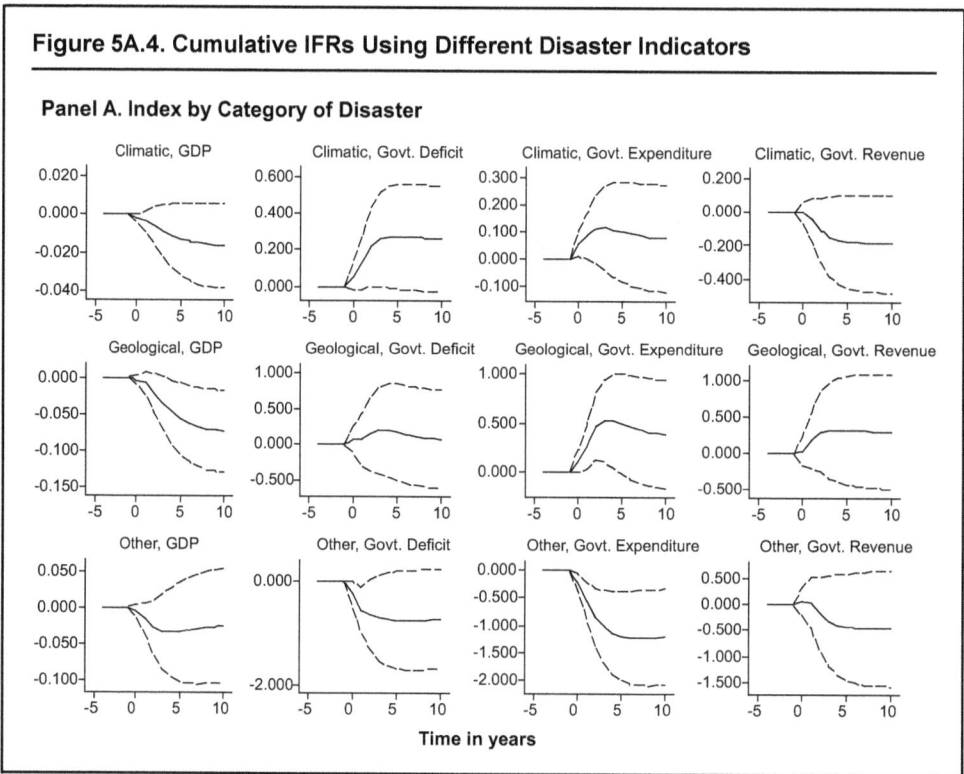

Time in years

(Figure continues on next page)

Figure 5A.4 *(continued)*

Panel B. Index Considering the Timing of the Disaster

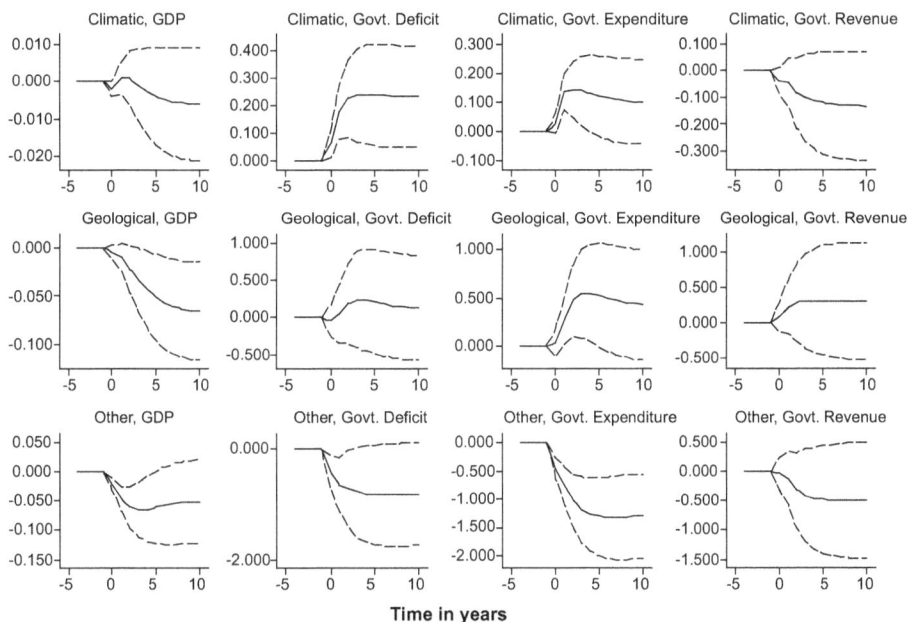

Time in years

Note: The figures show the cumulative impulse response functions (IRF) for GDP, government deficit, government expenditures, and government revenues. GDP and government deficit are expressed in real per capita terms; government expenditures and revenues are expressed as fractions of the long run government deficit. The parameters used to estimate the IRF come from the baseline specification with all variables expressed in levels (except the interest rate), and including two lags. The order of the endogenous variables entered in the VAR is the following: government expenditures, GDP, inflation, interest rate, and government revenues. The model also includes country specific means and trends, and with time fixed effects that capture global variables. The government deficit is obtained as the weighted difference of revenues and expenditures. In Panel A, the index used to show the occurrence of disasters takes the value 1 if at least one disaster of each category took place in a given year. In Panel B, this index takes into account the month when the disaster occurs. The solid lines show the cumulative percentage deviation of each variable from its trend resulting from a climatic, geological or other natural disasters occurred at time 0 (time in years). The dotted lines show one standard deviation confidence bands.

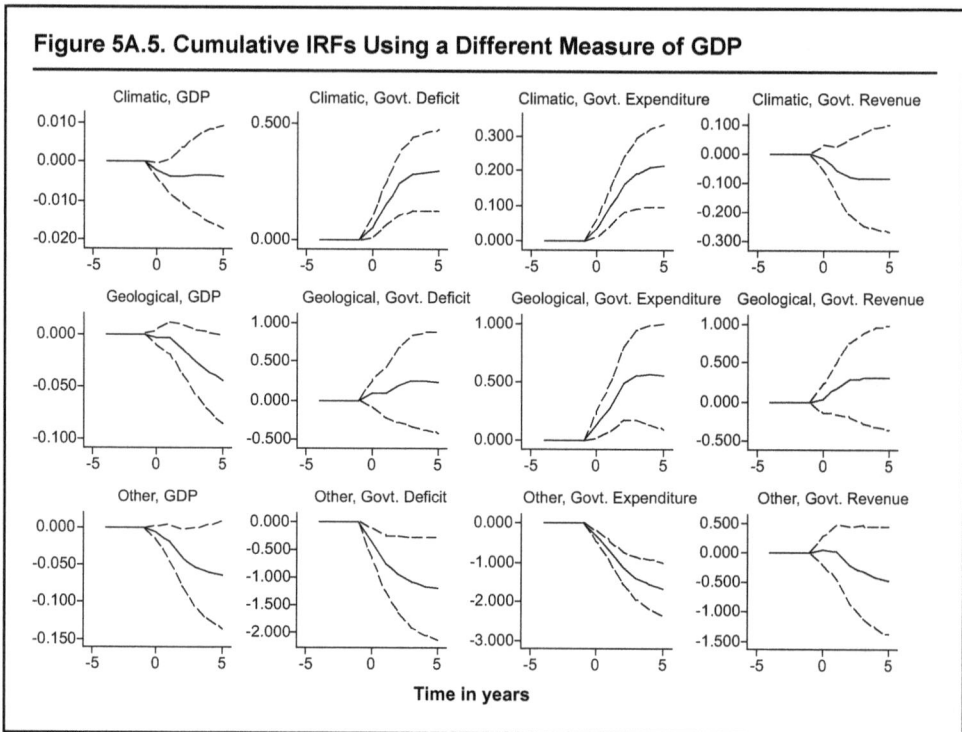

Figure 5A.5. Cumulative IRFs Using a Different Measure of GDP

Note: The figure shows the cumulative impulse response functions (IRF) for GDP, government deficit, government expenditures, and government revenues. GDP is expressed in real per capita terms and adjusted for purchasing power parity; government deficit is reported in real per capita terms; government expenditures and revenues are expressed as fractions of the long run government deficit. The parameters used to estimate the IRF come from the baseline specification with all variables expressed in levels (except the interest rate), and including two lags. The order of the endogenous variables entered in the VAR is the following: government expenditures, GDP, inflation, interest rate, and government revenues. The model also includes country specific means and trends, and with time fixed effects that capture global variables. The government deficit is obtained as the weighted difference of revenues and expenditures. The solid lines show the cumulative percentage deviation of each variable from its trend resulting from a climatic, geological or other natural disasters occurred at time 0 (time in years). The dotted lines show one standard deviation confidence bands.

Figure 5A.6. Cumulative IRFs Using Interest Rate Level

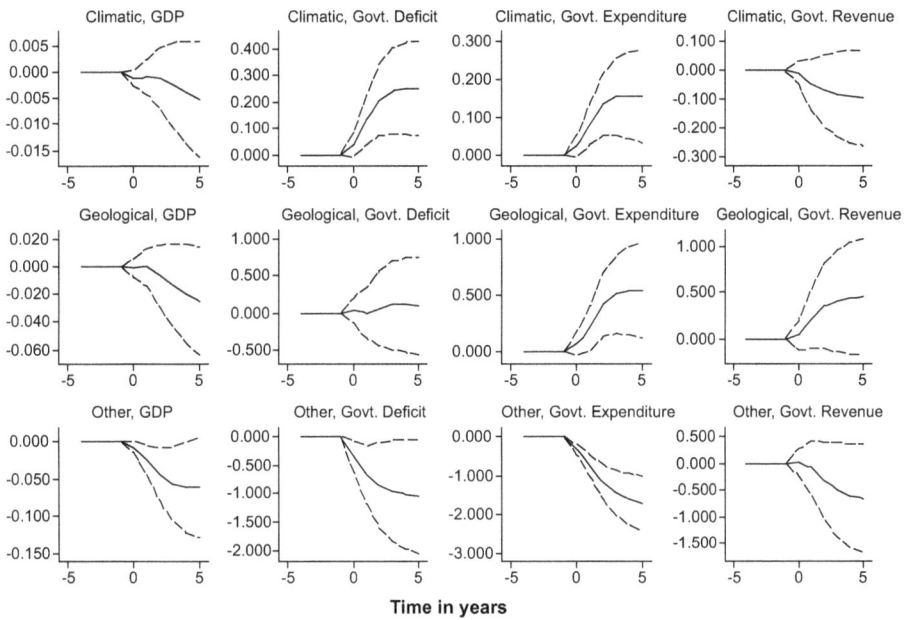

Note: The figure shows the cumulative impulse response functions (IRF) for GDP, government deficit, government expenditures, and government revenues. GDP and government deficit are expressed in real per capita terms; government expenditures and revenues are expressed as fractions of the long run government deficit. The parameters used to estimate the IRF come from the baseline specification with all variables expressed in levels, and including two lags. The order of the endogenous variables entered in the VAR is the following: government expenditures, GDP, inflation, interest rate, and government revenues. The model also includes country specific means and trends, and with time fixed effects that capture global variables. The government deficit is obtained as the weighted difference of revenues and expenditures. The solid lines show the cumulative percentage deviation of each variable from its trend resulting from a climatic, geological or other natural disasters occurred at time 0 (time in years). The dotted lines show one standard deviation confidence bands.

Figure 5A.7. Cumulative IRFs Changing Order in VAR

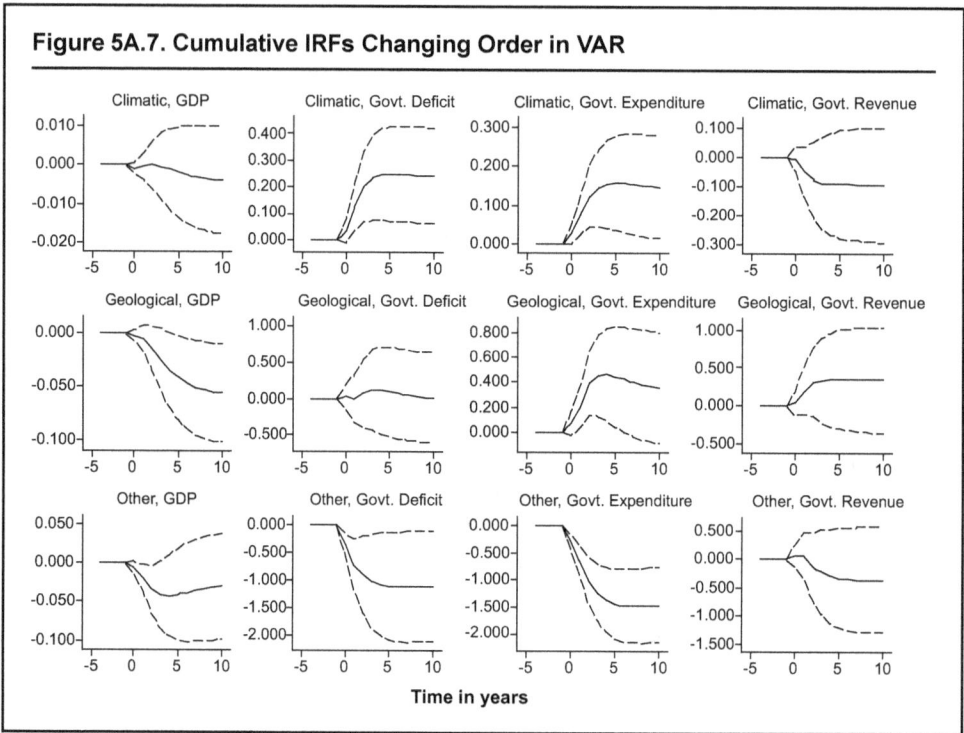

Note: The figure shows the cumulative impulse response functions (IRF) for GDP, government deficit, government expenditures, and government revenues. GDP and government deficit are expressed in real per capita terms; government expenditures and revenues are expressed as fractions of the long run government deficit. The parameters used to estimate the IRF come from the baseline specification with all variables expressed in levels (except the interest rate), and including two lags. The order of the endogenous variables entered in the VAR is the following: GDP, inflation, interest rate, government expenditures and government revenues. The model also includes country specific means and trends, and with time fixed effects that capture global variables. The government deficit is obtained as the weighted difference of revenues and expenditures. The solid lines show the cumulative percentage deviation of each variable from its trend resulting from a climatic, geological or other natural disasters occurred at time 0 (time in years). The dotted lines show one standard deviation confidence bands.

Figure 5A.8. Cumulative IRFs for High Income Countries

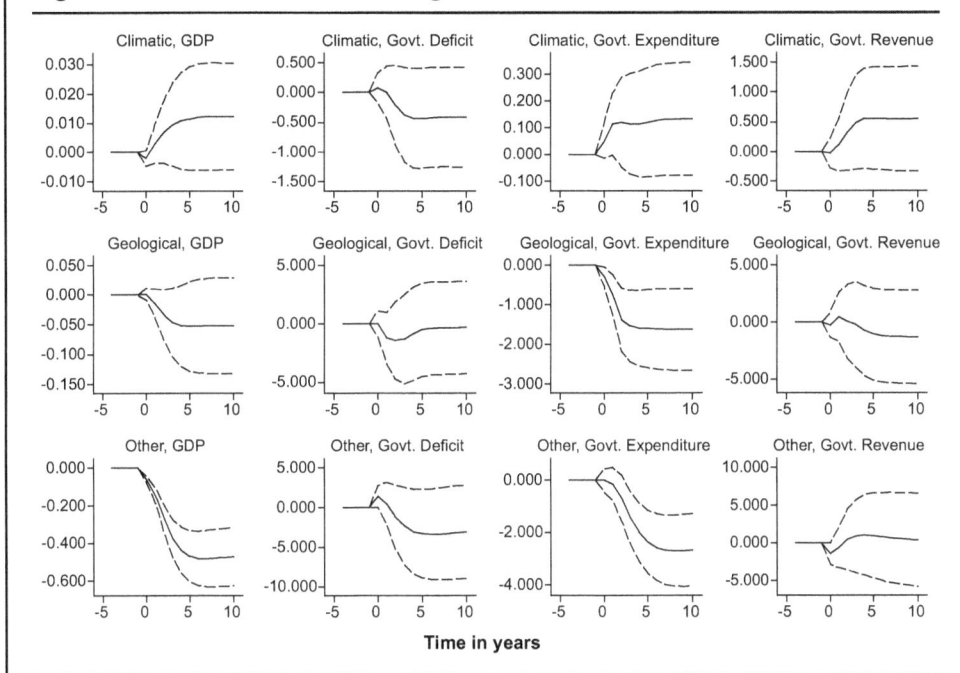

Time in years

Note: The figure shows the cumulative impulse response functions (IRF) for GDP, government deficit, government expenditures, and government revenues, for a sample of High Income countries according to the World Bank classification. GDP and government deficit are expressed in real per capita terms; government expenditures and revenues are expressed as fractions of the long run government deficit. The parameters used to estimate the IRF come from the baseline specification with all variables expressed in levels (except the interest rate), and including two lags. The order of the endogenous variables entered in the VAR is the following: government expenditures, GDP, inflation, interest rate, and government revenues. The model also includes country specific means and trends, and with time fixed effects that capture global variables. The government deficit is obtained as the weighted difference of revenues and expenditures. The solid lines show the cumulative percentage deviation of each variable from its trend resulting from a climatic, geological or other natural disasters occurred at time 0 (time in years). The dotted lines show one standard deviation confidence bands.

Figure 5A.9. Cumulative IRFs for Middle Income Countries

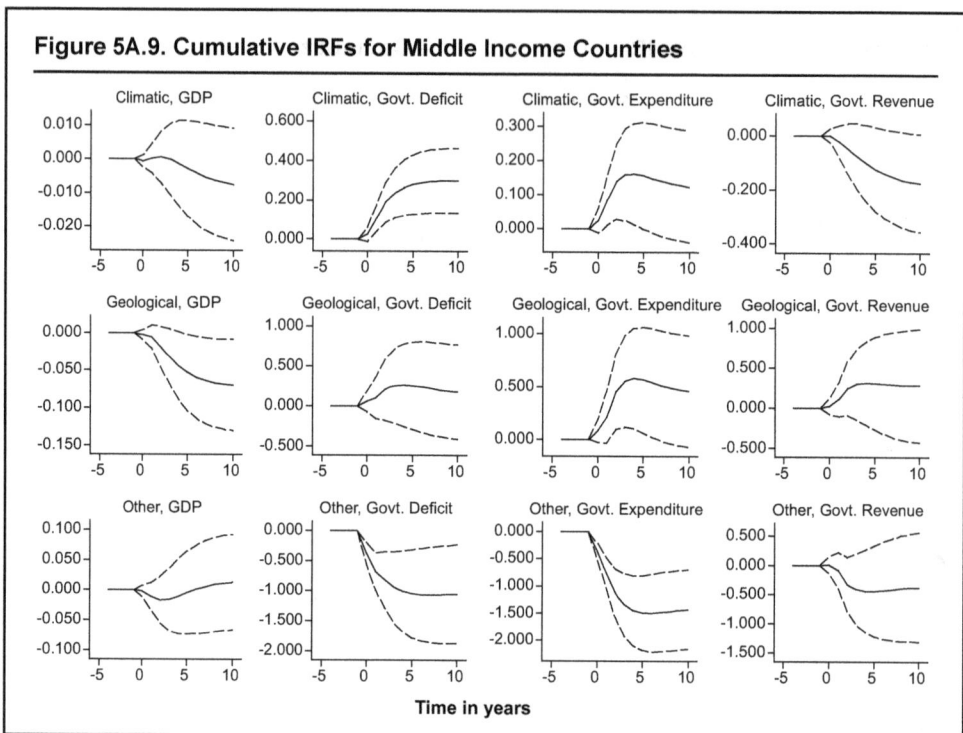

Time in years

Note: The figure shows the cumulative impulse response functions (IRF) for GDP, government deficit, government expenditures, and government revenues, for a sample of Middle Income countries according to the World Bank classification. GDP and government deficit are expressed in real per capita terms; government expenditures and revenues are expressed as fractions of the long run government deficit. The parameters used to estimate the IRF come from the baseline specification with all variables expressed in levels (except the interest rate), and including two lags. The order of the endogenous variables entered in the VAR is the following: government expenditures, GDP, inflation, interest rate, and government revenues. The model also includes country specific means and trends, and with time fixed effects that capture global variables. The government deficit is obtained as the weighted difference of revenues and expenditures. The solid lines show the cumulative percentage deviation of each variable from its trend resulting from a climatic, geological or other natural disasters occurred at time 0 (time in years). The dotted lines show one standard deviation confidence bands.

Figure 5A.10. Cumulative IRFs for Low and Middle Income Countries

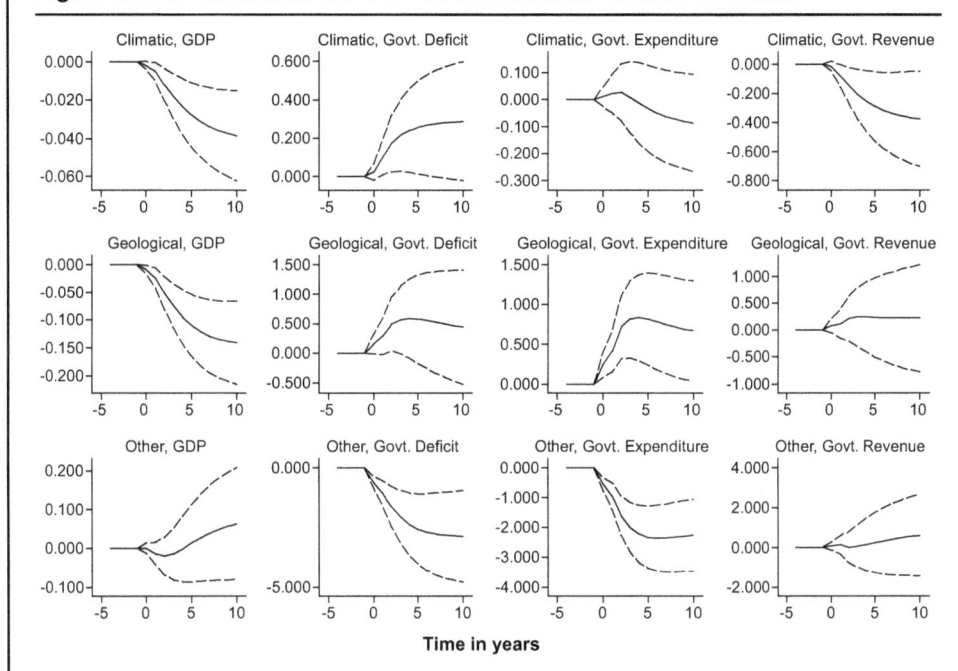

Note: The figure shows the cumulative impulse response functions (IRF) for GDP, government deficit, government expenditures, and government revenues, for a sample of Low and Middle Income countries according to the World Bank classification. GDP and government deficit are expressed in real per capita terms; government expenditures and revenues are expressed as fractions of the long run government deficit. The parameters used to estimate the IRF come from the baseline specification with all variables expressed in levels (except the interest rate), and including two lags. The order of the endogenous variables entered in the VAR is the following: government expenditures, GDP, inflation, interest rate, and government revenues. The model also includes country specific means and trends, and with time fixed effects that capture global variables. The government deficit is obtained as the weighted difference of revenues and expenditures. The solid lines show the cumulative percentage deviation of each variable from its trend resulting from a climatic, geological or other natural disasters occurred at time 0 (time in years). The dotted lines show one standard deviation confidence bands.

Figure 5A.11. Cumulative IRFs for Higher Middle Income Countries

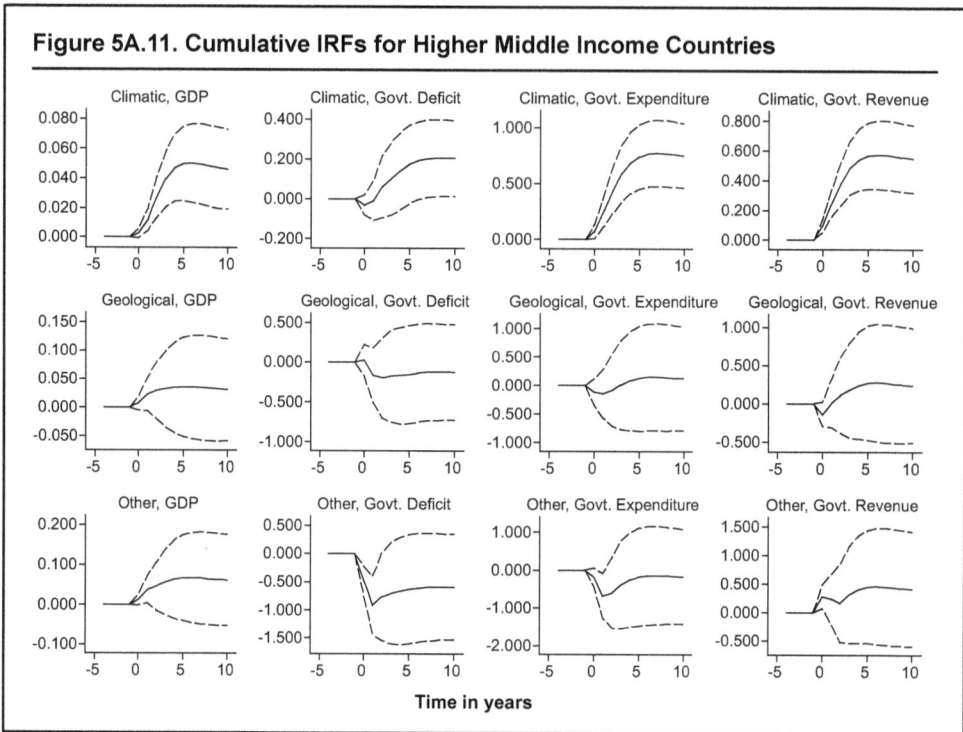

Note: The figure shows the cumulative impulse response functions (IRF) for GDP, government deficit, government expenditures, and government revenues, for a sample of High and Middle Income countries according to the World Bank classification. GDP and government deficit are expressed in real per capita terms; government expenditures and revenues are expressed as fractions of the long run government deficit. The parameters used to estimate the IRF come from the baseline specification with all variables expressed in levels (except the interest rate), and including two lags. The order of the endogenous variables entered in the VAR is the following: government expenditures, GDP, inflation, interest rate, and government revenues. The model also includes country specific means and trends, and with time fixed effects that capture global variables. The government deficit is obtained as the weighted difference of revenues and expenditures. The solid lines show the cumulative percentage deviation of each variable from its trend resulting from a climatic, geological or other natural disasters occurred at time 0 (time in years). The dotted lines show one standard deviation confidence bands.

Figure 5A.12. Cumulative IRFs for Different Debt Levels

Panel A. Low Debt Countries

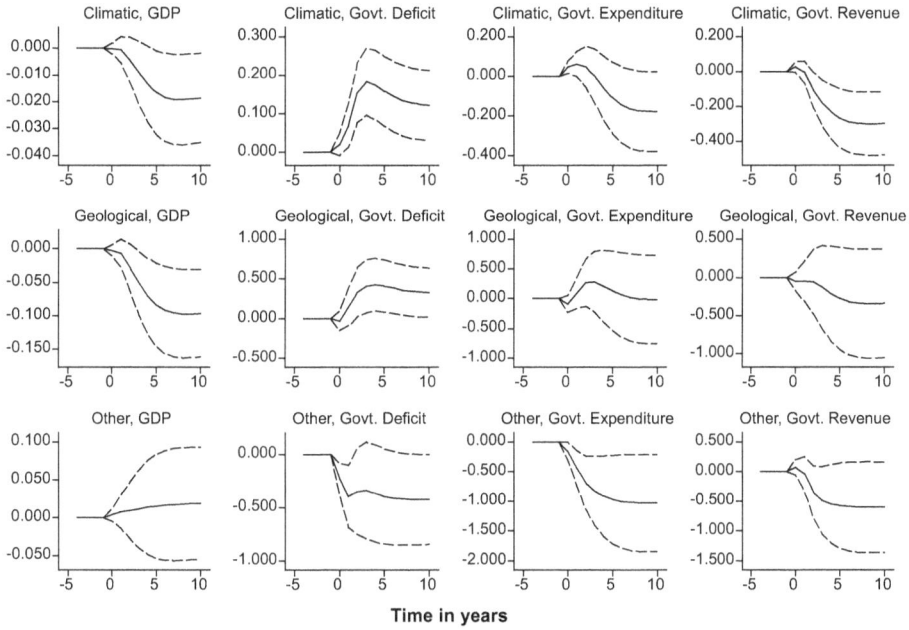

Time in years

(Figure continues on next page)

Figure 5A.12 *(continued)*

Panel B. High Debt Countries

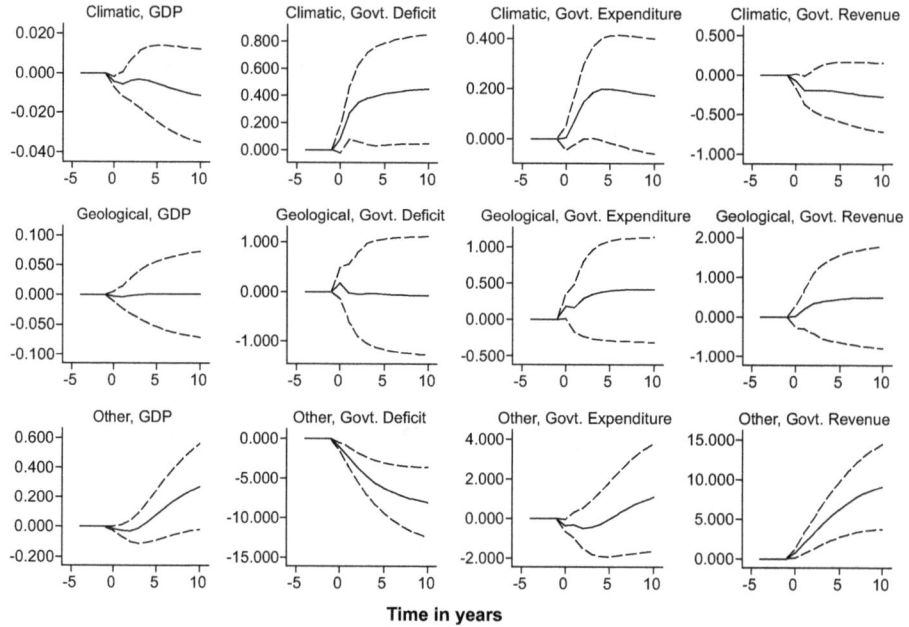

Time in years

Note: The figure shows the cumulative impulse response functions (IRF) for GDP, government deficit, government expenditures, and government revenues. Panels A and B reports the results for countries with debt to GDP ratio below and above the sample median respectively. GDP and government deficit are expressed in real per capita terms; government expenditures and revenues are expressed as fractions of the long run government deficit. The parameters used to estimate the IRF come from the baseline specification with all variables expressed in levels (except the interest rate), and including two lags. The order of the endogenous variables entered in the VAR is the following: government expenditures, GDP, inflation, interest rate, and government revenues. The model also includes country specific means and trends, and with time fixed effects that capture global variables. The government deficit is obtained as the weighted difference of revenues and expenditures. The solid lines show the cumulative percentage deviation of each variable from its trend resulting from a climatic, geological or other natural disasters occurred at time 0 (time in years). The dotted lines show one standard deviation confidence bands.

Figure 5A.13. Cumulative IRFs by Debt Controlling for Income Level

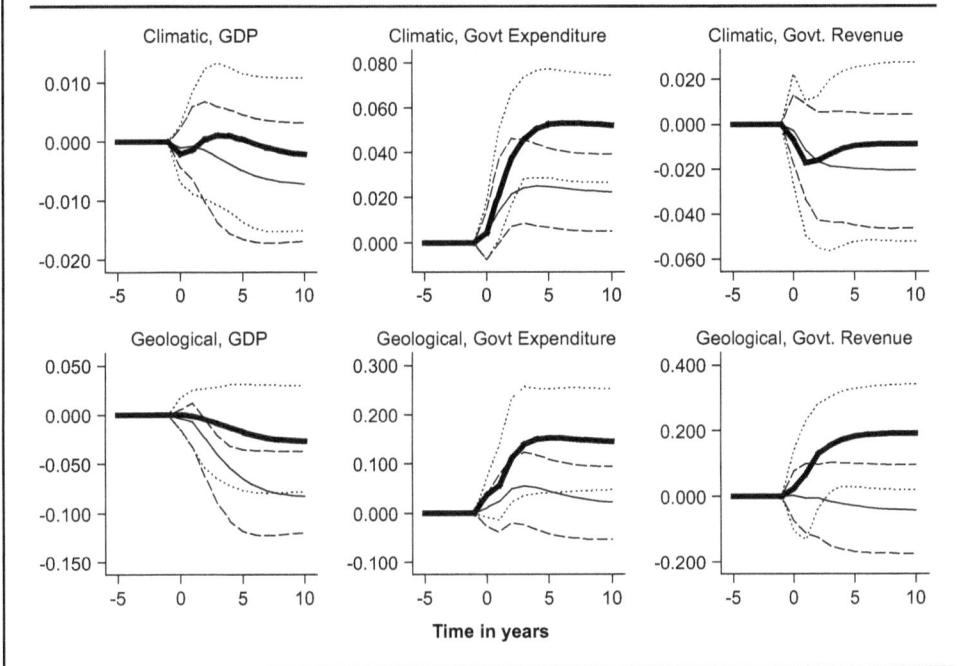

Note: The figure shows the cumulative impulse response functions (IRF) for GDP, government deficit, government expenditures, and government revenues, for countries with high and low levels of debt controlling for differences in income. The solid lines show the impact of a type of disaster, for countries with low (thin line) and high (thick line) debt levels (25th and 75th sample percentiles of debt to GDP ratio respectively). The dotted lines show one standard deviation confidence bands.

Figure 5A.14. Cumulative IRFs for Different Levels of Financial Development

Panel A. Financially Underdeveloped Countries

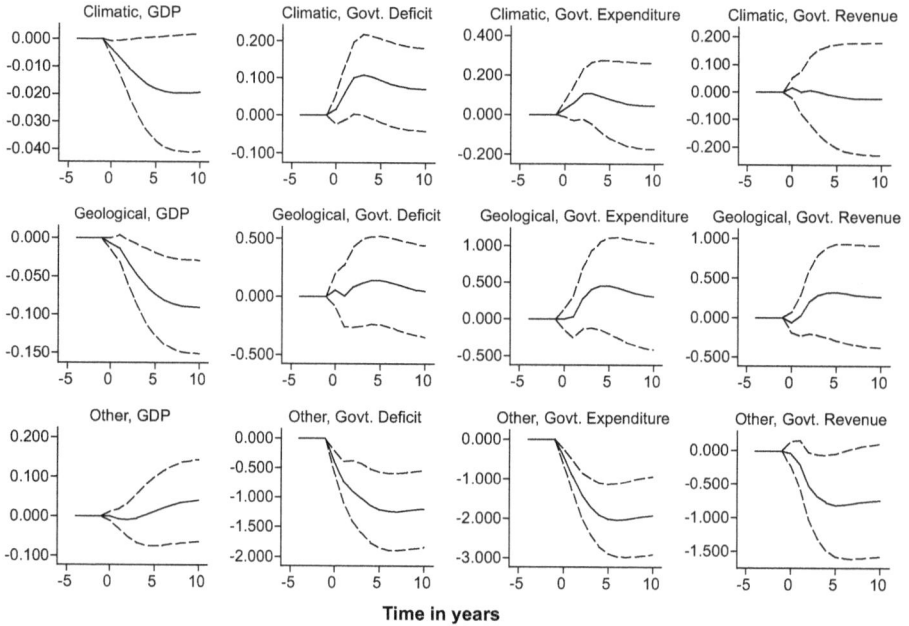

Time in years

(Figure continues on next page)

Figure 5A.14 *(continued)*

Panel B. Financially Developed Countries

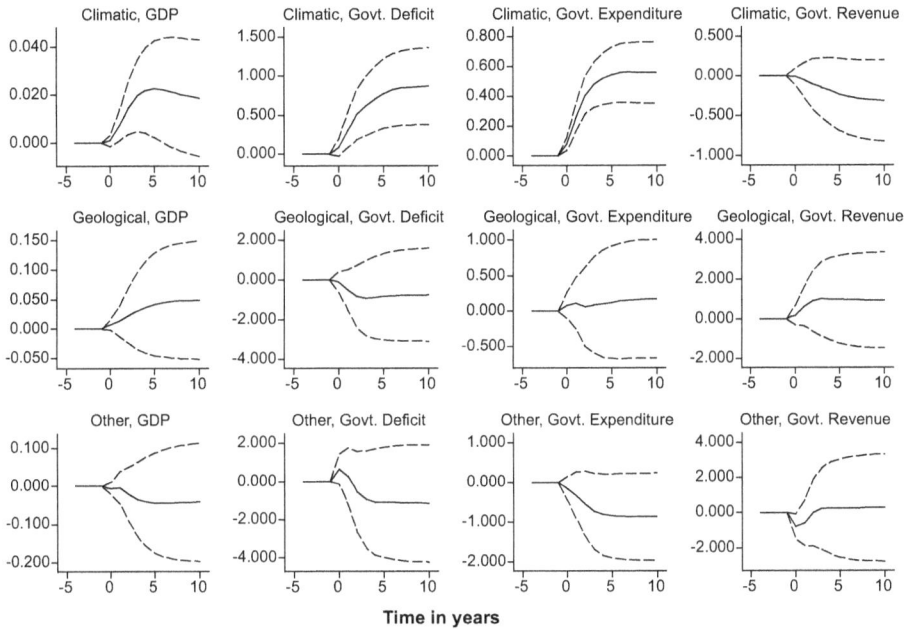

Note: The figure shows the cumulative impulse response functions (IRF) for GDP, government deficit, government expenditures, and government revenues. Panels A and B report the results for countries with the average ratio of private credit to GDP, below and above the sample median respectively. GDP and government deficit are expressed in real per capita terms; government expenditures and revenues are expressed as fractions of the long run government deficit. The parameters used to estimate the IRF come from the baseline specification with all variables expressed in levels (except the interest rate), and including two lags. The order of the endogenous variables entered in the VAR is the following: government expenditures, GDP, inflation, interest rate, and government revenues. The model also includes country specific means and trends, and with time fixed effects that capture global variables. The government deficit is obtained as the weighted difference of revenues and expenditures. The solid lines show the cumulative percentage deviation of each variable from its trend resulting from a climatic, geological or other natural disasters occurred at time 0 (time in years). The dotted lines show one standard deviation confidence bands.

Figure 5A.15. Cumulative IRFs by Financial Development Controlling for Income Level

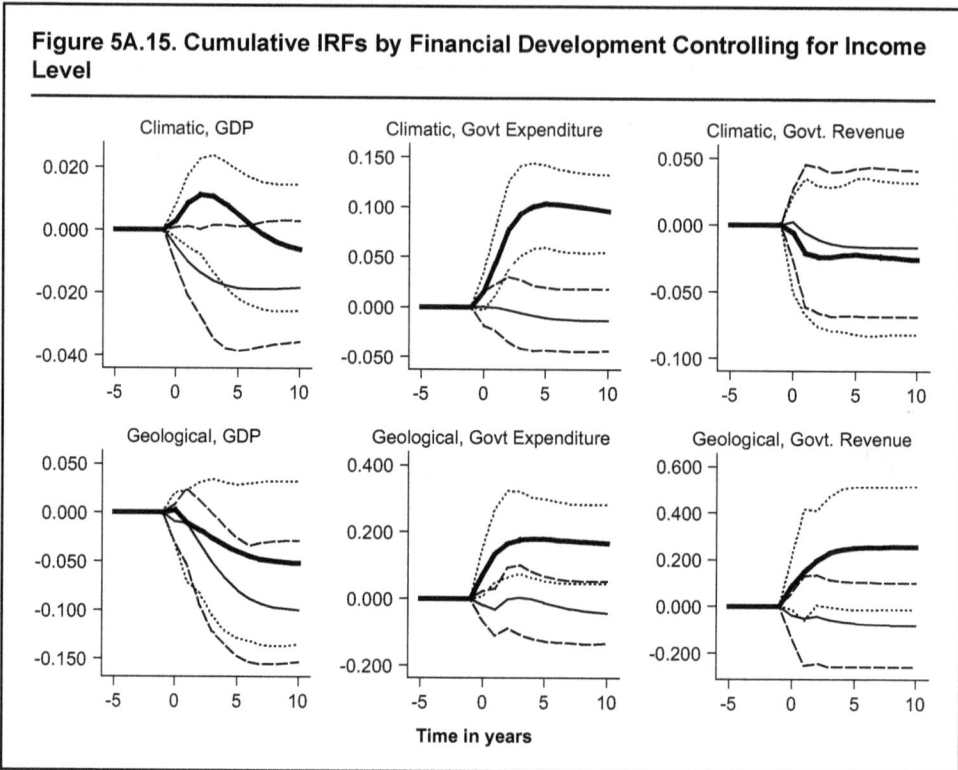

Note: The figure shows the cumulative impulse response functions (IRF) for GDP, government deficit, government expenditures, and government revenues, for countries with high and low levels of financial development controlling for differences in income. The solid lines show the impact of a type of disaster, for countries with low (thin line) and high (thick line) levels of financial development (25th and 75th sample percentiles of average ratio of private credit to GDP respectively). The dotted lines show one standard deviation confidence bands.

Figure 5A.16. Cumulative IRFs for Countries with Low Insurance Penetration

Panel A. Countries with Low Insurance Penetration

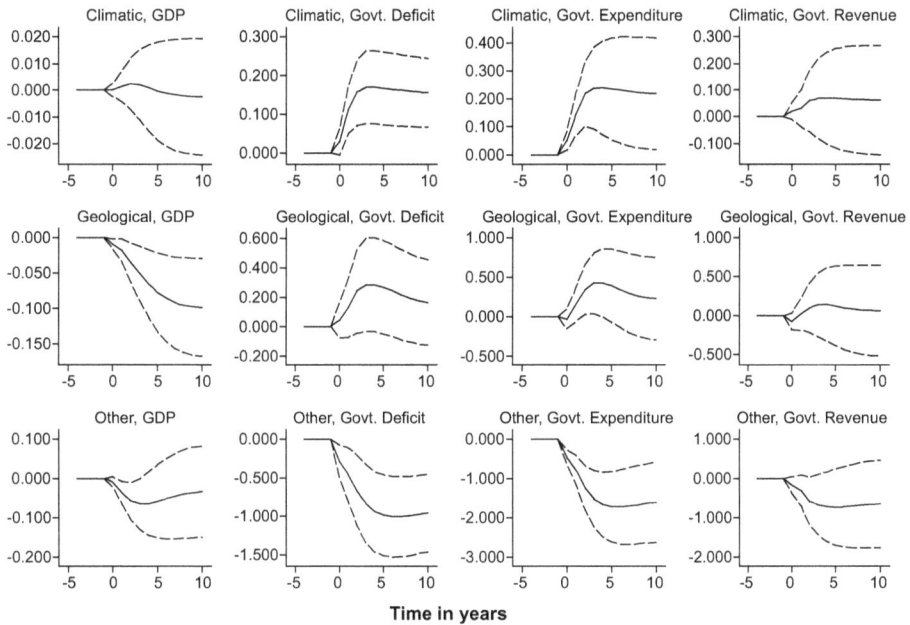

Time in years

(Figure continues on next page)

Figure 5A.16 (continued)

Panel B. Countries with High Insurance Penetration

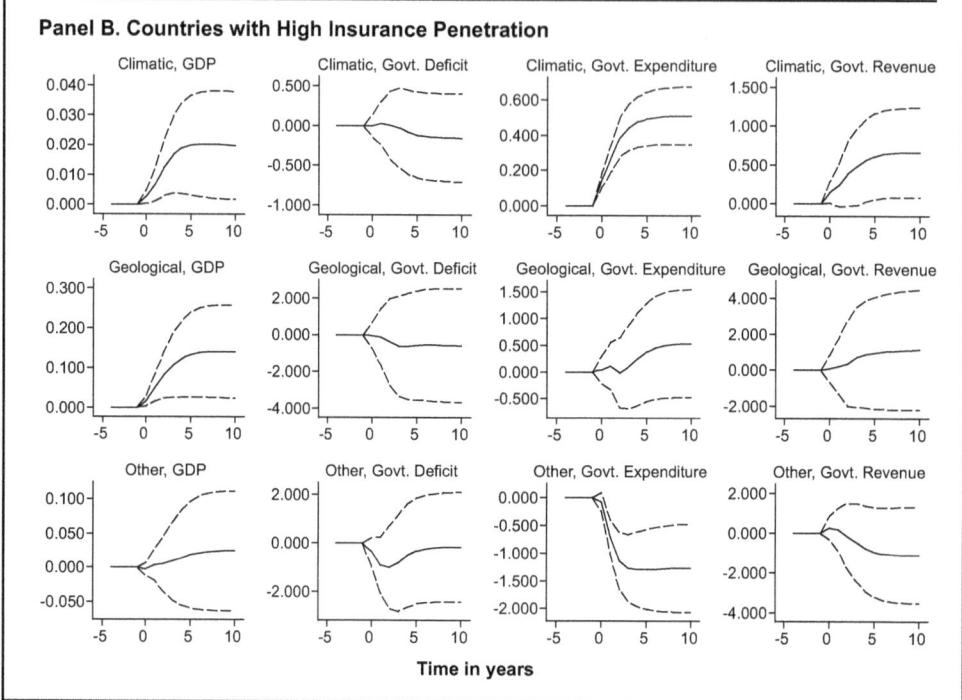

Time in years

Note: The figure shows the cumulative impulse response functions (IRF) for GDP, government deficit, government expenditures, and government revenues. Panels A and B report the results for countries with total value of premium to GDP ratio below and above the sample median respectively. GDP and government deficit are expressed in real per capita terms; government expenditures and revenues are expressed as fractions of the long run government deficit. The parameters used to estimate the IRF come from the baseline specification with all variables expressed in levels (except the interest rate), and including two lags. The order of the endogenous variables entered in the VAR is the following: government expenditures, GDP, inflation, interest rate, and government revenues. The model also includes country specific means and trends, and with time fixed effects that capture global variables. The government deficit is obtained as the weighted difference of revenues and expenditures. The solid lines show the cumulative percentage deviation of each variable from its trend resulting from a climatic, geological or other natural disasters occurred at time 0 (time in years). The dotted lines show one standard deviation confidence bands.

Figure 5A.17. Cumulative IRFs by Insurance Penetration Controlling for Income Level

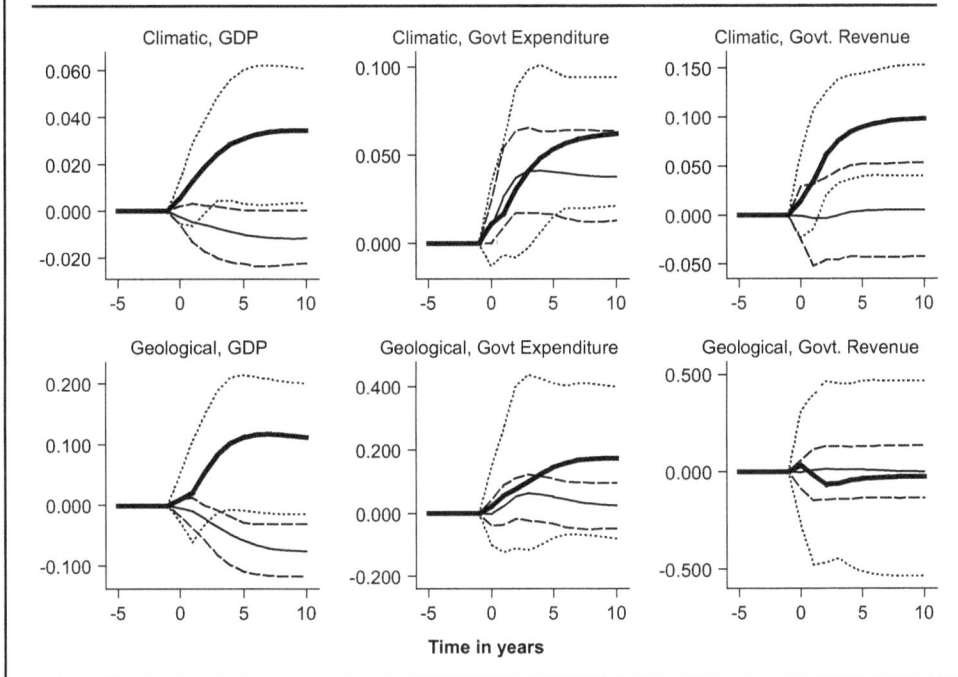

Note: The figure shows the cumulative impulse response functions (IRF) for GDP, government deficit, government expenditures, and government revenues, for countries with high and low levels of insurance penetration controlling for differences in income. The solid lines show the impact of a type of disaster, for countries with low (thin line) and high (thick line) levels of insurance penetration (25th and 75th sample percentiles of total value of premium to GDP ratio respectively). The dotted lines show one standard deviation confidence bands.

CHAPTER 6

Overall Conclusions of the Report

Megaflood disasters in the V-4 countries of Central and Eastern Europe (Poland, the Czech Republic, Hungary, and the Slovak Republic) have resulted in major losses in the last two decades. Based on historical and projected trends, future losses could easily represent significant shares of countries' GDP and government revenues, thus generating severe disruptions in fiscal finances and economic activity.

While there exist pan-European mechanisms such as the EU Solidarity Fund to help EU members fund mega disasters, these only kick in at extremely high loss levels. Such funds can also be delayed in terms of disbursing for several months and are not entirely suitable for immediate emergency funding. Coupled with the fact that V-4 government budgets which are reserved for natural catastrophes are modest, this calls for more state-of-the-art risk management arrangements for country governments to consider.

Given these issues, the governments of the V-4 countries should consider it a priority to set up risk transfer mechanisms to reduce fiscal volatility following natural catastrophes. Such mechanisms should count on joint country cooperation under collective risk pooling systems which will significantly reduce the costs of such instruments versus if each country arranged them on their own. In this regard, the report aims to provide the roadmap for policy makers in the Finance Ministries and other pertinent government offices, to understand the design parameters, costs, and benefits of establishing the pooled fiscal insurance mechanisms proposed for the V-4 region.

The private sector insurance markets in the V-4 countries appear adequate and reflect rather high levels of penetration in the economy and in the housing sector. In this regard, there does not appear to be a strong need to establish any catastrophe risk support mechanisms for the private sector or the insurance industry. However, for the government sector, there are significant exposures of properties, infrastructure, and other assets. While governments can always raise funds in the international bond markets following a disaster, it would be prudent to have pre-arranged mechanisms in place to provide quick liquidity to handle emergency needs and priority reconstruction of life lines and key infrastructure, as well as to ensure temporary shelter if required.

Economic and fiscal analyses based on global data also shows that countries with insurance mechanisms and markets show a stronger GDP recovery path and lower fiscal deficits following a disaster. The analysis is based on a large sample of countries including many with similar economic characteristics as the V-4 countries, and makes a strong case for relying on insurance and financial market mechanisms to achieve more sustainable economic and fiscal paths in natural disaster prone countries.

However, the V-4 countries, having a common hazard of flood, are in a unique position to develop highly cost effective flood insurance mechanisms. While these countries on their own, could design efficient financing and insurance structures to supplement fiscal resources in the event of major catastrophes, they would also obtain greater benefits from sharing risks under 'pooled' mechanisms that would better leverage the limited funds to support such schemes. Actuarial and portfolio risk analysis shows that all countries would benefit by lowering financing spreads if a pooled structure was used to insure fiscal resources against disaster losses.

As countries in general are more concerned with supplemental fiscal resources rather than individual property losses, the governments of the V-4 countries can consider parametric style contracts. This effectively means that contractual financial payments could be arranged and paid by insurers or investors (depending on the instrument used) and triggered by a physical measurement, for example, a threshold flood height in selected river catchments in the V-4 countries. Such contracts avoid any moral hazard in terms of measuring exact losses. This report has demonstrated how such "water level/flow" based contracts could be designed and provided several options.

Nevertheless, risk transfer or insurance mechanisms are not the only types that need to be considered. Government budget reserves for disaster financing (as currently practiced) should also constitute an important element in these risk financing strategies. Contingent prearranged loans may also be considered at upper loss levels since these carry close to a zero cost to have in place if no event occurs. But they should be used mainly for these higher level losses which occur infrequently, so as to avoid unnecessarily building up debt.

One of the options to consider is for the V-4 countries to jointly issue a catastrophe bond against flood risks. Such a bond would be purchased by investors and they would benefit from a bond return that is not correlated to the financial markets as it is based on unrelated flood risks. However, if the threshold flood event does occur, the principal proceeds of the bond would not be repaid by the governments and used for reconstruction. This would not constitute any default as such arrangements are standard contractual conditions for catastrophe bonds.

Another option that would likely lower costs for the V-4 governments would be the establishment of their own dedicated fiscal insurance fund. If adequately funded up-front, and with some reliance on the reinsurance market, this would reduce ongoing insurance costs substantially and provide a mechanism for fiscal compensation when the measured flood levels in the rivers of each of the countries, reached threshold heights.

The analysis in this report is meant to show, besides the financial mechanisms that would be beneficial for risk management, what large catastrophe exposures exist, and their relation to government finances and macroeconomic measures. While the analysis in this report was conducted by technical experts in the matter, governments should nevertheless engage in more detailed risk exposure analysis in each of their countries, to make a full assessment of level of the risks and losses they may be facing on account of recurrent flood hazards in the region.

Following a final phase of feasibility analysis and market testing, the V-4 countries should thus consider establishing a multicountry insurance pool to provide fast emergency funding after disasters. Such a pool can price member contributions based on their individual risk exposures while accruing large savings to all members by structuring it as a combined risk portfolio. An alternative innovative approach would be the joint issuance of a catastrophe bond to investors, which, besides not counting as public debt given its special insurance structure, would immediately compensate government with the bond proceeds held in trust, if a major catastrophe were to generate high losses.

Bibliography

Chapter 1 References

Canabarro, E., and M. Finkemeier. 1998. "Analyzing Insurance Linked Securities." *Goldman Sachs Fixed Income Research*, October.

Carpenter, Guy. 2010. "World Catastrophe Reinsurance Market." Available at: http://gcportal.guycarp.com/portal/extranet/popup/insights/reportsPDF/2010/World_Cat_2010.pdf.

CRED—Centre for Research on the Epidemiology of Disasters. 2010. Database on worldwide disasters.

Froot, K. 1999. "The Market for Catastrophic Risk: A Clinical Examination." National Bureau of Economic Research, Cambridge, MA. August.

International Monetary Fund (IMF). 2009. "International Financial Statistics." IMF, Washington, DC.

Melecky, Martin and Claudio Raddatz. 2011. "How Do Governments Respond after Catastrophes? Natural-Disaster Shocks and the Fiscal Stance." Policy Research Working Paper 5564. World Bank, Washington, DC.

Pollner, J. 2001. "Managing Catastrophic Disaster Risks Using Alternative Risk Financing and Pooled Insurance Structures." World Bank, Washington, DC.

Swiss Re and Sigma. 2010. "Natural Catastrophes and Man-Made Disasters in 2009." Available at: http://www.swissre.com/sigma/.

Chapter 2 References

[1] Catchment Characterisation and Modelling (CCM). European Commission, Joint Research Centre (JRC), Institute for Environment and Sustainability, (2007) (Update: July 16, 2008; quotation: June 20, 2009). Internet access: ccm.jrc.ec.europa.eu/php/index.php?action=view&id=23

[2] List of NACE codes. Brussels, EU: European Commission, (2009) (quotation: June 20, 2009). Internet access: ec.europa.eu/competition/mergers/cases/index/nace_all.html

[3] Main characteristics of the NUTS. Luxembourg, Luxembourg, EU: Eurostat, (2008) (quotation: June 20, 2009). Internet access: ec.europa.eu/eurostat/ramon/nuts/mainchar_regions_en.html

[4] Image 2000 & Corine Land Cover 2000 Project. Copenhagen, Denmark, EU: European Environmental Agency & Ispra, Italy, EU: European Commission - Joint Research Centre, (2009) (update: March 3, 2009; quotation: June 20, 2009). Internet access: image2000.jrc.ec.europa.eu

[5] European System of Accounts ESA 95. Luxembourg, Luxembourg, EU: Eurostat, (2006) (quotation: June 20, 2009). Internet access: circa.europa.eu/irc/dsis/nfaccount/info/data/esa95/en/titelen.htm

[6]   Multivariate Adaptive Regression Splines. Friedman, J.H. The Annals of Statistics, Vol. 19, No. 1, 1–141, Institute of Mathematical Statistics, 1991. Internet access: www.imstat.org/aos/

[7]   Digital Vector Map of Hungary 1:10,000. Gyula, Hungary: HISZI-Map Kft. (2008).

[8]   Digital Vector Map of Slovakia 1:50,000. Bratislava, Slovakia: MAPA Slovakia Plus, s.r.o. (2008). Internet access: www.mapa.sk

[9]   Digital Model of the Territory 1:25,000 (DMÚ-25). Dobruška, Czech Republic: Military Geographic and Hydro-meteorological Office (2007). Internet access: www.army.cz/acr/geos/htm/s_urad.html

[10]   Shuttle Radar Topography Mission. Pasadena, California, USA: Jet Propulsion Laboratory, California Institute of Technology, National Aeronautics and Space Administration (NASA-JPL), (2009) (update: June 17, 2009; quotation: June 20, 2009). Internet access: www2.jpl.nasa.gov/srtm

[11]   MONA Pro Europe. Gisat s.r.o, Praha. Internet access: www.gisat.cz/content/en/products/digital-elevation-model/mona-pro

[12]   FRAT 1.0 - Flood Risk Assessment Tool Czech Republic. Swiss Re, (2007) (quotation: October 20, 2009) Internet access: www.swissre.com/pws/business%20services/reinsurance/property%20and%20casualty/property/natural%20perils/frat%201%20%20flood%20risk%20assessment%20tool%20czech%20republic.html

[13]   Evaluation of the Catastrophic Flood in August 2002 (in Czech). T. G. Masaryk Water Research Institute, Public Research Institution, (2005) (quotation: June 20, 2009). Internet access: www.vuv.cz/povoden/index.html

[14]   Correspondence between ISIC Rev.3.1 and NACE Rev.1.1. New York, New York, USA: United Nations Statistics Division, (2009) (quotation: June 20, 2009). Internet access: unstats.un.org/unsd/cr/registry/regso.asp?Ci=26&Lg=1&Co=&T=0&

[15]   Method and System for Automated Location-Dependent Recognition of Flood Risks. Feyen, H., Mehlhorn, J., Oehy, C. In International Application Published under the Patent Cooperation Treaty (PCT): WO 2006 002566 A1, (on-line), Geneva, Switzerland: World Intelectual Property Organisation, 2006, (quotation: June 20, 2009). Internet access: www.wipo.int/pctdb/en/wads.jsp?IA=CH2005000365&LANGUAGE=EN&ID=id00000002383700&VOL=52&DOC=0004f3&WO=06/002566&WEEK=02/2006&TYPE=A1&DOC_TYPE=PAMPH&PAGE=1

[16]   Water Protection Maps of Hungary. 1:100,000 series. Budapest, Hungary: Environmental Protection and Water Management Research Institute—VITUKI, 1977. Internet access: www.vituki.hu

[17]   Statistical Yearbook of the Czech Republic 2008. Czech Statistical Office 2009. (quotation: October 19, 2009) Internet access: www.czso.cz/csu/2008edicniplan.nsf/engpubl/0001-08-2008

[18]   Regional Databank. Central Statistical Office of Poland. (quotation: October 19, 2009) Internet access: www.stat.gov.pl

[19]   Regional distribution of the fixed asset into NUTS-2 and NUTS-3 units, 2006. Czech Statistical Office (provided on request).

[20]   Eurostat, Statistical Database. (quotation: October 19, 2009) Internet access: epp.eurostat.ec.europa.eu

[21]   Regional Structure of the Fixed Asset Formation into NUTS-2 and NUTS-3 units, 1997-2006. Statistical Office of the Slovak Republic (provided on request).

[22]   Historical Fixed Asset Formation Data at LAU-1 Level, 1997-2006. Czech Statistical Office (unpublished data).

[23]   Statistical Yearbook of Slovakia 2007. Statistical Office of the Slovak Republic, 2008, Bratislava.

[24]   Regional Statistical Yearbook of Slovakia 2007. Statistical Office of the Slovak Republic, 2008, Bratislava

[25]   Evaluation of the Flood Situation in June 1997, Summary Report (in Czech), 1998. Czech Hydrometeorological Institute, Prague. (quotation: October 19, 2009) Internet access: www.chmu.cz/hydro/souhrn/obsah.html

[26]   Maximum monthly discharges in the selected 145 gauging stations for the period 12/1975−12/2004. Czech Hydrometeorological Institute, Prague. Commercially provided unpublished data.

[27]   N-years discharges in selected gauging stations. Czech Hydrometeorological Institute, Prague. (quotation: October 19, 2009) Internet access: hydro.chmi.cz/hpps/ and www.chmi.cz/hydro/opv/index.html (in Czech)

[28]   Kriging Interpolation. Chao-yi Lang, Dept. of Computer Science, Cornell University. (quotation: October 19, 2009) Internet access: www.nbb.cornell.edu/neurobio/land/OldStudentProjects/cs490-94to95/clang/kriging.html

[29]   Fixed Asset Structure for the Year 2006. Czech Statistical Office (provided on request).

[30]   Annual National Accounts 2006. Czech Statistical Office. (quotation: October 19, 2009) Internet access: apl.czso.cz/pll/rocenka/rocenka.indexnu_en

[31]   Fixed asset structure for the years 2006-2007. Statistical Office of the Slovak Republic (provided on request).

[32]   National Accounts, Hungary 2006-2007. Hungarian Central Statistical Office, Budapest 2009. (quotation: October 19, 2009) Internet access: portal.ksh.hu/pls/ksh/docs/hun/xftp/idoszaki/monsz/monsz0607.pdf

[33]   National Accounts, Hungary 2005-2006. Hungarian Central Statistical Office, Budapest 2008. (quotation: October 19, 2009) Internet access: portal.ksh.hu/pls/ksh/docs/hun/xftp/idoszaki/monsz/monsz0506.pdf

[34]   Capital Formation and Stock of Non-Financial Assets, 2000–2004. Hungarian Central Statistical Office, Budapest 2006

[35]   Statistical Yearbook of Poland 2008. Central Statistical Office of Poland. Warszawa 2008.

[36]   Census District Register (RSO) - database with information on houses and census districts including coordinates. Czech Statistical Office. (quotation: October 19, 2009) Internet access: www.czso.cz/eng/redakce.nsf/i/appendix_1_czso_basic_products_and_services (basic information in English) and www.czso.cz/csu/rso.nsf/i/prohlizeni_rso (On-Line version in Czech)

[37]   UIR-ADR (Territorial Identification Register of Buildings and Addresses) - database with information on build objects including classification in the classification into the administrative divisions. Ministry of Labor and Social Affairs of the Czech Republic. (quotation: October 19, 2009) Internet access: forms.mpsv.cz/uir/prohlizec/prohlizec.html (On-Line version in Czech)

[38]   Address Points of the Slovak Republic 2009. Mapa Slovakia Plus, s.r.o. (provided commercially)

[39]   Hungarian House Number Database 2008. HISZI-Map Kft. (provided commercially)

[40]   Built-up Area Polygons of Poland 1:200,000. Map of Europe 1:200,000. Mapa Slovakia Plus, s.r.o. 2009.

[41]   Regional Development in Hungary (regions, counties, districts). (in Hungarian, A Regionális Fejlődés Magyarországon (régiók, megyék, kistérségek). Mikroszkóp, 2003, February 27. EcoStat, Institute of Economic Analysis and Informatics, Budapest. www.ecostat.hu/kiadvanyok/mikroszkop-kulonszam.pdf

[42]   Detailed Gazetteer of the Republic of Hungary, 2009. Hungarian Central Statistical Office, Budapest 2009. (quotation: October 19, 2009) Internet access: portal.ksh.hu/pls/portal/cp.gazetteer (information on population for individual settlements/municipalities)

[43]   Antecedent Precipitation Index (API). University of Arizona 1998. (quotation: October 19, 2009) Internet access: web.hwr.arizona.edu/globe/globe3/api512.html

[44]   Flood Losses and Instruments for their Reduction (in Czech, Povodňové škody a nástroje k jejich snížení). Lenka Čamrová, Jiřina Jílková, and col. University of Economics, Prague. 2006. (quotation: October 19, 2009) Internet access: www.ieep.cz/editor/assets/publikace/pdf/pub036.pdf

[45]   Roads and Motorways in the Czech Republic 2009. The Road and Motorway Directorate of the Czech Republic. (quotation: October 19, 2009) Internet access: www.rsd.cz/doc/Silnicni-a-dalnicni-sit/silnice-a-dalnice-v-ceske-republice-2009

[46]   Motorways and Speedways Backbone Network in the Czech Republic (In Czech, Páteřní síť dálnic a rychlostních silnic v ČR). The Road and Motorway Directorate of the Czech Republic 2009. (quotation: October 19, 2009) Internet access: www.rsd.cz/doc/Stavime-pro-vas/paterni-sit-dalnic.

[47]   Annual Report 2008 (in Czech). The Road and Motorway Directorate of the Czech Republic. (quotation: October 19, 2009) Internet access: www.rsd.cz/doc/Organizace-RSD-CR/Vyrocni-zpravy/vyrocni-zprava-2008

[48]   Annual Report 2008 (in Czech). Railway Infrastructure Administration of the Czech Republic. (quotation: October 19, 2009) Internet access: www.szdc.cz/o-nas/vysledky-szdc.html

[49]   Railway Transport (in Czech, Drážní doprava). Czech Ministry of Transport 2004. (quotation: October 19, 2009) Internet access: www.mdcr.cz/cs/Media/Faq/Drazni_doprava.htm

[50]   Current practice in the field of protection against the effects of floods in the world and European Union rules (in Polish, Obecna praktyka działania w zakresie ochrony przed skutkami powodzi na świecie i przepisy Unii Europejskiej). Roman Konieczny, Paweł Madej, Centrum Edukacji Hydrologiczno Meteorologicznej (IMGW), Krakow. 2009. (quotation: October 19, 2009) Internet access: www.gdansk.uw.gov.pl/download_attachment.php?f=pl.attachment_10835891634b068fde3f89a.pdf

Chapter 3 References

Demarta, S., and A. J. McNeil. 2005. "The t Copula and Related Copulas." *International Statistical Review* 73(1): 111–129.

Embrechts, P., A. McNeil, and D. Straumann. 2002. "Correlation and Dependence in Risk Management: Properties and Pitfalls." In *Risk Management: Value at Risk and Beyond*, ed. M.A.H. Dempster, 176–223. Cambridge: Cambridge University Press.

Chapter 5 References

Adolfson, M. 2001. "Monetary Policy with Incomplete Exchange Rate Pass-Through." Working Paper No. 127, Sveriges Riksbank.

Ahmed, S. 2003. "Sources of Macroeconomic Fluctuations in Latin America and Implications for Choice of Exchange Rate Regime." *Journal of Development Economics* 72:181–202.

Benson, C., and E. Clay. 2003. "Bangladesh: Disasters and Public Finance." Disaster Risk Management Working Paper Series 6. World Bank, Washington, DC.

———. 2004. "Understanding the Economic and Financial Impacts of Natural Disasters." World Bank, Washington, DC.

Blanchard, O., and R. Perotti. 2002. "An Empirical Characterization of the Dynamic Effects of Changes in Government Spending and Taxes On Output." *The Quarterly Journal of Economics* 117(4): 1329–1368.

Borensztein, E., E. Cavallo, and P. Valenzuela. 2007. "Debt Sustainability under Catastrophic Risk: the Case for Government Budget Insurance." IADB Working Paper, WP607. Inter-American Development Bank (IADB), Washington, DC.

Broda, C. 2004. "Terms of Trade and Exchange Rate Regimes in Developing Countries." *Journal of International Economics* 63(1): 31–58.

Centre for Research on the Epidemiology of Disasters. 2008. Em-dat, the ofda/cred international disaster database. Universite Catholique de Louvain, Brussels, Belgium. www.em-dat.net.

Christiano, L. J., M. Eichenbaum, and C. L. Evans. 1998. "Monetary Policy Shocks: What Have We Learned and to What End?" In J. B. Taylor and M. Woodford, eds., *Handbook of Macroeconomics*, volume 1A, 65–148. Handbooks in Economics 15. North-Holland.

Hoppe, P., and T. Grimm. 2008. "Rising Natural Catastrophe Losses—What is the Role of Climate Change?" In *Economics and Management of Climate Change Risks, Mitigation and Adaptation*, B. Hansjürgens and R. Antes, eds. New York: Springer.

Ilzetzki, E., E. Mendoza, and C. Vegh. 2010. "How Big (Small?) are Fiscal Multipliers?" Mimeo, University of Maryland.

Inter-American Development Bank (IADB). 2009. Fiscal Sustainability II. Programmatic Policy Based Grant, Grant Proposal. IADB, Washington, DC.

International Monetary Fund (IMF). 2009. "Fiscal Rules—Anchoring Expectations for Sustainable Public Finances." Staff Paper, Fiscal Affairs Department. IMF, Washington, DC.

———. 2003. Fund Assistance for Countries Facing Exogenous Shocks. Policy Development and Review Department. IMF, Washington, DC.

Levin, A., C. Lin, and J. Chu. 2002. "Unit Root Tests in Panel Data: Asymptotic and Finite-Sample Properties." *Journal of Econometrics* 108(1): 1–24.

Linde, J., M. Nessén, and U. Söderström. 2009. "Monetary Policy in an Estimated Open Economy Model with Imperfect Pass-Through." *International Journal of Finance and Economics* 14(4): 301–333.

Loayza, N., and C. Raddatz. 2007. "The Structural Determinants of External Vulnerability." *World Bank Economic Review* 21(3): 359.

Monacelli, T. 2005. "Monetary Policy in a Low Pass-Through Environment." *Journal of Money Credit and Banking* 37(6): 1047–66.

Noy, I. 2009. "The Macroeconomic Consequences of Disasters." *Journal of Development Economics* 88(2): 221–31.

Panizza, U., F. Sturzenegger, and J. Zettelmeyer. 2009. "The Economics and Law of Sovereign Debt and Default." *Journal of Economic Literature* 47(3): 651–98.

Pedroni, P. 1999. "Critical Values for Cointegration Tests in Heterogeneous Panels with Multiple Regressors." *Oxford Bulletin of Economics and Statistics* 61(S1): 653–670.

———. 2004. "Panel Cointegration: Asymptotic and Nite Sample Properties of Pooled Time Series Tests with an Application to the PPP Hypothesis." *Econometric Theory* 20(03): 597–625.

Perotti, R. 2007. "Fiscal Policy in Developing Countries: A Framework and Some Questions." World Bank Policy Research Paper 4365. World Bank, Washington, DC.

Pesaran, M., and R. Smith. 1995. "Estimating Long Run Relationships from Dynamic Heterogeneous Panels." *Journal of Econometrics* 68: 79–113.

Pollner, J. 2001. "Catastrophe Risk Management: Using Alternative Risk Financing and Insurance Pooling Mechanisms." World Bank Policy Research Working Paper No. 2560. World Bank, Washington, DC.

Raddatz, C. 2007. "Are External Shocks Responsible for the Instability of Output in Low-Income Countries?" *Journal of Development Economics* 84(1): 155–87.

———. 2009. "The Wrath of God. Macroeconomics Costs of Natural Disasters." World Bank Policy Research Working Paper No. 5039. World Bank, Washington, DC.

Ramcharan, R. 2007. "Does the Exchange Rate Regime Matter for Real Shocks? Evidence from Windstorms and Earthquakes." *Journal of International Economics* 73(1): 31–47.

Rasmussen, T. 2004. "Macroeconomic Implications of Natural Disasters in the Caribbean." Technical report, IMF Working Papers WP/04/224. IMF, Washington, DC.

Robertson, D., and J. Symons. 1992. "Some Strange Properties of Panel Data Estimators." *Journal of Applied Econometrics* 7(2): 175–89.

Skidmore, M., and H. Toya. 2002. "Do Natural Disasters Promote Long-Run Growth?" *Economic Inquiry* 40(4): 664–87.

Toya, H., and M. Skidmore. 2007. "Economic Development and the Impacts of Natural Disasters." *Economics Letters* 94(1): 20–25.

United Nations Environment Programme (UNEP). 2005. "Environmental Management and Disaster Reduction." Session Concept Paper, UNEP Thematic Session on Environmental Management and Disaster Reduction: Building a Multi-Stakeholder Partnership. World Conference on Disaster Reduction.

Uribe, M., and V. Yue. 2006. "Country Spreads and Emerging Countries: Who Drives Whom?" *Journal of International Economics* 69(1): 6–36.

World Bank. 2001. "Kyrgyz Republic: Fiscal Sustainability Study. A World Bank Country Study." World Bank, Washington, DC.

———. 2010. World Development Indicators. CD-ROM. World Bank, Washington, DC.

www.ingramcontent.com/pod-product-compliance
Lightning Source LLC
Chambersburg PA
CBHW080610270326
41928CB00016B/2992